OpenGL®
Distilled

OpenGL® Distilled

Paul Martz

✦ Addison-Wesley

Upper Saddle River, NJ • Boston • Indianapolis • San Francisco
New York • Toronto • Montreal • London • Munich • Paris • Madrid
Capetown • Sydney • Tokyo • Singapore • Mexico City

Many of the designations used by manufacturers and sellers to distinguish their products are claimed as trademarks. Where those designations appear in this book, and the publisher was aware of a trademark claim, the designations have been printed with initial capital letters or in all capitals.

The author and publisher have taken care in the preparation of this book, but make no expressed or implied warranty of any kind and assume no responsibility for errors or omissions. No liability is assumed for incidental or consequential damages in connection with or arising out of the use of the information or programs contained herein.

The publisher offers excellent discounts on this book when ordered in quantity for bulk purchases or special sales, which may include electronic versions and/or custom covers and content particular to your business, training goals, marketing focus, and branding interests. For more information, please contact:

U.S. Corporate and Government Sales
(800) 382-3419
corpsales@pearsontechgroup.com

For sales outside the U.S., please contact:

International Sales
international@pearsoned.com

Visit us on the Web: www.awprofessional.com

 This Book Is Safari Enabled

The Safari® Enabled icon on the cover of your favorite technology book means the book is available through Safari Bookshelf. When you buy this book, you get free access to the online edition for 45 days.

Safari Bookshelf is an electronic reference library that lets you easily search thousands of technical books, find code samples, download chapters, and access technical information whenever and wherever you need it.

To gain 45-day Safari Enabled access to this book:

• Go to http://www.awprofessional.com/safarienabled

• Complete the brief registration form

• Enter the coupon code L5HJ-8WYI-KFHW-UJIP-34ZE

If you have difficulty registering on Safari Bookshelf or accessing the online edition, please e-mail customer-service@safaribooksonline.com.

Library of Congress Cataloging-in-Publication Data

Martz, Paul.
  OpenGL distilled / Paul Martz.
      p. cm.
  Includes bibliographical references and index.
  ISBN 0-321-33679-8 (pbk. : alk. paper)
  1. Computer graphics. 2. OpenGL. I. Title.

  T385.M3666 2006
  006.6'6—dc22

                              2005036423

ISBN 0-321-33679-8
Text printed in the United States on recycled paper at Courier in Stoughton, Massachusetts.
First printing, February 2006

Computer graphics programming isn't much fun without good eyesight.

*This book is dedicated to the doctors and researchers
battling retinitis pigmentosa.*

Contents

Foreword

A long time ago, in terms of the innovation of computers (which is about fifteen years for those of us stuck in the real world), deploying a cross-platform application that rendered graphics was challenging, to put it mildly. At that time, one could argue that the problem was less about computer hardware, and much more about software and APIs. Vendors had their own libraries and methods for coercing hardware into drawing pictures for us, but they were all proprietary, and the applications that were deployed on multiple vendors' hardware had huge swaths of code living within the confines of #ifdef blocks. Okay, so that part hasn't been totally eliminated, but for graphics, the situation has clearly improved.

Around that time, a group of smart folks with lots of experience in creating computer hardware and the interfaces that drove them attempted to address the problem. While the library proposed was designed and implemented by a single company, Silicon Graphics Computer Systems, Inc., perhaps their most innovative idea was to share this interface with direct competitors, accepting and integrating their ideas and methods into the library. Hence, OpenGL was born into a large, loving family called the OpenGL Architecture Review Board (the "ARB"), which understood that computers and graphics were nothing without the applications that drive them.

If you consider the prospect of designing a programming interface that abstracts away all the differences that might exist between different implementations of graphics algorithms, this was no small task. Furthermore, for the interface to be accepted and used, it had to be simple enough to get tasks done, but also had to meet the requirements of interactive, 3D computer graphics, which is to be as efficient as possible. Rarely is it easy to be both simple to use and highly efficient. In a way, that's the essence of software engineering, and this interface was being designed while that discipline was still formulating its basic principles.

To make matters more complicated, the authors of OpenGL knew that the computer graphics field was barely out of its infancy at that point. The rapid evolution of graphics techniques and their hardware implementations was already in full swing; if OpenGL were to be a contender, it would need to evolve with the field.

All heady stuff, to say the least.

Now, fast-forward to the present. The book you're holding is about OpenGL, the dominant programming interface for cross-platform, 3D computer graphics and image processing—the same interface that was designed those many years ago. It's remained true to its heritage, and is easy for novices to use to create interactive applications using 3D graphics, but powerful enough to drive the most performance-sensitive graphics applications. To that end, however, the interface (at version 2.0 at the time of this writing), has more than 800 entry points exposing current features of computer graphics in OpenGL parlance. Navigating through all those functions and methods is a daunting task, and an experienced guide would be very helpful.

Enter Paul Martz, who's been a long-time member of the graphics community, watching and contributing to OpenGL's evolution. He's offered to share his experience to help make your path to OpenGL mastery as painless as possible. Paul has considered the entirety of OpenGL and then distilled the essential elements of modern OpenGL programming and best practices into these pages to be your guide. I congratulate him on his accomplishment, and wish you the best of luck with OpenGL.

Happy rendering!

Dave Shreiner
Mountain View, CA
January 2006

Preface

"NVIDIA's core strategy is to deliver a breakthrough product every six months, doubling performance with each generation at a rate of essentially Moore's Law cubed." —Jen-Hsun Huang

"Children crawl before they walk, walk before they run—each generally a precondition for the other." —Lillian Breslow Rubin

Computer graphics technology, like all computer technology, advances at a staggering rate. In the late 1990s, the first hardware-accelerated 3D graphics cards for consumers signaled the dawn of a new age in 3D graphics software development. Already, these cards are gathering in landfills, superseded by more powerful and advanced hardware.

If you're new to OpenGL, you probably wish you could dive in and start writing advanced OpenGL applications. Although many advanced graphics programming books exist, most assume familiarity with OpenGL or some other 3D graphics Application Programmer Interface (API). Before you tackle more advanced programming tasks, you need a way to get up to speed on OpenGL quickly.

About the Book

OpenGL® Distilled is a concise book about the essential, commonly used features of modern OpenGL, the industry-standard cross-platform API for high-performance 3D computer graphics. By focusing on essential OpenGL features, eliminating discussion of algorithms, and pointing the reader to sources of additional information, *OpenGL® Distilled* provides useful information quickly and concisely.

OpenGL version 1.0 was introduced by SGI in 1992 and quickly dominated the 3D software development industry. It is available for several versions of Microsoft Windows, Linux, and Unix, and for Apple Mac OS. Graphics hardware manufacturers supporting OpenGL include 3Dlabs, ATI, Intel, Matrox, NVIDIA, and SGI.

The fact that OpenGL is an open standard is certainly one reason for its popularity. The OpenGL feature set is determined by the OpenGL Architecture Review Board (ARB), a governing body composed of representatives from several major hardware and software companies.[1] This group meets regularly to discuss and approve additions and modifications to the OpenGL specification. The ARB's multivendor nature ensures that OpenGL runs equally well on a wide variety of graphics architectures.

This book documents OpenGL version 2.0, released in September 2004. Although OpenGL has evolved significantly since its initial release, each version has remained compatible with previous versions. The benefits of backward compatibility are obvious, and several companies have taken advantage of OpenGL's stability to amortize the expense of software development.

Over time, some older OpenGL features fell into disfavor as the ARB added new rendering methods and paradigms to the OpenGL standard. Still other features never quite caught on with the developer community for a variety of reasons, such as corner-case or platform-specific applicability, overlapping or limited functionality, or nearly universal inefficient implementation.

The addition of new functionality, while continuing to keep older (and increasingly obsolete) features for backward compatibility, has resulted in a bulky and more complex OpenGL specification. Consider:

- In 1992, the original OpenGL version 1.0 specification contained 163 pages. Today, the OpenGL version 2.0 specification contains 368 pages, and the OpenGL Shading Language supplement increases this page count to a total of 474.

- Addison-Wesley's definitive *OpenGL® Programming Guide* and *OpenGL® Reference Manual* (the *red* and *blue* books), first published in 1993 to document the OpenGL version 1.0 standard, totaled 960 pages. In their most recent editions, documenting OpenGL versions 1.4 and 2.0, they total more than 1,600 pages. With the addition of the recently published *OpenGL® Shading Language, Second Edition* (the *orange* book), the page count tops 2,400.

Although such comprehensive documentation is indispensable for experienced programmers, the documentation's growth in size and complexity

---

1. The voting members of the ARB as of January 2006 are 3Dlabs, Apple, ATI, Dell, IBM, Intel, NVIDIA, SGI, and Sun.

over the years has increased the learning curve for new OpenGL developers. Furthermore, finding advice on accepted modern usage is difficult for new OpenGL programmers due to the sheer magnitude of information or time wasted learning outdated methodologies and paradigms.

OpenGL® Distilled addresses these issues by presenting only the essential elements of modern OpenGL used in current 3D software development. To meet this goal, several features of OpenGL have been left out of this book. *OpenGL® Distilled* presents the commonly used features and accepted practices in modern OpenGL programming. Features that have fallen into disfavor are omitted except where they help illustrate accepted practices or important concepts. Each chapter begins with a summary of what is and what is not covered.

To reduce the learning curve further, *OpenGL® Distilled* presents information in a direct, how-to style so that readers can find information quickly without wading through extraneous information. For this reason, there is little explanation or discussion of graphics algorithms. Shadow algorithms (discussed in Chapter 6) are the exception because of their almost-universal applicability and lack of direct OpenGL support. For other algorithms, *OpenGL® Distilled* assumes that the reader is familiar with computer graphics or is reading *OpenGL® Distilled* as part of a university-level computer graphics course.

This book presents the subset of OpenGL that most programmers can use to do the majority of their OpenGL programming. Because this material is a subset, the reader will likely desire access to more information. For this reason, *OpenGL® Distilled* serves as a gateway or road map to additional OpenGL and 3D graphics programming information. This book will frequently refer to the following resources:

- The official OpenGL Web site, http://www.opengl.org, is home to several developer forums, example programs, utility libraries, white papers, documentation, hyperlinks, and other valuable OpenGL resources.

- *The OpenGL Graphics System: A Specification,* by Mark Segal and Kurt Akeley, edited by Jon Leech, is OpenGL's complete and formal specification. Though intended for OpenGL implementers, its information is indispensable for application programmers. It's freely available as a PDF file from the OpenGL Web site.

- *OpenGL® Programming Guide, Fifth Edition,* by OpenGL ARB, Dave Shreiner, Mason Woo, Jackie Neider, and Tom Davis (Addison-Wesley), better known as the *red book,* is the definitive OpenGL programming guide. Furthermore, it contains extensive discussions of graphics algorithms and their implementation in OpenGL.

- *OpenGL® Reference Manual, Fourth Edition,* by OpenGL ARB and Dave Shreiner (Addison-Wesley), better known as the *blue book,* is the definitive OpenGL programmer's reference.

- *OpenGL® Shading Language, Second Edition,* by Randi Rost (Addison-Wesley), better known as the *orange book,* documents OpenGL's interface to programmable graphics hardware. This functionality is part of the OpenGL version 2.0 specification.

- *Computer Graphics: Principles and Practice, Second Edition,* by James D. Foley, Andries van Dam, Steven K. Feiner, and John F. Hughes (Addison-Wesley), and *3D Computer Graphics,* by Alan Watt (Addison-Wesley), are both excellent general 2D and 3D computer graphics texts.

Intended Audience

OpenGL® Distilled is intended for C++ programmers who are new to OpenGL.

This book assumes moderate familiarity with computer graphics. The reader should be familiar with graphics resources, texts, and algorithms. Graphics expertise is not required to make use of this book. The reader doesn't need to know how to code Bresenham's algorithm, for example, but should be familiar with the concept of scan conversion. Experience with another graphics API is helpful but isn't a prerequisite.

The reader should be familiar with the C++ programming language. The example source code on the book's Web site is in C++, and will build and run in Microsoft Windows, Apple Mac OS, and most flavors of Linux and Unix. Many of the code snippets in the book should be comprehensible to any programmer who is familiar with C and who has access to a C++ reference manual.

The reader should be familiar with vector and matrix mathematics as covered in a typical linear-algebra course. The reader should understand matrix concatenation and vector-matrix multiplication. Readers already familiar with transformation and coordinate systems from another 3D graphics API will find *OpenGL® Distilled* an easy read. For readers unfamiliar with this subject, many general 3D graphics texts cover the subject adequately, such as Chapter 5, "Geometrical Transformations," in *Computer Graphics: Principles and Practice.*

The reader should, of course, be familiar with basic mathematics such as algebra, geometry, and trigonometry.

Format of the Book

OpenGL® Distilled consists of eight chapters followed by four appendices and an index.

Chapter 1, "An Introduction to OpenGL," presents OpenGL architecture and concepts in broad terms. It also introduces the GLUT and GLU support libraries, discusses setting up an OpenGL development environment, and presents a simple OpenGL example. This chapter concludes with an extensive history of the OpenGL API.

Chapter 2, "Drawing Primitives," covers how to use OpenGL to render geometric data. It describes the OpenGL drawing primitive types and how to render them by using the vertex array and buffer object features. This chapter also presents other drawing details, such as clearing the framebuffer, order dependence, and the depth test.

Chapter 3, "Transformation and Viewing," describes the OpenGL transformation pipeline. This chapter covers how to position and orient views, set perspective and orthographic projections, and control the Viewport. It also covers interactive view manipulation using the mouse.

Chapter 4, "Lighting," explains how to set lighting parameters, which control light position, direction, and color, as well as material reflectance.

Chapter 5, "Pixel Rectangles," introduces the OpenGL paradigm for drawing, reading, and copying blocks of pixel data.

Chapter 6, "Texture Mapping," tells you how to create texture objects and apply them to rendered geometry. Texture mapping is a powerful tool for increasing the realism of rendered images. This chapter describes techniques for improving specular highlights, environment mapping, and creating shadows.

Chapter 7, "Extensions and Versions," describes how to write version-safe, platform-independent code that uses implementation-specific graphics hardware functionality.

Chapter 8, "Platform-Specific Interfaces," describes OpenGL interfaces specific to Apple Mac OS, Linux, and Microsoft Windows. This chapter describes how to create and use multiple OpenGL rendering contexts and share objects between them.

Appendix A, "Other Features," briefly covers several OpenGL features outside the scope of this book, such as the OpenGL Shading Language, clip planes, fog, multisampling, and stencil.

Appendix B, "Best Practices," enumerates generally accepted good OpenGL programming practices that help ensure a robust and portable OpenGL application.

Appendix C, "Performance," describes how to take accurate timing measurements and how to identify and eliminate performance bottlenecks.

Appendix D, "Troubleshooting and Debugging," assists in resolving commonly encountered issues.

Each chapter opens with a quick summary of what the reader will learn, as well as topics that aren't covered. Each chapter concludes with pointers to further reading related to the chapter subject.

Conventions

After reading *OpenGL® Distilled,* many readers will purchase *OpenGL® Programming Guide.* To ease the transition from one book to another, the same style conventions are used where possible.

This book uses the following style conventions:

- **Bold**—OpenGL entry points, function names, and matrices

- *Italics*—Variables, arguments, parameter names, spatial dimensions, and matrix components

- `Regular`—Enumerant types and values, defined constants, source code, references, file names, and system paths

Blocks of code are set aside from the text and use a monospace font.

This book presents OpenGL commands by using a command summary, which includes function prototypes, descriptions of the command parameters, and OpenGL version information. Here's the template for a command summary:

Function prototype for the command

A description of the command and its parameters.

▶ OpenGL version: Versions of OpenGL that support the command

In the function prototype, braces indicate a set of options. As an example, consider the **glLight*v** () set of functions.

---

void **glLight**[fd]**v**(GLenum *light*, GLenum *pname*, const *TYPE* param*);

This prototype defines two functions: **glLightfv** () and **glLightdv** (). f and d identify the parameter data type—GLfloat or GLdouble, respectively. In the function prototype parameter list, replace *TYPE* with the actual data type.

The command summary can be used as a concise reference for the command. *OpenGL® Reference Manual,* however, typically contains a more exhaustive reference.

OpenGL® Distilled Web Site

The book's Web site, http://www.opengldistilled.com, provides access to all the code in the book. Click the Download link to get at the files. All code was built and tested on the following platforms: Microsoft Windows XP using Visual Studio version 6.0, .NET 2003, and the Cygwin development environment; Apple Mac OS X using Xcode version 2.0; and Red Hat Linux using the GNU compilers.

The sample code requires GLUT, the TIFF library, and GNU Make. The Web site provides links for downloading these libraries and utilities.

OpenGL® Distilled contains references to color plates. These color plates are available as a PDF file from the book's Web site and also from Addison-Wesley's Web site: http://www.awprofessional.com/title/0321336798.

If errors are found in this book, corrections will be posted to the Web site.

Acknowledgments

Creating a book is too large a task for a single person. This book wouldn't exist if it weren't for the hard work of several people.

Thanks to Brenda Mulligan, formerly of Addison-Wesley, for the initial concept plus lots of other early help; this book would never have gotten off the ground without her. Thanks to my entire Addison-Wesley team—Debra Williams Cauley; Mary O'Brien; Marty Rabinowitz; Curt Johnson; Tyrrell Albaugh, Noreen Regina; Julie Nahil; Jessica D'Amico; and especially Chris Zahn for reading every word, which would undoubtedly put most nonprogrammers into a coma.

Addison-Wesley also put together a stellar technical-review team. I'd like to thank Eric Chan, Martin Ecker, Jeffery Galinovsky, Bill Licea-Kane, Scott Nations, Marc Olano, Randi Rost, Jeremy Sandmel, Dave Shreiner, and others for lending their expertise and providing insightful feedback and suggestions on the book proposal, sample chapter, and first draft.

Several people enabled the example code. I'm deeply indebted to Hewlett-Packard and my former co-workers Courtney Goeltzenleuchter and Jeff Burrell for providing a Linux box during example source-code development. Thanks to Brian Stempel, who wrote the AGL example code, tested all the example code on the Apple platform, and acted as a consultant on all things Apple. I owe you a beer, Brian. Thanks to artist and travel companion Dean Randazzo, who provided one of his awesome photographs for use as a texture map in the SecondaryColor example. And thanks to my employer, SimAuthor, for the elevation and texture map data of the Grand Teton region used in the TextureMapping example.

SimAuthor also gets my thanks for its support and use of its resources. A further tip of my panama hat to John Platt and Charlie Douglas; playing poker every other week helped keep me sane.

I sincerely appreciate the help of luminaries like Jon Leech at SGI, Mesa creator Brian Paul, Bill Licea-Kane, and several others for patiently answering my questions on OpenGL.

Alex Berry at Seven21 Productions did a great job of converting my child-like scribbles into professional-looking diagrams. Fellow OpenGL developer Chris Hansen at 3D Nature and Matt Gadda at SimAuthor both reviewed sections of the book and provided insightful feedback. Thanks to all of you.

I really have to thank my wife, Deedre Martz. Like any author's spouse, Dee supported me fully while I spent nights and weekends writing this book. But beyond that, she lent her technical-writing expertise. Her feedback is responsible for the professional tone of this book. In fact, I owe most of what I know about technical writing to Dee.

Finally, I'm indebted to Andy Goodrich, Spencer Thomas, and Bert Herzog, who collectively got me started down the 3D graphics path many years ago. Thanks for opening the door to a fascinating career.

About the Author

Paul Martz is a senior software engineer at SimAuthor, Inc., in Boulder, Colorado, where he creates OpenGL-based flight-data visualization software. Before working at SimAuthor, Paul worked in the Graphics Software Lab at Hewlett-Packard and the Workstation Graphics Division at Evans & Sutherland.

Paul has been involved in computer graphics since 1986, with 3D graphics systems software and OpenGL device driver development at the heart of his career. In 1993, Paul developed performance-sensitive code for Evans & Sutherland's first OpenGL product. In the late 1990s, Paul contributed to HP-UX and Microsoft Windows OpenGL device driver development for Hewlett-Packard's OpenGL-based workstation graphics hardware. Paul has helped review revisions to the OpenGL specification and is currently an individual contributor to the OpenGL ARB.

Paul led the effort to create the OpenGL Technical FAQ, available at the official OpenGL Web site: `http://www.opengl.org`. He has also written several technical white papers, Internet tutorials, and computer graphics book reviews.

When not doing something OpenGL-related, Paul can usually be found with an ace in his hat at a poker game or making lots of noise playing drums.

An Introduction to OpenGL

OpenGL is a good 3D graphics API.

When asked "What makes a good 3D graphics API?", most software developers will probably mention the following:

- It must allow real-time rendering—that is, it must be efficient.

- It must be widely supported.

- It must be easy to use.

Efficiency is often in the eye of the beholder. Many applications require frame rates that allow real-time interactivity, whereas significantly lower frame rates suffice for applications such as offline video production and visualizing terabytes of scientific data. If the application isn't the bottleneck, and the API is well designed, API efficiency should always be an implementation issue. A good API design should facilitate and never hinder efficient implementations.

In general, an API whose design facilitates efficiency allows implementation on a wide variety of graphics hardware architectures and computing platforms. Moreover, well-designed APIs remain popular for years and run on several generations of graphics hardware architectures (Lichtenbelt 1997). But for most software developers, the question of API support boils down to "Is it available on my development platform?" or, more important, "Is it available on my customers' platforms?" OpenGL implementations on a wide variety of hardware architectures are well documented (Cojot 1996, Carson 1997, Kilgard 1997, McCormack 1998).

Defining and measuring *ease of use* is somewhat subjective. Does the API provide a rich feature set? Does it allow flexible usage? Is it self-consistent?

After you've learned how to use the API to solve one rendering problem, can you draw upon what you've learned to solve other rendering problems? A majority of "yes" answers indicates that the API is easy to use.

If you assume that efficiency and availability are givens, your primary concern as a new programmer is ease of use. This introductory chapter outlines the overall design of OpenGL and shows you how easy it is to put together a simple test program.

What You'll Learn

Chapter 1 presents the following topics:

- A high-level description of OpenGL—This section defines OpenGL and covers architecture, syntax, features, and paradigms for querying state.

- Support libraries—These sections introduce two common support libraries, GLUT and GLU, that most OpenGL programmers will encounter.

- Development environment—This section details the header files and libraries you'll need to develop OpenGL applications.

- Example—This section provides a small example program to present the "look and feel" of an OpenGL program.

- History—This section discusses the origins of OpenGL.

What You Won't Learn

Keep this in mind as you read this chapter:

- As this chapter enumerates OpenGL features, it also notes features and topics that aren't covered in *OpenGL® Distilled*.

1.1   What Is OpenGL?

OpenGL is the graphics API defined by *The OpenGL Graphics System: A Specification*. OpenGL programs use implementations of this specification for display of 2D and 3D geometric data and images.

According to the OpenGL specification, "To the programmer, OpenGL is a set of commands that allow the specification of geometric objects in two or three dimensions, together with commands that control how these objects are rendered into the framebuffer."[1] OpenGL is typically implemented as a library of entry points (the *GL* in *OpenGL* stands for *Graphics Library* [Kilgard 1997]) and graphics hardware to support that library, as Figure 1-1 shows.

In computer systems designed for 3D graphics, the hardware directly supports almost all OpenGL features. As a result, the OpenGL library is merely a thin layer, allowing the application to access hardware functionality efficiently. High-level features that are difficult to implement in hardware—such as support for high-level primitive types, scene graphs, and utility functions—are not part of the OpenGL specification (Carson 1997). Several libraries to support such high-level functionality are available, however. See the section "GLU" later in this chapter for an overview of one such library.

OpenGL doesn't include support for windowing, input (mouse, keyboard, and so on), or user interface functionality, as computer systems typically

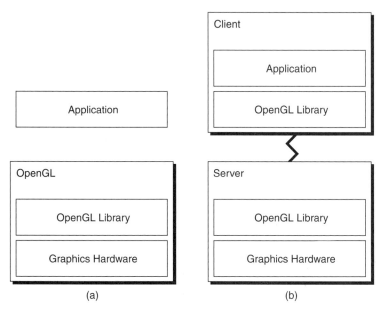

Figure 1-1   Two typical OpenGL implementations. In (a), applications link with a library of OpenGL entry points that pass commands to OpenGL-based graphics hardware. (b) illustrates a client–server implementation. Applications link with a library of OpenGL entry points that pass commands over network protocol. A server (local or remote) receives the commands and renders using server hardware.

1. Segal, Mark and Kurt Akeley, *The OpenGL Graphics System: A Specification*, version 2.0, September 2004, p. 2.

provide platform-specific support for these features. The GLUT library (see the section "GLUT" later in this chapter) provides platform-independent support for this functionality and is sufficient for most small-application and demo-program needs. This book covers platform-specific libraries in Chapter 8, "Platform-Specific Interfaces."

1.1.1   Fundamentals and Architecture

OpenGL is a state machine. Applications call OpenGL functions to set OpenGL state, which in turn determines the final appearance of a primitive in the framebuffer. An application might set the color to red, draw a point primitive, set the color to blue, and draw a second and third point primitive, as follows:

```
glColor3f( 1.f, 0.f, 0.f ); // red as an RGB triple
glBegin( GL_POINTS );
  glVertex3f( -.5f, 0.f, 0.f ); // XYZ coordinates of first point
glEnd();

glColor3f( 0.f, 0.f, 1.f ); // blue as an RGB triple
glBegin( GL_POINTS );
  glVertex3f( 0.f, 0.f, 0.f ); // XYZ coordinates of second point
glEnd();

glBegin( GL_POINTS );
  glVertex3f( .5f, 0.f, 0.f ); // XYZ coordinates of third point
glEnd();
```

In this case, OpenGL displays the first point red and the second point blue. Because the code doesn't change the color state before the third point, OpenGL also draws it blue. (**glColor3f**() specifies an RGB color value. **glVertex3f**() specifies an *xyz* vertex location. This code uses **glBegin**() and **glEnd**() to denote individual primitives, but more efficient methods are covered in Chapter 2.)

Primitives are groups of one or more vertices. In the example above, a single vertex is used for each point. Line and fill primitives require two or more vertices. Vertices have their own color, texture coordinates, and normal state (as well as other per-vertex states). You could rewrite the above code for drawing a red and blue point as follows:

```
glBegin( GL_POINTS );
  glColor3f( 1.f, 0.f, 0.f ); // red as an RGB triple
  glVertex3f( -.5f, 0.f, 0.f ); // XYZ coordinates of first point
  glColor3f( 0.f, 0.f, 1.f ); // blue as an RGB triple
  glVertex3f( .5f, 0.f, 0.f ); // XYZ coordinates of second point
glEnd();
```

OpenGL always executes commands in the order in which the application sends them. In a client–server implementation (refer to Figure 1-1), these commands can be buffered on the client side and might not execute immediately, but applications can force OpenGL to execute buffered commands by calling **glFlush**() or swapping buffers.

Like modern CPUs, OpenGL rendering uses a pipeline architecture. OpenGL processes pixel and vertex data using four main stages—per-vertex operations, pixel operations, rasterization, and per-fragment operations—and stores the results in the framebuffer or texture memory (see Figure 1-2).

Applications pass two types of data to OpenGL for rendering: vertex data and pixel data. They use vertex data to render 2D and 3D geometric primitives, such as points, lines, and filled primitives. (See Chapter 2, "Drawing Primitives," for more information.) Applications specify pixel data as arrays of pixels and can direct OpenGL to display the pixels directly to the framebuffer or copy them to texture memory for later use as texture maps. Additionally, applications can read pixel data from the framebuffer or copy portions of the framebuffer into texture memory. Chapter 5, "Pixel Rectangles," and Chapter 6, "Texture Mapping," cover this subject in greater depth.

Note   OpenGL has always featured a *fixed-function* pipeline—a fixed set of functionality controlled by the application via OpenGL state. Starting with version 2.0, however, OpenGL allows applications to override certain per-vertex and per-fragment operations with vertex and fragment *shaders*—small programs written using a shading language. *OpenGL® Shading Language* is the definitive resource for writing shaders in OpenGL, and Appendix A, "Other Features," briefly discusses this subject.

OpenGL® Distilled covers only the fixed-function pipeline; it doesn't cover shaders, which are beyond the scope of this book.

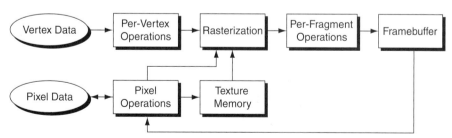

Figure 1-2   The OpenGL pipeline architecture.

1.1.1.1   Per-Vertex Operations

OpenGL performs the following operations on each vertex it receives from your application:

- Transformation—OpenGL transforms each vertex from object-coordinate space to window-coordinate space. This is a gross oversimplification of the transformation process, which is covered in detail in Chapter 3, "Transformation and Viewing."

- Lighting—If the application has enabled lighting, OpenGL calculates a lighting value at each vertex. Lighting is discussed in Chapter 4, "Lighting."

- Clipping—When OpenGL determines that an entire primitive is not visible because it is outside the view volume, OpenGL discards all vertices. If a primitive is partially visible, OpenGL clips the primitive so that only the visible portion is rasterized.

After per-vertex operations, OpenGL rasterizes the primitive and performs per-fragment operations on the result.

1.1.1.2   Pixel Operations

OpenGL performs pixel storage operations on all blocks of pixel data that applications send to and receive from OpenGL. These operations control byte swapping, padding, and offsets into blocks of pixel data to support sending and receiving pixels in a wide variety of formats.

Other pixel operations, such as pixel transfer (mapping, scaling, and biasing) and the optional imaging subset, are outside the scope of this book. See Chapter 8, "Drawing Pixels, Bitmaps, Fonts, and Images," in *OpenGL®* *Programming Guide* for more information.

1.1.1.3   Rasterization

Rasterization converts geometric data into fragments. *Fragments* are position, color, depth, texture coordinate, and other data that OpenGL processes before eventually writing into the framebuffer. Contrast this with pixels, which are the physical locations in framebuffer memory where fragments are stored. Typically, OpenGL associates a fragment with a single pixel location. OpenGL implementations that support multisampling, however, store fragments in subpixel locations.

Rasterization rules are covered in Chapter 3, "Rasterization," of *The OpenGL Graphics System*. Most programmers won't need to know these rules unless they're developing applications that require exact pixelization.

OpenGL specifies rasterization at the subpixel level; it treats point primitives as mathematical points, line primitives as mathematical lines, and filled primitives as areas bounded by mathematical lines. Multisampling aside, the programmer should visualize window-coordinate space as a Cartesian grid in which each grid cell corresponds to a pixel on the screen. With this in mind, OpenGL performs rasterization as follows:

- When rasterizing point primitives, OpenGL produces a fragment if the point lies within the pixel boundary.

- OpenGL rasterizes a line by producing fragments that lie between its endpoints. As a general rule, OpenGL doesn't produce a fragment corresponding to the second, or *triggering,* vertex in a line segment. This ensures that connected line segments with the same slope won't paint the same pixel twice.

- OpenGL produces fragments for filled primitives if the pixel center lies within the mathematical boundary of the primitive. Special rules for pixel centers that lie on the mathematical boundary ensure that two nonoverlapping filled primitives sharing an edge won't paint the same pixel twice.

- When rasterizing blocks of pixel data at the default zoom level, OpenGL produces a fragment for each pixel in the pixel block.

This is a simplification of the rasterization process. *OpenGL® Distilled* doesn't cover features such as smooth points, lines, and polygons; wide points and lines; and pixel zoom, all of which affect the rasterization stage. *OpenGL® Programming Guide* covers these features in detail.

1.1.1.4 Per-Fragment Operations

OpenGL performs significant processing on each fragment to determine its final framebuffer values and whether or not to write it into the framebuffer.

For every fragment produced by rasterization, OpenGL performs the following operations:

- *Pixel ownership test*—This test allows OpenGL to display correctly in the presence of multiple overlapping windows. Fragments corresponding to framebuffer locations that are obscured by an overlapping window can be discarded or saved in a backing store.

- *Scissor test*—If the framebuffer location lies outside an application-defined window-coordinate rectangle, OpenGL discards the fragment.

- *Multisample fragment operations*—OpenGL modifies fragment alpha and coverage values according to multisampling rules.

- *Alpha test*—If the fragment alpha value does not pass application-specified criteria, OpenGL discards it. This is useful for discarding completely or partially transparent fragments.

- *Stencil test*—OpenGL compares the stored stencil value at the framebuffer location and uses the current application state to determine what to do with the fragment and how to modify the stored stencil value. The stencil test has many uses, including nonrectangular clipping, shadows, and constructive solid geometry (CSG).

- *Depth test*—The depth test discards a fragment if a comparison between the fragment depth value and the value stored in the depth buffer fails. The OpenGL depth test is a form of *z*-buffering.

- *Occlusion query*—When an occlusion query is active, OpenGL increments a count for each fragment that passes the depth test. Occlusion queries allow fast visibility testing in complex scenes.

- *Blending*—Blending combines the fragment RGB color and alpha values with the RGB and alpha values stored at the framebuffer location. Applications typically use blending to simulate translucent objects.

- *Dithering*—When the framebuffer has less color precision than the fragment RGB and alpha values, OpenGL dithers the fragment color and alpha, using a repeatable algorithm. This feature is rarely used due to the widespread availability of 24-bit framebuffers.

- *Logical operation*—OpenGL writes the final color value into the framebuffer according to an application-specified logical operation.

As a concise guide to OpenGL, *OpenGL® Distilled* doesn't cover all fragment operations. For information on scissor, multisample, stencil, occlusion query, dithering, and logical operations, see *OpenGL® Programming Guide*.

1.1.2 Syntax

OpenGL is supported by several programming languages, each with its own binding. This book and the C++ example code use the C-binding.

The C-binding syntax rules are as follows.

1.1.2.1 Types

The C-binding prefixes all OpenGL type names with *GL*. The Boolean type is GLboolean, for example, and the double-precision floating-point type is

GLdouble. The GLbyte, GLshort, and GLint types have unsigned analogues: GLubyte, GLushort, and GLuint.

Table 1-1 summarizes some common OpenGL data types.

Table 1-1   OpenGL Data Types

OpenGL Type	Minimum Number of Bits	Command Suffix	Description
GLboolean	1	NA	Boolean
GLbyte	8	**b**	Signed integer
GLubyte	8	**ub**	Unsigned integer
GLshort	16	**s**	Signed integer
GLushort	16	**us**	Unsigned integer
GLsizei	32	NA	Non-negative integer size
GLsizeiptr	Number of bits in a pointer	NA	Pointer to a non-negative integer size
GLint	32	**i**	Signed integer
GLuint	32	**ui**	Unsigned integer
GLfloat	32	**f**	Floating point
GLclampf	32	NA	Floating point clamped to the range [0, 1].
GLenum	32	NA	Enumerant
GLbitfield	32	NA	Packed bits
GLdouble	64	**d**	Floating point
GLvoid*	Number of bits in a pointer	NA	Pointer to any data type; equivalent to "void*" in C/C++.

1.1.2.2 Commands

The C-binding implements OpenGL commands as C-callable functions prefixed with **gl**. To execute the OpenGL Enable command, for example, your application calls the **glEnable**() function. *OpenGL® Distilled* uses the phrases "OpenGL commands" and "OpenGL function calls" synonymously.

In general, OpenGL doesn't overload commands.[2] To support commands with identical functionality but different numbers and types of argument, OpenGL suffixes command names with up to four characters. The first character indicates the number of arguments; the second character or pair of characters indicates the parameter type; and the final character, if present, is **v**, which indicates that the function takes an address as an argument.

For example:

```
// Specify an RGB color value with three floats:
GLfloat red=1.f, green=1.f, blue=1.f;
glColor3f( red, green, blue );

// Specify an RGBA color value with four unsigned bytes:
GLubyte r=255, g=255, b=255, a=255;
glColor4ub( r, g, b, a );

// Specify an RGB value with the address of three shorts:
GLshort white[3] = { 32767, 32767, 32767 };
glColor3sv( white );
```

1.1.2.3 Enumerants

The C-binding defines OpenGL enumerants using the C preprocessor and prefixes enumerant names with *GL_*. To query OpenGL for its version string using the VERSION enumerant, for example, your application calls **glGetString**(GL_VERSION);.

1.1.3 State and Queries

As a state machine, OpenGL won't function without a place to store current state values. OpenGL stores its state in a *GL context*. Platform-specific interfaces allow you to create, destroy, and copy *rendering contexts* that embody the GL context. Chapter 8, "Platform-Specific Interfaces," covers how to manage rendering contexts. This book, however, uses the GLUT

---

2. OpenGL version 1.5 overloads commands that access buffer objects. Chapter 2, "Drawing Primitives," and Chapter 7, "Extensions and Versions," demonstrate this.

library, which implicitly manages rendering contexts. See the section "GLUT" later in this chapter for more information. For now, all you need to know is that OpenGL stores state in a rendering context. As your application issues commands that change OpenGL state, those changes are kept in the current rendering context.

OpenGL provides several commands for setting state. The most common commands programmers encounter are **glEnable**() and **glDisable**().

---

void **glEnable**(GLenum *target*);
void **glDisable**(GLenum *target*);

Use these commands to set the enable state of OpenGL features. *target* specifies which feature to enable or disable. This book describes relevant *target* enumerants as it covers various features throughout the book. For a complete list of valid *target* enumerants, see "glEnable" in *OpenGL® Reference Manual*.

▶ OpenGL version: 1.0 and later.

As an example, call **glEnable**(GL_DEPTH_TEST) to enable the depth test (or *z*-buffering) feature. After your application issues this command, OpenGL renders subsequent primitives using the depth test. Later, if your code calls **glDisable**(GL_DEPTH_TEST) to disable the feature, followed by other primitives, OpenGL won't use the depth test to render them.

Most OpenGL features are disabled by default. In fact, only two features are enabled by default: dithering (GL_DITHER) and multisampling (GL_MULTISAMPLE).

1.1.3.1 Using glIsEnabled

Query whether a feature is currently enabled or disabled with the **glIsEnabled**() command.

GLboolean **glIsEnabled**(GLenum *value*);

Returns whether an OpenGL feature is enabled or disabled. *value* is any OpenGL enumerant that is valid as the *target* parameter in **glEnable**()/**glDisable**(). **glIsEnabled**() returns GL_TRUE if *value* is enabled and GL_FALSE if *value* is disabled.

▶ OpenGL version: 1.0 and later.

Your application enables and disables lighting with **glEnable**
(GL_LIGHTING) and **glDisable**(GL_LIGHTING), respectively. To
query the current state of lighting, call **glIsEnabled**(GL_LIGHTING).

1.1.3.2   Using glGet

Applications might need to query OpenGL state for any number of reasons.
Usually, applications query OpenGL at init time to obtain implementation-
specific values, such as GL_MAX_ATTRIB_STACK_DEPTH or GL_MAX_LIGHTS.
OpenGL lets the application query any value that the application can set.
The application could obtain the current color (set with **glColor3f**()) by
querying GL_CURRENT_COLOR.

OpenGL provides a general mechanism for querying various state values.

---

void **glGetBooleanv**(GLenum *pname*, GLboolean* *param*);
void **glGetDoublev**(GLenum *pname*, GLdouble* *param*);
void **glGetFloatv**(GLenum *pname*, GLfloat* *param*);
void **glGetIntegerv**(GLenum *pname*, GLint* *param*);

This set of routines allows you to query OpenGL state values by type.

pname designates the state item to query, and *param* points to a GLboolean,
GLdouble, GLfloat, or GLint location in memory to hold the state
value.

▶ OpenGL version: 1.0 and later.

Use the function that fits the type of the state item being queried. GL_MAX_
LIGHTS is an integer value, so your code would use **glGetIntegerv**():

```
GLint maxLights;
glGetIntegerv( GL_MAX_LIGHTS, &maxLights );
```

Throughout the book, *OpenGL® Distilled* describes various state items that
your application can query. For a complete list, see "glGet" in *OpenGL® Reference Manual* and Chapter 6, "State and State Requests," in *The OpenGL
Graphics System.*

| Note | Applications should use queries sparingly in performance-sensitive code sections.[3] |

---

3. Occlusion queries can actually boost application performance, however. See Appendix A,
   "Other Features," for more information.

1.1.3.3   The Attribute Stack

OpenGL features stack data structures for saving and restoring state changes. The top of the attribute stacks contain the current OpenGL state. After your application has pushed the stack and made state changes, popping the stack restores OpenGL to its state before the push command.

There is one stack for OpenGL server state, and another for OpenGL client state. Chapter 2, "Drawing Primitives," describes the differences between client and server state.

---

void **glPushAttrib**(GLbitfield *mask*);
void **glPopAttrib**(void);
void **glPushClientAttrib**(GLbitfield *mask*);
void **glPopClientAttrib**(void);

Pushes and pops OpenGL state stacks. *mask* is a bitwise OR of OpenGL-defined bit values representing groups of state to be pushed. The server and client stacks save and restore different state values. `glPushAttrib`()/`glPopAttrib`() affect the server stack, whereas `glPushClientAttrib`()/`glPopClientAttrib`() affect the client stack.

▶ OpenGL version: `glPushAttrib`()/`glPopAttrib`(),1.0 and later;
            `glPushClientAttrib`()/`glPopClientAttrib`(),1.1 and later.

The *mask* parameter allows your application to specify which sets of state values are saved and restored by the push/pop commands. Calling `glPushAttrib`(GL_LIGHTING_BIT) causes the corresponding `glPopAttrib`() to restore only state values that affect OpenGL lighting, such as changes to material and light properties.

To push all stackable server state, call `glPushAttrib`() with a *mask* of GL_ALL_ATTRIB_BITS. Likewise, push all stackable client state by calling `glPushClientAttrib`(GL_CLIENT_ALL_ATTRIB_BITS).

Although the OpenGL specification states that `glPushAttrib`()/`glPushClientAttrib`() act as though they were copying the current OpenGL state onto the new top of stack, most modern OpenGL products implement this with minimal data copying. As a result, pushing all state is not as expensive as you might expect. Although pushing all state is certainly more expensive than pushing some state, developers often find that the reusability benefits of GL_ALL_ATTRIB_BITS and GL_CLIENT_ALL_ATTRIB_BITS outweigh the performance cost. For information on all the valid *mask* values, see "glPushAttrib" and "glPushClientAttrib" in *OpenGL*®

Reference Manual and Chapter 6, "State and State Requests," in *The OpenGL Graphics System.*

The attribute stacks have an implementation-specific depth of at least 16. Your application can query the maximum attribute stack depths by calling **glGetIntegerv**(GL_MAX_ATTRIB_STACK_DEPTH, ...) and **glGetIntegerv**(GL_MAX_CLIENT_ATTRIB_STACK_DEPTH, ...).

1.1.3.4   Using glGetString

OpenGL provides information about the implementation in string form. Use **glGetString**() to query these values.

---

const GLubyte* **glGetString**(GLenum *name*);

Returns OpenGL string-based state values. *name* is the string state item to query.

▶ OpenGL version: 1.0 and later.

glGetString() returns different values depending on the value of *name:*

- GL_VENDOR—Returns the manufacturer of the OpenGL implementation

- GL_VERSION—Returns the OpenGL version

- GL_EXTENSIONS—Returns extensions available in the OpenGL implementation

- GL_RENDERER—Returns vendor-specific renderer information

(GL_SHADING_LANGUAGE_VERSION is another possible value for *name;* for more information, see *OpenGL® Shading Language.*)

Applications typically query GL_VERSION and GL_EXTENSIONS at init time to determine the supported feature set. GL_EXTENSIONS will be covered in more detail in Chapter 7, "Extensions and Versions."

Note   As described in the section "State and Queries" earlier in this chapter, OpenGL stores state in a rendering context. It's common for beginners to call **glGetString**() accidentally to query OpenGL's version and supported extensions at init time without a current rendering context. In this case, behavior is undefined, and **glGetString**() commonly returns NULL. To prevent this, don't call **glGetString**() until after calling **glutCreateWindow**(), which creates a rendering context and makes it current in GLUT.

The version string returned by **glGetString**(GL_VERSION) is either *major_number.minor_number* or *major_number.minor_number.release_number* and is optionally followed by a space and additional vendor-specific information. Applications can parse the version string to obtain the major and minor version numbers with the following code:

```
std::string ver((const char*) glGetString(GL_VERSION));
assert( !ver.empty() );
std::istringstream verStream( ver );

int major, minor;
char dummySep;
verStream >> major >> dummySep >> minor;
```

After parsing the version string, applications can determine what OpenGL feature set to use based on the major and minor version numbers. Because *major_version* 1 and *minor_version* 4 indicate OpenGL version 1.4, for example, you wouldn't be able to use the OpenGL version 1.5 core interface for features like buffer objects and occlusion queries in your application.

As of this printing, the possible version numbers for OpenGL are 1.0, 1.1, 1.2, 1.3, 1.4, 1.5, and 2.0.

1.1.3.5 Querying Identifiers

OpenGL generates identifiers for buffers, display lists, and textures. Your application can query whether an identifier is a valid buffer, display list, or texture by calling **glIsBuffer**(), **glIsList**(), and **glIsTexture**(), respectively. These functions are covered in later chapters.

1.1.3.6 Other Query Functions

Other OpenGL query functions allow the application to obtain lighting and texture mapping-specific values. Chapter 4, "Lighting," and Chapter 6, "Texture Mapping," discuss setting lighting and texture mapping state parameters, but *OpenGL® Distilled* doesn't cover querying these values. See "glGetLight," "glGetMaterial," "glGetTexEnv," "glGetTexGen," "glGetTexImage," and "glGetTexParameter" in *OpenGL® Reference Manual*.

1.1.3.7 Errors

There are several ways for your application to generate errors in OpenGL. If your application generates an error that OpenGL detects, you can query the error with **glGetError**().

GLenum **glGetError**(void);

Returns the current error state. Error values returned by **glGetError**()
are summarized in Table 1-2. If OpenGL hasn't recorded an error,
glGetError() will return GL_NO_ERROR.

▶ OpenGL version: 1.0 and later.

When OpenGL detects an error, it records an error code and continues processing commands. Your application can retrieve the recorded error code
by calling **glGetError**(). It returns the error code as a GLenum.

Table 1-2 summarizes OpenGL errors.

For example, if your application calls

```
glEnable( GL_MAX_LIGHTS );
```

OpenGL records the error GL_INVALID_ENUM, because GL_MAX_LIGHTS is
a valid enumerant for **glGetIntegerv**(), not for **glEnable**().

OpenGL saves error codes until they are retrieved with **glGetError**(). If
your application retrieves an error from **glGetError**(), any of several preceding OpenGL commands could have generated it.

Table 1-2   OpenGL Error Codes Returned by **glGetError**()[a]

GLenum Error Code	Description
GL_INVALID_ENUM	An invalid enumerant was passed to an OpenGL command.
GL_INVALID_OPERATION	An OpenGL command was issued that was invalid or inappropriate for the current state.
GL_INVALID_VALUE	A value was passed to OpenGL that was outside the allowed range.
GL_OUT_OF_MEMORY	OpenGL was unable to allocate enough memory to process a command.
GL_STACK_OVERFLOW	A command caused an OpenGL stack to overflow.
GL_STACK_UNDERFLOW	A command caused an OpenGL stack to underflow.

a. In addition to the errors listed, OpenGL might return the error GL_TABLE_TOO_LARGE.
   See *The OpenGL Graphics System* for more information.

When an OpenGL command generates an error, OpenGL behavior is usually well defined: The offending call acts as a no-op (the function has no effect on OpenGL state or the framebuffer), and if it returns a value, it returns zero. If the error GL_OUT_OF_MEMORY occurs, however, OpenGL is left in an undefined state.[4]

Typical Usage

Treat OpenGL errors as bugs in your application that you need to fix. Production code shouldn't generate OpenGL errors.

Applications typically call **glGetError**() after any OpenGL initialization code and at the end of each rendered frame in an animation. Programmers typically only call **glGetError**() in nonproduction code to avoid negatively affecting application performance. This can be done with an assert() call:

```
assert( glGetError() == GL_NO_ERROR );
```

Programmers typically use CPP macros to check OpenGL errors and take some action, such as display an error dialog box or throw an exception, with the macro defined as a no-op in production code. The example code that comes with this book demonstrates this strategy with the OGLDIF_ CHECK_ERROR CPP macro. Appendix D, "Troubleshooting and Debugging," shows the declaration of this macro and also provides debugging tips for code that generates OpenGL errors.

1.2   GLUT

The "State and Queries" section earlier in this chapter mentions that platform-specific window libraries are responsible for creating OpenGL rendering contexts to encapsulate state. Sadly, this impedes platform-independent code.

The OpenGL Utility Toolkit (GLUT) is a platform-independent library for managing windows, input, and rendering contexts. It isn't a complete replacement for platform-specific code, but it does implement a subset of functionality that is useful for examples and demos, as well as some simple applications.

---

4. If **glEndList**() generates GL_OUT_OF_MEMORY, OpenGL state is defined. See "glEndList" in the *OpenGL Reference Manual* for details.

GLUT function names have the form **glut***(). The GLUT function for swapping buffers, for example, is **glutSwapBuffers**().The current GLUT version is 3.7.

GLUT allows *OpenGL® Distilled* to focus on OpenGL rather than the details of platform-specific window and rendering context creation and management. Chapter 8, "Platform-Specific Interfaces," covers these details after you've become more comfortable with OpenGL concepts.

The definitive guide to GLUT (and also GLX) is *OpenGL Programming for the X Window System* (Kilgard 1996). GLUT information is also available from the OpenGL Web site.

```
http://www.opengl.org/resources/libraries/index.html
```

The section "A Simple Example" later in this chapter describes the use of some basic GLUT functions.

1.3   GLU

GLU is the OpenGL Utility Library. It's an ARB-approved library that is available with most OpenGL implementations. It provides support for higher-order operations not directly available in OpenGL, such as control over camera position and orientation, higher-order curves and surfaces, multipolygonal primitives such as cylinders and spheres, projection to and from window-coordinate space, and polygon tessellation.

GLU function names have the form **glu***(). The function to create a view transform, for example, is called **gluLookAt**(). The current version of GLU is 1.3.

OpenGL® Distilled covers only a few common GLU routines. For complete information on GLU, download the GLU specification, *The OpenGL Graphics System Utility Library,* from the OpenGL Web site, www.opengl.org/resources/libraries/index.html. Also, *OpenGL® Reference Manual* is a good reference for GLU.

1.4   Development Environment

To develop OpenGL software, you need a development environment with the necessary libraries and header files:

- The OpenGL header file and library

- The GLU header file and library

- The GLUT header file and library or platform-specific header files and libraries for your specific window system

How you obtain these components varies according to your chosen development platform. *OpenGL® Distilled* includes information on three popular development platforms: Apple Mac OS X, Linux, and Microsoft Windows.

To build the example source code, you'll also need to obtain libTIFF and GNU Make. See the book's Web site for information on obtaining these components for your specific development platform.

If you purchase from a reputable computer manufacturer a new computer with a graphics card that supports OpenGL, chances are that the system is already configured to run OpenGL with hardware acceleration. Graphics card manufacturers, however, frequently upgrade their device drivers to add features, fix issues, and enhance performance. To upgrade your graphics card's device driver, download the new version from the computer manufacturer's or graphics card manufacturer's Web site, and follow the installation instructions.

1.4.1 Apple Mac OS X

The Apple Developer Connection contains links to an extensive amount of OpenGL information, including documentation devoted to developing OpenGL applications in Mac OS X and tools for debugging and optimizing your Mac OS X OpenGL applications.

The *Macintosh OpenGL Programming Guide,* available from the following Web site, is an excellent source of information on developing OpenGL applications on Apple platforms:

```
http://developer.apple.com/graphicsimaging/opengl
```

OpenGL header and library files are located in the OpenGL framework directory on your Mac OS X system:

```
/System/Library/Frameworks/OpenGL.framework
```

AGL is one of Apple's platform-specific OpenGL interfaces and is discussed in Chapter 8, "Platform-Specific Interfaces." To build code that uses AGL, use the headers and libraries in the AGL framework directory:

```
/System/Library/Framework/AGL.framework
```

Most of the examples use the platform-independent GLUT interface, but this is also a supported interface on Apple platforms.

```
/System/Library/Framework/GLUT.framework
```

You can develop OpenGL applications on a Macintosh by using either the Xcode IDE or a makefile system that uses the GNU compilers directly. The example source code uses a makefile system and should compile from a shell prompt without modification. If you want to use Xcode, you'll have to configure it to use the appropriate frameworks. There are several OpenGL example programs that use Xcode on your Apple Mac OS X system.

```
/Developer/Examples/OpenGL/GLUT
```

Use these examples as a guide if you wish to develop using Xcode.

Visit the *OpenGL® Distilled* Web site to download the example code and view updated information on building it in Apple Mac OS X.

1.4.2   Linux

Example source code for *OpenGL® Distilled* was developed on a Red Hat Linux Enterprise WS system, but developing OpenGL in other Linux and many Unix systems should be similar.

Full Linux distributions typically include a development environment with OpenGL, GLU, GLUT or freeglut, and GLX headers and libraries. If your Linux system is missing these components, you should obtain Mesa. Mesa is a 3D API with an interface that is very similar to OpenGL. Many Linux distributions use Mesa for hardware-accelerated OpenGL. Mesa includes the OpenGL, GLU, GLUT, and GLX headers and libraries. For more information and to download the Mesa source, visit the Mesa Web site:

```
http://www.mesa3d.org
```

If you purchased your Linux system from a reputable computer manufacturer, it's probably configured for full hardware acceleration. Verify this with the `glxinfo` program. If you are installing a Linux system from scratch and your graphics card doesn't have an open-source driver, you'll need to visit your graphics card manufacturer's Web site to obtain a Linux driver. Otherwise, OpenGL rendering will be unaccelerated.

If your OpenGL header files are installed in the typical location (`/usr/include/GL`), you don't need a `-I` option to specify their location; the compiler should find them automatically. Typical link options for an OpenGL program include: `-L/usr/X11R6/lib -lglut -lglu -lgl`.

1.4.3 Microsoft Windows

The OpenGL development environment for Microsoft Windows has remained stable since Windows 98.[5] The following information is valid for Windows 98, Windows ME, Windows 2000, Windows XP, and Windows NT version 3.5 and later.

Microsoft Visual Studio .NET includes OpenGL version 1.1 headers and export stub library files. When linking your application, you'll need to specify `opengl32.lib` as an input library. Microsoft distributes the runtime dynamic link library `opengl32.dll` with the operating system.

In addition to the version 1.1 header file, you need `glext.h` to access post-1.1 features and extensions. Obtain the latest version of `glext.h` from the OpenGL Extension Registry Web site:

```
http://oss.sgi.com/projects/ogl-sample/ABI/glxext.h
```

Microsoft compilers include the GLU 1.2 header and export stub library files. Your application needs to link with `glu32.lib`. Microsoft Windows includes the runtime GLU dynamic link library as part of the operating system.

Download GLUT from the OpenGL Web site, `http://www.opengl.org`. Because there are many download options, be sure to download the precompiled binaries for Microsoft Windows, not the source code or binaries for another platform.

After downloading GLUT, you need to install it manually. You should have the following files:

- `glut.h`, the GLUT header file
- `glut32.lib`, the export stub library
- `glut32.dll`, the runtime dynamic link library

Move `glut.h` into the `GL` subdirectory of the default include directory for your compiler. This varies from compiler to compiler but will always end in `...\include\GL`. The files `gl.h` and `glu.h` should already be in this directory.

---

5. Microsoft has announced plans to provide an updated OpenGL in future operating systems.

Move `glut32.lib` into the default `lib` directory for your compiler.

Finally, move `glut32.dll` into the `System32` directory for your operating system (for example, `C:\Windows\System32`) or any directory within your DLL search path.

1.5   A Simple Example

The OpenGL code shown in Listing 1-1, although very simple, should serve as a good introduction. This program, called SimpleExample, is available from the book's Web site. It draws a white triangle on a black background, as shown in Figure 1-3.

Listing 1-1   SimpleExample program

```
#include <GL/glut.h>
#include <GL/glu.h>
#include <GL/gl.h>
#include <string>
#include <sstream>
#include <assert.h>

// Define an ID for the "Quit" menu item.
static const int QUIT_VALUE( 99 );

// Global variable to hold display list ID
GLuint listID;


//
// GLUT display callback. Called by GLUT when the window
// needs redrawing.
static void display()
{
    glClear( GL_COLOR_BUFFER_BIT );

    // Modeling transform, move geometry 4 units back in Z.
    glLoadIdentity();
    glTranslatef( 0.f, 0.f, -4.f );

    // Draw the geometry
    glCallList( listID );

    // Swap buffers (display the rendered image).
    glutSwapBuffers();

    assert( glGetError() == GL_NO_ERROR );
}
```

```
//
// GLUT resize callback, called when window size changes.
static void reshape( int w, int h )
{
    // Update the viewport to draw to the full window
    glViewport( 0, 0, w, h );

    // Update the projection matrix / aspect ratio
    glMatrixMode( GL_PROJECTION );
    glLoadIdentity();
    gluPerspective( 50., (double)w/(double)h, 1., 10. );

    // Leave us in model-view mode for our display routine
    glMatrixMode( GL_MODELVIEW );

    assert( glGetError() == GL_NO_ERROR );
}


//
// GLUT menu callback, called when user selects a menu item.
static void mainMenuCB( int value )
{
    if (value == QUIT_VALUE)
        exit( 0 );
}


static void init()
{
    // Dither is on by default but not needed, disable it.
    glDisable( GL_DITHER );

    // Determine whether or not vertex arrays are available.
    // In other words, check for OpenGL v1.1...
    std::string ver((const char*) glGetString( GL_VERSION ));
    assert( !ver.empty() );
    std::istringstream verStream( ver );

    int major, minor;
    char dummySep;
    verStream >> major >> dummySep >> minor;
    const bool useVertexArrays = ( (major >= 1) && (minor >= 1) );

    const GLfloat data[] = {
        -1.f, -1.f, 0.f,
        1.f, -1.f, 0.f,
        0.f, 1.f, 0.f };

    if (useVertexArrays)
    {
        // Set up for using vertex arrays.
        glEnableClientState( GL_VERTEX_ARRAY );
```

```
        glVertexPointer( 3, GL_FLOAT, 0, data );
    }

    // Create a new display list.
    listID = glGenLists( 1 );
    glNewList( listID, GL_COMPILE );

    if (useVertexArrays)
        // Vertex arrays are available in OpenGL 1.1, use them.
        glDrawArrays( GL_TRIANGLES, 0, 3 );

    else
    {
        // Use OpenGL 1.0 Begin/End interface.
        glBegin( GL_TRIANGLES );
        glVertex3fv( &data[0] );
        glVertex3fv( &data[3] );
        glVertex3fv( &data[6] );
        glEnd();
    }

    glEndList();

    assert( glGetError() == GL_NO_ERROR );

    // Register our display and resize callbacks with GLUT.
    glutDisplayFunc( display );
    glutReshapeFunc( reshape );

    // Create a right-mouse menu to allow users to exit.
    int mainMenu = glutCreateMenu( mainMenuCB );
    glutAddMenuEntry( "Quit", QUIT_VALUE );
    glutAttachMenu( GLUT_RIGHT_BUTTON );
}

int main( int argc, char** argv )
{
    glutInit( &argc, argv );

    // Create a single GLUT window, 300x300 pixels, RGB mode,
    // and double-buffered. Call it "Simple Example".
    glutInitDisplayMode( GLUT_RGB | GLUT_DOUBLE );
    glutInitWindowSize( 300, 300 );
    glutCreateWindow( "Simple Example" );

    init();

    // Loop for events.
    glutMainLoop();

    return 0;
}
```

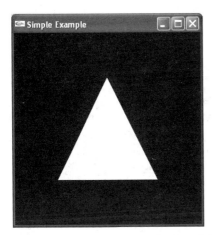

Figure 1-3   Output from the SimpleExample program.

The first three header files—<GL/glut.h>, <GL/glu.h>, and <GL/gl.h>—contain definitions for GLUT, GLU, and OpenGL, respectively. They're followed by some standard C/C++ header files.

This code uses the C preprocessor to define a value that identifies the Quit menu option. When the user opens the menu and selects the Quit option, GLUT passes this identifier to the menu callback function.

Modern programming style avoids use of global variables, but they are still useful and acceptable for small demos such as this. In this case, the code defines an OpenGL display list identifier as a global. The application initializes it in the init() function and references it in the display() callback. OpenGL display lists can store many types of OpenGL commands, but this list holds only drawing commands. For more information on display lists, see Chapter 2, "Drawing Primitives."

GLUT calls the display() callback function when necessary to refresh the window. In this example, this function includes OpenGL calls to clear the window, load a transformation matrix, call the display list that contains the commands to draw the triangle, and check for errors. It also contains a GLUT call to swap buffers.

The next function, reshape(), also a GLUT callback, is executed when the user resizes the window. The function issues OpenGL commands to draw to the full window and maintain the correct aspect ratio and projection. It, too, checks for errors.

GLUT calls the `mainMenuCB()` function when the user selects an item from the pop-up menu. This function checks only to see whether the item selected is the Quit item, and if so, it causes the application to exit.

The `init()` function configures OpenGL and creates the display list.

There are many ways to draw primitives in OpenGL. To keep this example simple, it demonstrates only two methods: the **glBegin**()/**glEnd**() method and vertex arrays. Because the vertex arrays feature isn't available in OpenGL version 1.0, the code queries OpenGL for its version. If the version is 1.1 or later, the code uses a vertex array rendering command to draw the triangle; otherwise, it uses **glBegin**()/**glEnd**(). It's common for OpenGL applications to choose which features to use based on the OpenGL version.

Regardless of the method, the application stores the drawing commands in a display list. Note that display lists store only OpenGL commands. The conditional to check the version gets executed only when the display list is constructed, to determine its contents. When the `display()` function executes (or calls) the list, only the stored OpenGL commands are executed—either the vertex array call or the **glBegin**()/**glEnd**() calls, but not the conditional. Display lists are an effective way to both reduce the number of function calls, as well as eliminate conditionals that are constant at runtime.

Finally, the `init()` function registers the callback functions and creates the GLUT pop-up menu.

The `main()` routine performs GLUT initialization to create a window and rendering context. After creating the window, `main()` calls `init()` to perform further initialization. Finally, it calls **glutMainLoop**(), which waits for events and messages, and calls back to the application when necessary.

1.6 History of OpenGL

To understand how and why OpenGL was developed, it's important to consider the graphics landscape before OpenGL.

1.6.1 Before 1992

In 1980, the SIGGRAPH Core group reorganized to develop a new ANSI standard graphics API, called PHIGS (Programmer's Hierarchical Interactive Graphics System). By the late 1980s, PHIGS/PHIGS+ was supported on most graphics terminals and workstations. Implementations varied widely from platform to platform, however, impeding independent software vendor (ISV) production of platform-independent applications.

Silicon Graphics, Inc.,[6] began developing its proprietary API, Iris GL, in 1982. Throughout the development of PHIGS in the 1980s, SGI's Iris GL grew in popularity. SGI clearly dominated the interactive 3D computer graphics market for both developers and end users. This was in part because developers felt that Iris GL was more flexible and intuitive than other APIs of the era. By the late 1980s, SGI began licensing Iris GL to companies such as IBM and Nth Portable Graphics. A lack of uniform implementations and uniform performance was an issue for ISVs, however.

Yet another problem for ISVs was the lack of uniformity in windowing systems. Many workstation manufacturers had their own proprietary windowing system, such as NeWS or OpenWindows. But by 1985, the industry had arrived at a common windowing system: the X Window System (Scheifler 1986). X Windows promised to alleviate some of the portability issues for ISVs by making networks transparent to the application. Any computer supporting the X Windows protocol could display output from any X Windows application.

In 1987, DEC and Sun jointly proposed an extension to X Windows called X3D,[7] more commonly known as PEX,[8] to enable network-transparent interactive 3D graphics applications. The extension was initially intended to support networked PHIGS applications. Later, however, it evolved into the PEXlib API, a thin layer over the X3D protocol. Full PEX implementations were available by the late 1980s (Rost 1989).

By the late 1980s, ISVs with Iris GL-based applications demanded that SGI turn Iris GL into a uniform open standard. Allen Akin, engineering manager of SGI's OpenGL group, recalls the impetus for developing OpenGL: "The main reason was that software vendors said they had to expand their hardware base in order to survive, so they gave SGI the choice of opening up [Iris] GL in some form, or they'd drop support for SGI hardware and go for the higher-volume workstations. PEXlib was one of several alternative APIs that would have competed for those software vendors if OpenGL hadn't been created."[9]

---

6. Popularly referred to as "SGI" for years, Silicon Graphics, Inc., officially changed its corporate identity to SGI in 1999.

7. Not to be confused with Web3D's VRML successor with the same name.

8. PEX is an acronym for the PHIGS Extension to X Windows, but the actual extension name is X3D.

9. comp.graphics.api.opengl Usenet newsgroup post, March 6, 2001.

SGI started the OpenGL project in 1989. In 1991, it formed the OpenGL ARB, which is composed of representatives from several companies, to oversee its design.

The ARB released the OpenGL version 1.0 specification in June 1992. Commercial implementations from DEC, IBM, and SGI soon followed. OpenGL was designed based on the needs of SGI's large ISV base, so version 1.0 came out with a feature set capable of supporting a wide variety of 3D graphics applications.

1.6.2   OpenGL Compared with Iris GL

SGI used Iris GL as a base for OpenGL development, and there are many similarities between them. Consider this snippet of Iris GL code for drawing a five-sided polygon:

```
bgnpolygon();
   c3s( red ); v3f( v0 );
   c3s( green ); v3f( v1 );
   c3s( blue ); v3f( v2 );
   c3s( black ); v3f( v3 );
   c3s( white ); v3f( v4 );
endpolygon();
```

This code encloses commands for colors and vertices with a `bgnpolygon()`/ `endpolygon()` pair. The code specifies vertices by passing their address to `v3f()` (the function name implies a vertex composed of three floats) and specifies the color of each vertex with `c3s()` (a color composed of three shorts).

Note the similarities between this and its OpenGL version 1.0 equivalent:

```
glBegin( GL_POLYGON );
   glColor3sv( red ); glVertex3fv( v0 );
   glColor3sv( green ); glVertex3fv( v1 );
   glColor3sv( blue ); glVertex3fv( v2 );
   glColor3sv( black ); glVertex3fv( v3 );
   glColor3sv( white ); glVertex3fv( v4 );
glEnd();
```

1.6.3   OpenGL Compared with PEX

SGI's technical white paper, *Analysis of PEX 5.1 and OpenGL 1.0* (Akin 1992), examined the differences between OpenGL and PEX. Some feature differences were significant. For example, PEX didn't include support for features such as texture mapping or alpha blending when OpenGL version 1.0 was released.

OpenGL also departed from PEX at a philosophical level:

- OpenGL specifies an API and also includes a wire protocol for networked operation (GLX). PEX, on the other hand, specifies only a wire protocol, originally intended to support the PHIGS API.

- OpenGL version 1.0 requires all implementations to support all functionality, whereas the PEX subset paradigm allowed implementations to support only one of three mutually exclusive operational modes. PEX subsets impeded portable application development. Many PEX features are optional, further impeding portability.

- PEX was designed solely for an X Windows environment. OpenGL is separate from the windowing system, allowing OpenGL implementations in X Windows, Microsoft Windows, Apple Mac OS X, and even nonwindowed environments.

By the late 1990s, most ISVs had ported their PHIGS- and PEXlib-based applications to OpenGL. Today, there is little, if any, PHIGS or PEX development.

1.6.4 Continued Evolution of OpenGL

The OpenGL extension mechanism allows vendors and the ARB to add new features in response to advances in graphics technology (see Chapter 7, "Extensions and Versions"). Texture mapping made extensive use of the extension mechanism, as it was an active area of research and development in the early 1990s. Many OpenGL implementations soon supported extensions for texture objects, copying to textures and subtextures, querying for texture hardware support, and additional texture formats. In January 1996, the ARB released OpenGL version 1.1, formalizing many of these extensions.

Throughout the 1990s, low-cost commercial desktop PCs increased in power and correspondingly consumed more of the traditional workstation market share. Advances in technology also drove the development of single-chip, low-cost graphics hardware, first accelerating only OpenGL fragment operations but later accelerating the full OpenGL pipeline (Geist 1998, McCormack 1998).

By the late 1990s, advances in graphics hardware technology resulted in an increasing number of extensions to OpenGL, making OpenGL application development more complex. To address this issue, the ARB committed to a more aggressive release schedule for new OpenGL versions. OpenGL version 1.2 and the minor release of OpenGL version 1.2.1 both occurred in 1998, with many new texture mapping enhancements. Since the August 2001 release of OpenGL version 1.3, the ARB has released new versions annually, with version 2.0 released in 2004.

In 2002, the release of OpenGL ES (OpenGL for embedded systems) made OpenGL available on handheld devices, appliances, and other platforms with limited memory or computing power. It supports a subset of OpenGL functionality and also supports fixed-point data types.

1.7   More Information

Chapter 1, "Introduction to OpenGL," of *OpenGL® Programming Guide* complements this chapter with additional high-level OpenGL information. The OpenGL Web site, `http://www.opengl.org`, contains both technical and nontechnical overviews of OpenGL. Both *Computer Graphics: Principles and Practice* and *3D Computer Graphics* contain general 3D graphics information that explains topics mentioned in this chapter, such as lighting, rasterization, texture mapping, and depth buffering.

For history buffs, *OpenGL Programming for the X Window System* (Kilgard 1996) contains a well-written history of OpenGL, as well as additional OpenGL overview information. This book is also the definitive programming guide and reference for GLUT.

See the book's Web site for source code that appears in the section "A Simple Example" earlier in this chapter, as well as other complete example programs. Also, the OpenGL Web site has several coding resources.

1.8   References

(Akin 1992) Akin, Allen. "Analysis of PEX 5.1 and OpenGL 1.0." SGI technical white paper, August 1992.

(Carson 1997) Carson, George S. "Standards Pipeline: The OpenGL Specification." *ACM SIGGRAPH Computer Graphics* 31:2 (May 1997).

(Cojot 1996) Cojot, Vincent S. "OpenGL Programming on Linux." *Linux Journal* (November 1996).

(Geist 1998) Geist, Robert and James Westall. "Bringing the High End to the Low End: High Performance Device Drivers of the Linux PC." ACM Southeast Regional Conference Proceedings, April 1998.

(Kilgard 1996) Kilgard, Mark J. *OpenGL Programming for the X Window System.* Reading, MA: Addison-Wesley, 1996.

(Kilgard 1997) Kilgard, Mark J. "Realizing OpenGL: Two Implementations of One Architecture." Proceedings of the ACM SIGGRAPH/EUROGRAPHICS Workshop on Graphics Hardware, August 1997.

(Lichtenbelt 1997) Lichtenbelt, Barthold. "Design of a High Performance Volume Visualization System." Proceedings of the ACM SIGGRAPH/ EUROGRAPHICS Workshop on Graphics Hardware, August 1997.

(McCormack 1998) McCormack, Joel, et al. "Neon: A Single-Chip 3D Workstation Graphics Accelerator." Proceedings of the ACM SIGGRAPH/ EUROGRAPHICS Workshop on Graphics Hardware, August 1998.

(Rost 1989) Rost, Randi J., Jeffrey D. Friedberg, and Peter L. Nishimoto. "PEX: A Network-Transparent 3D Graphics System." *IEEE Computer Graphics and Applications* (1989).

(Scheifler 1986) Scheifler, Robert W., and Jim Gettys. "The X Window System." *ACM Transactions on Graphics* (April 1986).

Chapter 2

Drawing Primitives

Computer-generated animation in film and television, as well as state-of-the-art video games, features realistic water, fire, and other natural effects. Many people new to computer graphics are astounded to learn that these realistic and complex models are simple triangles and pixels as far as computer graphics hardware is concerned.

OpenGL is often referred to as a low-level API because of its minimal support for higher-order primitives, data structures such as scene graphs, or support for loading 2D image files or 3D model files. Instead, OpenGL focuses on rendering low-level primitives efficiently and with a variety of basic, yet flexible, rendering features. As a result of this "tools not rules" approach, OpenGL is the preferred low-level API for a variety of middleware and applications that feature higher-order primitives, scene graph data structures, and file loaders.

In this chapter, *OpenGL® Distilled* covers the OpenGL primitive types and how to control their appearance with several basic rendering features.

What You'll Learn

This chapter covers the following aspects of primitive rendering:

- Primitive types—The ten primitive types for rendering point, line, and polygonal primitives.

- Buffer objects and vertex arrays—Generally recognized as the most efficient method for specifying geometry.

- Rendering details—OpenGL commands for hidden surface removal, transparency, and displaying co-planar primitives.

- Performance issues—Some tips to help your application run as efficiently as possible on most OpenGL implementations.

What You Won't Learn

Because this book presents only OpenGL's most essential commands, several aspects of primitive rendering aren't covered in this chapter:

- The **glBegin()**/**glEnd()** paradigm—*OpenGL® Distilled* covers the **glBegin()**/**glEnd()** paradigm for illustrative purposes only. Most OpenGL implementations avoid using **glBegin()**/**glEnd()** to specify geometry due to its inherent performance issues.

- Vertex data—This chapter covers normal and texture-coordinate data and omits other vertex data, such as vertex attributes (used in vertex shaders), edge flags, and fog coordinates.

- Mapping and unmapping buffer objects—This chapter doesn't discuss the interface for dynamically altering portions of buffer object data.

- Evaluators—OpenGL allows programmers to render implicit curves and surfaces from control points.

- Rectangles—Because you can specify vertices to render any desired shape, this shorthand interface for drawing rectangles in the $z=0$ plane is rarely used.

- Full vertex array functionality—This book presents a subset of the vertex array interface and doesn't cover interleaved arrays; vertex array data types other than GL_FLOAT and GL_DOUBLE; and some vertex array rendering commands, such as **glDrawArrays()**.

- This book doesn't cover all features that affect the final color and appearance of rendered geometry, such as fog, stencil, vertex and fragment shaders, and other related features.

Though useful in many rendering circumstances, these features aren't essential for OpenGL programming. If your application requires this functionality, see *OpenGL® Programming Guide, OpenGL® Reference Manual,* and *OpenGL® Shading Language.*

2.1 OpenGL Primitives

In OpenGL, applications render primitives by specifying a primitive type and a sequence of vertices with associated data. The primitive type determines how OpenGL interprets and renders the sequence of vertices.

2.1.1 Primitive Types

OpenGL provides ten different primitive types for drawing points, lines, and polygons, as shown in Figure 2-1.

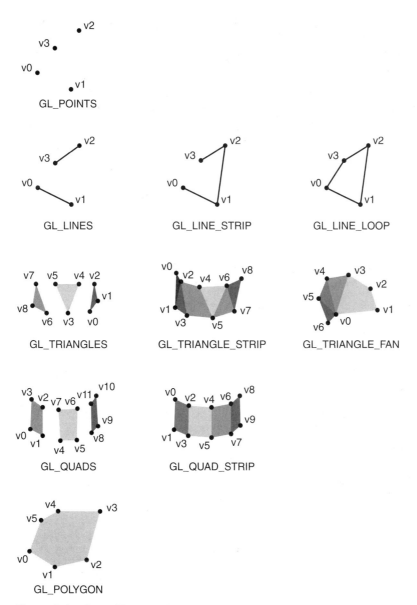

Figure 2-1 OpenGL primitive types.

OpenGL interprets the vertices and renders each primitive using the following rules:

- GL_POINTS—Use this primitive type to render mathematical points. OpenGL renders a point for each vertex specified.

- GL_LINES—Use this primitive to draw unconnected line segments. OpenGL draws a line segment for each group of two vertices. If the application specifies n vertices, OpenGL renders $n/2$ line segments. If n is odd, OpenGL ignores the final vertex.

- GL_LINE_STRIP—Use this primitive to draw a sequence of connected line segments. OpenGL renders a line segment between the first and second vertices, between the second and third, between the third and fourth, and so on. If the application specifies n vertices, OpenGL renders $n-1$ line segments.

- GL_LINE_LOOP—Use this primitive to close a line strip. OpenGL renders this primitive like a GL_LINE_STRIP with the addition of a closing line segment between the final and first vertices.

- GL_TRIANGLES—Use this primitive to draw individual triangles. OpenGL renders a triangle for each group of three vertices. If your application specifies n vertices, OpenGL renders $n/3$ triangles. If n isn't a multiple of 3, OpenGL ignores the excess vertices.

- GL_TRIANGLE_STRIP—Use this primitive to draw a sequence of triangles that share edges. OpenGL renders a triangle using the first, second, and third vertices, and then another using the second, third, and fourth vertices, and so on. If the application specifies n vertices, OpenGL renders $n-2$ connected triangles. If n is less than 3, OpenGL renders nothing.

- GL_TRIANGLE_FAN—Use this primitive to draw a fan of triangles that share edges and also share a vertex. Each triangle shares the first vertex specified. If the application specifies a sequence of vertices v, OpenGL renders a triangle using v_0, v_1, and v_2; another triangle using v_0, v_2, and v_3; another triangle using v_0, v_3, and v_4; and so on. If the application specifies n vertices, OpenGL renders $n-2$ connected triangles. If n is less than 3, OpenGL renders nothing.

- GL_QUADS—Use this primitive to draw individual convex quadrilaterals. OpenGL renders a quadrilateral for each group of four vertices. If the application specifies n vertices, OpenGL renders $n/4$ quadrilaterals. If n isn't a multiple of 4, OpenGL ignores the excess vertices.

- GL_QUAD_STRIP—Use this primitive to draw a sequence of quadrilaterals that share edges. If the application specifies a sequence of vertices v, OpenGL renders a quadrilateral using v_0, v_1, v_3, and v_2; another quadrilateral using v_2, v_3, v_5, and v_4; and so on. If the application specifies n vertices, OpenGL renders $(n-2)/2$ quadrilaterals. If n is less than 4, OpenGL renders nothing.

- GL_POLYGON—Use GL_POLYGON to draw a single filled convex n-gon primitive. OpenGL renders an n-sided polygon, where n is the number of vertices specified by the application. If n is less than 3, OpenGL renders nothing.

For GL_QUADS, GL_QUAD_STRIP, and GL_POLYGON, all primitives must be both planar and convex. Otherwise, OpenGL behavior is undefined. The GLU library supports polygon tessellation, which allows applications to render filled primitives that are nonconvex or self-intersecting, or that contain holes. See the "gluTess" set of functions in *OpenGL® Reference Manual* for more information.

2.1.2   Vertex Sharing

Note that GL_LINE_STRIP, GL_LINE_LOOP, GL_TRIANGLE_STRIP, GL_TRIANGLE_FAN, and GL_QUAD_STRIP all share vertices among their component line segments, triangles, and quadrilaterals. In general, you should use these primitives when possible and practical to reduce redundant per-vertex computation.

You could render a two-quadrilateral GL_QUAD_STRIP primitive by using GL_QUADS, for example. Rendered as a GL_QUAD_STRIP, your application would need to send only six unique vertices. The GL_QUADS version of this primitive, however, would require eight vertices, two of which are redundant. Passing identical vertices to OpenGL increases the number of per-vertex operations and could create a performance bottleneck in the rendering pipeline.

2.2   Specifying Vertex Data

OpenGL allows the application to specify primitives in several ways. *OpenGL® Distilled* briefly covers the **glBegin**()/**glEnd**() paradigm for illustrative purposes only. You should avoid using **glBegin**()/**glEnd**() because of its inherent call overhead, which inhibits application performance. Instead, use buffer objects and vertex arrays, presented later in this chapter. Vertex arrays dramatically reduce function call overhead compared with **glBegin**()/**glEnd**() and also allow vertex sharing. Using buffer objects causes OpenGL to store vertex data in high-performance server memory, which allows your application to avoid expensive data copies at render time.

2.2.1   Drawing Primitives Using glBegin()/glEnd()

OpenGL version 1.0 features a flexible interface for primitive rendering called the **glBegin**()/**glEnd**() paradigm. Contemporary OpenGL features more efficient rendering mechanisms, which are the focus of this chapter. Because OpenGL is backward compatible with older versions, however, many applications still use the **glBegin**()/**glEnd**() paradigm in spite of its inherent performance issues. This chapter covers **glBegin**()/**glEnd**() briefly because it illustrates the OpenGL concept of per-vertex state.

Applications render primitives by surrounding vertices with a pair of functions, **glBegin**() and **glEnd**(). Applications specify the primitive type by passing it as a parameter to **glBegin**().

---

void **glBegin**(GLenum *mode*);
void **glEnd**(void);

---

glBegin() and **glEnd**() surround commands that specify vertices and vertex data. *mode* specifies the primitive type to draw and must be one of GL_POINTS, GL_LINES, GL_LINE_STRIP, GL_LINE_LOOP, GL_TRIANGLES, GL_TRIANGLE_STRIP, GL_TRIANGLE_FAN, GL_QUADS, GL_QUAD_STRIP, or GL_POLYGON.

▶ OpenGL version: 1.0 and later.

Between **glBegin**() and **glEnd**(), applications specify vertices and vertex states such as the current primary color, current normal and material properties (for lighting), and current texture coordinates (for texture mapping).[1] Applications specify colors, normals, material properties, texture coordinates, and vertices each with individual function calls. *OpenGL® Distilled* doesn't cover these function calls in detail, but their names are self-explanatory, as you'll see in the following examples.

---

1. OpenGL allows the application to specify a large amount of per-vertex states not covered in this book, such as color indices, fog coordinates, edge flags, and vertex attributes. See *OpenGL® Programming Guide* for more information.

The **glBegin**()/**glEnd**() paradigm serves as an excellent illustration of OpenGL per-vertex state. The following code, for example, demonstrates how to draw a red triangle:

```
glBegin( GL_TRIANGLES );
  glColor3f( 1.f, 0.f, 0.f ); // Sets current primary color to red
  glVertex3f( 0.f, 0.f, 0.f ); // Specify three vertices
  glVertex3f( 1.f, 0.f, 0.f );
  glVertex3f( 0.f, 1.f, 0.f );
glEnd();
```

Recall that OpenGL is a state machine. The **glColor3f**() command sets the current primary color state using the RGBA value (1.0, 0.0, 0.0, 1.0) for red (the alpha value 1.0 is implicit in the **glColor3f**() command). As OpenGL receives **glVertex3f**() commands, it copies the current primary color state into the state associated with each vertex.

An application can set different states at each vertex. Consider the following example, which draws a triangle with red, green, and blue vertices:

```
glBegin( GL_TRIANGLES );
  glColor3f( 1.f, 0.f, 0.f );
  glVertex3f( 0.f, 0.f, 0.f );
  glColor3f( 0.f, 1.f, 0.f );
  glVertex3f( 1.f, 0.f, 0.f );
  glColor3f( 0.f, 0.f, 1.f );
  glVertex3f( 0.f, 1.f, 0.f );
glEnd();
```

In this case, the current primary color state is different at the time OpenGL receives each **glVertex3f**() command. As a result, the state associated with the first vertex has red stored in its primary color, with green and blue stored in the state for the subsequent vertices.

> **Note**   When specifying a primitive with different primary colors at each vertex, your application can direct OpenGL to interpolate those colors linearly or render the primitive using only the final vertex color. For more information, see "Smooth and Flat Shading" later in this chapter.

OpenGL doesn't limit the number of vertices an application can specify between **glBegin**() and **glEnd**(). If your application calls **glBegin**(GL_QUADS), followed by four million vertices and **glEnd**(), for example, OpenGL renders 1 million individual quadrilaterals from your vertex data.

Individual function calls to specify vertices and vertex states provide great flexibility for the application developer. The function call overhead inherent in this interface, however, dramatically limits application performance. Even though display lists (see "Performance Issues" later in this chapter) allow implementations to optimize data sent using the **glBegin**()/**glEnd**()

paradigm, many OpenGL vendors expect that developers will simply use mechanisms that are inherently more efficient and easier to optimize, such as buffer objects and vertex arrays. For this reason, avoid using the **glBegin**()/**glEnd**() paradigm.

Regardless, many applications use **glBegin**()/**glEnd**() extensively, possibly for historical reasons. Before OpenGL version 1.1 was released, the **glBegin**()/**glEnd**() paradigm was the only option available. Performance may be another reason; **glBegin**()/**glEnd**() is perfectly adequate for applications that have extremely light rendering requirements or are not performance critical.

2.2.2   Drawing Primitives Using Vertex Arrays

Vertex arrays allow applications to render primitives from vertex and vertex state data stored in blocks of memory. Under some circumstances, OpenGL implementations can process the vertices and cache the results for efficient reuse. Applications specify primitives by indexing into the vertex array data.

Vertex arrays, a common OpenGL extension in version 1.0, became part of the OpenGL core in version 1.1, with additional feature enhancements through version 1.4. Before version 1.5, applications using vertex arrays could store data only in client storage. Version 1.5 introduced the buffer object feature, allowing applications to store data in high-performance server memory.

This book focuses primarily on using buffer objects. The section "Vertex Array Data" later in this chapter, however, shows how to specify blocks of data with and without buffer objects. The example source code uses buffer objects when the OpenGL runtime version is 1.5 or later and uses the pre-1.5 interface otherwise.

2.2.2.1   Buffer Objects

Applications use buffer objects to store vertex data[2] in server memory.

Each buffer object requires a unique identifier. Obtain a buffer object identifier with **glGenBuffers**().

---

2. The GL_ARB_pixel_buffer_object extension allows buffer objects to contain pixel data so that applications can store blocks of pixel data in server memory. See Chapter 7, "Extensions and Versions," for an example. This functionality may become part of OpenGL version 2.1.

void **glGenBuffers**(GLsizei *n*, GLuint* *buffers*);
GLboolean **glIsBuffer**(GLuint *buffer*);

glGenBuffers() obtains *n* buffer identifiers from its pool of unused buffers. *n* is the number of buffer identifiers desired by the application. **glGenBuffers**() stores the identifiers in *buffers*.

glIsBuffer() returns GL_TRUE if *buffer* is an existing buffer object.

▶ OpenGL version: 1.5 and later.

You might need to create four buffer objects to store vertex data, normal data, texture coordinate data, and indices in vertex arrays. The following code obtains identifiers for four buffer objects:

```
GLuint bufObjects[4];
glGenBuffers( 4, bufObjects );
```

Before you can store data in the buffer object, your application must bind it using **glBindBuffer**().

void **glBindBuffer**(GLenum *target*, GLuint *buffer*);

Specifies the active buffer object and initializes it if it's new. Pass a *target* value of GL_ARRAY_BUFFER to use the buffer object as vertex array data, and pass a *target* value of GL_ELEMENT_ARRAY_BUFFER to use the buffer object as vertex array indices. *buffer* is the identifier of the buffer object to bind.

▶ OpenGL version: 1.5 and later.

The command **glBindBuffer**(GL_ARRAY_BUFFER, bufObjects[0]) binds the first buffer object ID obtained in the previous code listing, bufObjects[0], for use with vertex array data. If a buffer object is already bound, **glBindBuffer**() unbinds it and then binds *buffer*.

To unbind a buffer object, call **glBindBuffer**() with a buffer ID of zero. After **glBindBuffer**(GL_ARRAY_BUFFER, 0) is called, for example, no buffer is associated with vertex array data.

When an application binds a buffer object for the first time, OpenGL creates an empty buffer object. To load the buffer object with data, call **glBufferData**().

> void **glBufferData**(GLenum *target*, GLsizeiptr *size*, const GLvoid* *data*,
>   GLenum *usage*);
>
> ---
>
> Copies data from host memory to the active buffer object. *target* must be
> GL_ARRAY_BUFFER or GL_ELEMENT_ARRAY_BUFFER; *size* indicates the
> size of the data in bytes; and *data* points to the data.
>
> *usage* is a hint to OpenGL, stating the application's intended usage of
> the buffer data. A *usage* parameter of GL_STATIC_DRAW indicates that
> the application intends to specify the data once and use it to draw sev-
> eral times. Other values for *usage* are described in Section 2.9, "Buffer
> Objects," of *The OpenGL Graphics System*.
>
> ▶ OpenGL version: 1.5 and later.

OpenGL doesn't limit the amount of data you can store in a buffer object.
Some implementations, however, can provide maximum performance
only if buffer object data is below an implementation-specific size and
must fall back to a slower rendering path when buffer objects are too large.
Currently, OpenGL doesn't provide a mechanism to query this implementation-specific limit. OpenGL vendors often make this type of information
available to developers in implementation-specific documentation, however.

Applications typically create buffer objects and load them with data at initialization time. You might create a single buffer object and load it with
three vertices by using the following code:

```
// Obtain a buffer identifier from OpenGL
GLuint bufferID;
glGenBuffers( 1, &bufferID );

// Define three vertices to draw a right triangle.
const GLfloat vertices[] = {
    0.f, 0.f, 0.f,
    1.f, 0.f, 0.f,
    0.f, 1.f, 0.f };

// Bind the buffer object, OpenGL initially creates it empty.
glBindBuffer( GL_ARRAY_BUFFER, bufferID );
// Tell OpenGL to copy data from the 'vertices' pointer into
//   the buffer object.
glBufferData( GL_ARRAY_BUFFER, 3*3*sizeof(GLfloat), vertices,
    GL_STATIC_DRAW );
```

To render the three vertices stored in this buffer object as a triangle, your
application must bind the buffer object before issuing the appropriate ver-

tex array pointer commands. See the next section, "Vertex Array Data," for additional information.

Some applications need to specify dynamic data. Because buffer objects exist in server memory, OpenGL provides an interface that allows applications to map the buffer object in client memory. This interface isn't covered in this book. For more information, see Section 2.9, "Buffer Objects," of *The OpenGL Graphics System*. Applications can replace all data in a buffer object with the **glBufferData**() command.

When your application no longer needs the buffer object, call **glDelete-Buffers**(). This command empties the specified buffers and places their IDs in OpenGL's pool of unused buffer object IDs.

---

void **glDeleteBuffers**(GLsizei *n*, const GLuint* *buffers*);

Returns buffer object identifiers to the unused pool and deletes buffer object resources. The parameters are the same as for **glGenBuffers**().

▶ OpenGL version: 1.5 and later.

Applications typically delete buffers when the application exits but should delete buffers to conserve server memory whenever the application no longer needs the buffer object.

2.2.2.2 Vertex Array Data

When rendering primitives with vertex arrays, your application must tell OpenGL where to obtain vertex array data. You can either submit the data directly or bind a buffer object, which tells OpenGL to obtain the data from that buffer. Both methods use the same interface.

---

void **glVertexPointer**(GLint *size*, GLenum *type*, GLsizei *stride*, const GLvoid* *pointer*);
void **glNormalPointer**(GLenum *type*, GLsizei *stride*, const GLvoid* *pointer*);
void **glTexCoordPointer**(GLint *size*, GLenum *type*, GLsizei *stride*, const GLvoid* *pointer*);

Submits arrays of vertices, normals, and texture coordinates to OpenGL for use with vertex arrays. *type* indicates the type of data being submitted. Applications typically use GL_FLOAT for single-precision vertices, normals, and texture coordinates. If your application uses buffer objects, most OpenGL implementations optimize for GL_FLOAT data.[3]

stride lets you interleave data. If your data is tightly packed (noninterleaved), specify a *stride* of zero. Otherwise, specify a byte distance between the vertices, normals, or texture coordinates.

pointer points to your data or indicates an offset into a buffer object.

glVertexPointer() and **glTexCoordPointer**() additionally take a *size* parameter. Use a *size* of 3 when sending 3D (*xyz*) vertices with **glVertexPointer**(). For 2D (*st*) texture coordinates, specify a *size* of 2 to **glTexCoordPointer**(). Because normals always consist of three elements, **glNormalPointer**() doesn't require a *size* parameter.

OpenGL supports sending other vertex data besides normals and texture coordinates. See *OpenGL® Programming Guide* for more information.

▶ OpenGL version: 1.1 and later.

To enable and disable vertex, normal, and texture coordinate arrays, call **glEnableClientState**() and **glDisableClientState**() with the parameters GL_VERTEX_ARRAY, GL_NORMAL_ARRAY, and GL_TEXTURE_COORD_ARRAY, respectively. If your application renders a vertex array primitive without enabling the normal or texture coordinate arrays, OpenGL renders the primitive without that data. Note that if your application fails to call **glEnableClientState**(GL_VERTEX_ARRAY), OpenGL will render nothing; the vertex array must be enabled to render geometry with vertex arrays.

glEnableClientState() and **glDisableClientState**() are similar in concept to **glEnable**() and **glDisable**(), except that the former enables and disables OpenGL client state features, whereas the latter enables and disables OpenGL server state features. See "glEnableClientState" in *OpenGL® Reference Manual* for more information.

Without Buffer Objects

Most programmers will code their applications to use buffer objects but also need to allow for the case in which buffer objects are unavailable, such

---

3. For color data, implementations typically optimize for GL_UNSIGNED_BYTE. See "glColorPointer" in *OpenGL® Reference Manual* for details on specifying color values per-vertex by using vertex arrays.

as when running on a pre-1.5 version of OpenGL. The example code that accompanies this book demonstrates both methods.

When not using buffer objects, the *pointer* parameter is a simple GLvoid* address of array data. The following code demonstrates how to enable and specify a vertex array by using **glVertexPointer**():

```
const GLfloat data[] = {
    -1.f, -1.f, 0.f,
    1.f, -1.f, 0.f,
    0.f, 1.f, 0.f };

// Enable the vertex array and specify the data.
glEnableClientState( GL_VERTEX_ARRAY );
glVertexPointer( 3, GL_FLOAT, 0, data );
```

Although this may be simpler than using buffer objects, it requires OpenGL to copy the vertex array from client memory each time the application renders a primitive that uses it. This is illustrated in Figure 2-2.

The next section discusses buffer objects (the preferred method), which eliminate the copy from client memory to server memory. Buffer objects allow vertex array rendering commands to source vertex array data directly from high-performance server memory.

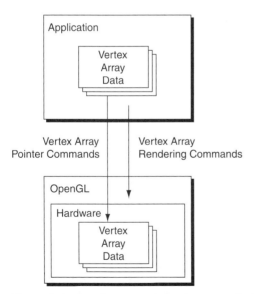

Figure 2-2   Rendering with vertex arrays before OpenGL version 1.5. OpenGL must copy the vertex array data each time the application renders primitives that use it.

With Buffer Objects

As shown in the preceding section, "Without Buffer Objects," before OpenGL version 1.5, applications could submit data only directly with these functions; the *pointer* parameter could only be an address in application-accessible memory, and OpenGL accessed the data from client memory to render primitives. OpenGL version 1.5 overloads these functions, however. If your application has bound a buffer object to GL_ARRAY_BUFFER, OpenGL interprets *pointer* as an offset into the buffer object data.

Because C doesn't allow function overloading, *pointer* must still be a GLvoid* address, even though the buffer object feature requires an offset. When obtaining data from a buffer object, OpenGL computes this offset by subtracting a pointer to NULL from *pointer,* where both addresses are treated as char*.

Applications commonly direct OpenGL to use buffer object data from the start of the buffer, for example. In this case, the offset into the buffer is 0. If you store vertices in the buffer object as tightly packed single-precision floats, call **glVertexPointer**() as follows:

```
glVertexPointer( 3, GL_FLOAT, 0, (GLvoid*)((char*)NULL) );
```

Here, *pointer* is a char* pointer to NULL, typecast as a GLvoid*. To determine the offset into the buffer object, OpenGL subtracts a pointer to NULL from *pointer*, and in this case, the result is an offset of 0.

As a second example, consider how you would call **glVertexPointer**() if you wanted to skip the first vertex in the buffer object. Because a single vertex is 12 bytes long (3 * sizeof(GLfloat)) on most 32-bit systems, this requires an offset of 12 bytes into the buffer object. Your application would call **glVertexPointer**() as follows:

```
glVertexPointer( 3, GL_FLOAT, 0, (GLvoid*)(((char*)NULL) + 12) );
```

pointer is a char* pointer to NULL plus 12 bytes, so when OpenGL subtracts a pointer to NULL from *pointer,* it obtains a result of 12. When rendering, OpenGL uses this as an offset into the buffer object before obtaining vertex data, effectively skipping the first vertex.

Note   When you use a vertex array pointer command with buffer objects, the data stored in the buffer object must meet alignment requirements as determined by the *type* parameter. GLfloat data is typically aligned on 4-byte boundaries, for example. If your application calls **glVertexPointer**() with the *type* parameter set to GL_FLOAT, each float element stored in the corresponding buffer object must lie on a 4-byte boundary.

The following code shows a convenience routine that takes the desired off-set in bytes as a parameter and returns a GLvoid* value to use as the *pointer* parameter to the vertex array pointer functions:

```
inline GLvoid* bufferObjectPtr( unsigned int idx )
{
    return (GLvoid*)( ((char*)NULL) + idx );
}
```

The example code uses this function when using vertex arrays with buffer objects. Using this function, your application would call **glVertex-Pointer**() as follows to specify a 12-byte buffer object offset:

```
glVertexPointer( 3, GL_FLOAT, 0, bufferObjectPtr( 12 ) );
```

Without buffer objects, the vertex array pointer commands incur the expense of copying vertex array data each time the vertex array rendering commands are issued. With buffer objects, OpenGL copies this data at initialization time, when the application calls **glBufferData**(). At render time, the vertex array pointer commands simply pass in an offset to the bound buffer object, eliminating render-time copies from client memory to server memory. This is illustrated in Figure 2-3.

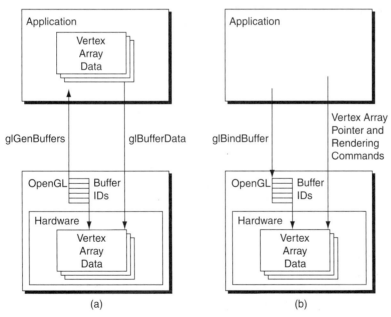

Figure 2-3 Vertex arrays with buffer objects. Initialization operations are shown in (a). The application allocates a buffer object ID with **glGenBuffers**() and stores vertex array data with **glBufferData**(). At render time (b), the application binds the buffer object and sends vertex array pointer and rendering commands.

2.2.2.3   Vertex Array Rendering Commands

So far, this chapter has covered creating and using buffer objects, and specifying vertex arrays with and without buffer objects. OpenGL doesn't draw anything, however, until your application issues vertex array rendering commands that tell OpenGL what primitives to draw from the vertex array data. This section covers those commands.

OpenGL provides several commands for drawing primitives with vertex arrays; *OpenGL® Distilled* covers three of them. (See *OpenGL® Programming Guide, OpenGL® Reference Manual,* and *The OpenGL Graphics System* for information on other vertex array commands.) These three commands are:

- **glDrawElements**()—This command renders a single OpenGL primitive with vertices and vertex data specified by vertex array indices.

- **glDrawRangeElements**()—This optimized form of **glDrawElements**() restricts selected vertex data to a specified range of index values.

- **glMultiDrawElements**()—This command renders multiple OpenGL primitives of the same type. It, too, uses indices to obtain vertex data from vertex arrays.

All three commands use indices to obtain vertices, normals, and texture coordinates from the data specified by your application in **glVertexPointer**(), **glNormalPointer**(), and **glTexCoordPointer**(). Before OpenGL version 1.5, copying these indices was a potential performance bottleneck for large blocks of static indices. Buffer objects, however, allow the application to store the indices in high-performance server memory. The following sections demonstrate this technique.

Using glDrawElements()

Applications should use **glDrawElements**() to draw a single OpenGL primitive. **glDrawElements**() was added to OpenGL in version 1.1. The example code that comes with this book falls back to using this command in versions of OpenGL that don't support more-preferred interfaces.

---

void **glDrawElements**(GLenum *mode*, GLsizei *count*, GLenum *type*,
    const GLvoid* *indices*);

Draws a single primitive from vertex array data. *mode* is any valid OpenGL primitive type, as listed in the section "Primitive Types" earlier in this chapter and illustrated in Figure 2-1. *count* is the number of vertices to render.

indices is an array of indices into the enabled vertex arrays. *type* is the data type of the *indices* array and must be GL_UNSIGNED_BYTE, GL_UNSIGNED_SHORT, or GL_UNSIGNED_INT.

▶ OpenGL version: 1.1 and later.

This command causes OpenGL to read *count* indices from the *indices* array and use them to index into the enabled vertex arrays to obtain vertices and vertex data. Then it uses that data to render a primitive of type *mode*. Using **glDrawElements**() vastly reduces the number of function calls made by applications using the **glBegin**()/**glEnd**() paradigm.

If a buffer object is bound to GL_ELEMENT_ARRAY_BUFFER when the **glDrawElements**() command is issued, OpenGL interprets *indices* as an offset into that buffer and obtains the indices from the bound buffer object. This is more common with **glDrawRangeElements**() and **glMultiDrawElements**(), because an OpenGL implementation that supports buffer objects also supports these more efficient interfaces.

Calling **glDrawElements**() with enabled normal and texture coordinate arrays leaves the current normal and current texture-coordinate states undefined.

> **Note**   **glDrawElements**() should be used only when the OpenGL implementation doesn't provide higher-performance rendering commands such as **glDrawRangeElements**() and **glMultiDrawElements**(), described next.

Using glDrawRangeElements()

The **glDrawRangeElements**() command is identical to **glDrawElements**() but requires the application to specify the minimum and maximum values of the indices. Using this command often results in better performance than **glDrawElements**() because it allows OpenGL to make better use of internal vertex array data caches.

---

void **glDrawRangeElements**(GLenum *mode*, GLuint *start*, GLuint *end*, GLsizei *count*, GLenum *type*, const GLvoid* *indices*);

Draws a single primitive using a range of vertex array data. *mode*, *count*, *type*, and *indices* mean the same as in **glDrawElements**(). *start* and *end* denote lower and upper limits on the *count* index values that are used in the *indices* array.

▶ OpenGL version: 1.2 and later.

When **glDrawRangeElements**() was introduced in OpenGL version 1.2, it clearly outperformed **glDrawElements**() because it allowed OpenGL to process a single block of vertex data rather than element by element. Although buffer objects somewhat level the performance of these two commands, **glDrawRangeElements**() still largely replaces **glDrawElements**() in cases where the application knows the range of its indices.

If a buffer object is bound to GL_ELEMENT_ARRAY_BUFFER when the **glDrawRangeElements**() command is issued, OpenGL interprets *indices* as an offset into that buffer and obtains the indices from the bound buffer object. The example source code makes extensive use of this feature. See the section "Vertex Arrays Example Code" later in this chapter.

Like **glDrawElements**(), vertex states that are modified by enabled vertex arrays (such as the current normal and current texture coordinate) are left undefined after a call to **glDrawRangeElements**().

Using glMultiDrawElements()

The **glMultiDrawElements**() command draws multiple primitives of the same type. It's comparable to calling **glDrawElements**() repeatedly with the same *mode* parameter.

---

void **glMultiDrawElements**(GLenum *mode*, const GLsizei* *count*, GLenum *type*, const GLvoid** *indices*, GLsizei *primcount*);

Draws multiple primitives of the same type from vertex array data. *primcount* is the number of primitives to draw. All primitives drawn are of type *mode*.

indices is a two-dimensional array of type *type*. Each subarray in *indices* contains the indices for one of the primitives. The number of indices in the subarray is specified by the corresponding element of the *count* array.

▶ OpenGL version: 1.4 and later.

This command is simple in concept, yet difficult to explain in plain English text. As an illustration, consider that **glMultiDrawElements**() behaves as though it were executing the following code:

```
for ( int i=0; i<primcount; i++ )
  if (count[i] > 0)
    glDrawElements( mode, count[i], type, indices[i] );
```

If a buffer object is bound to GL_ELEMENT_ARRAY_BUFFER when the **glMultiDrawElements**() command is issued, OpenGL interprets *indices* as an offset into that buffer and obtains the indices from the bound buffer object. The example source code makes extensive use of this feature. See the next section, "Vertex Arrays Example Code," for an example.

Like **glDrawElements**() and **glDrawRangeElements**(), vertex states that are modified by enabled vertex arrays (such as the current normal and current texture coordinate) are left undefined after a call to **glMultiDrawElements**().

2.2.2.4 Vertex Arrays Example Code

The example code, available from this book's Web site, contains C++ objects for rendering cylinders, spheres, planes, and tori. The code uses different rendering paradigms and issues different OpenGL commands depending on the OpenGL version; your application needs to do the same to run on a wide variety of OpenGL implementations:

- If the OpenGL version is 1.5 or later, the example code creates and uses buffer objects. Otherwise, it passes vertex data directly when issuing the vertex pointer commands.

- All objects require either **glDrawRangeElements**() or **glMulti-DrawElements**() and use this interface if the OpenGL version is 1.2 or 1.4 or later, respectively. Otherwise, the code uses the **glDrawElements**() interface.

- The example code requires at least OpenGL version 1.1; it never falls back to using the **glBegin**()/**glEnd**() paradigm. This should be sufficient because OpenGL version 1.0 implementations are rarely encountered today.

To branch efficiently in the OpenGL version, the example code uses a singleton instance that queries the OpenGL version string by using **glGetString**(GL_VERSION) once and encodes it as an enum: Ver11 for version 1.1, Ver12 for version 1.2, and so on.

Listing 2-1 shows the draw() method of the Cylinder object. This code draws the cylinder body as a quad strip and optionally caps the ends of the cylinder with triangle fans. (Note that this example doesn't use display lists. Later in this chapter, "Performance Issues" covers this topic.)

Listing 2-1 Drawing with vertex arrays and buffer objects

```
void Cylinder::draw()
{
    if (!_valid)
    {
        if (!init())
            return;
    }

    glPushClientAttrib( GL_CLIENT_VERTEX_ARRAY_BIT );

    glEnableClientState( GL_VERTEX_ARRAY );
    glEnableClientState( GL_NORMAL_ARRAY );

    if (OGLDif::instance()->getVersion() >= Ver15)
    {
        glBindBuffer( GL_ARRAY_BUFFER, _vbo[1] );
        glNormalPointer( GL_FLOAT, 0, bufferObjectPtr( 0 ) );
        glBindBuffer( GL_ARRAY_BUFFER, _vbo[0] );
        glVertexPointer( 3, GL_FLOAT, 0, bufferObjectPtr( 0 ) );

        glBindBuffer( GL_ELEMENT_ARRAY_BUFFER, _vbo[2] );
        glDrawRangeElements( GL_QUAD_STRIP, _idxStart,
                _cap1Idx, _numVerts, GL_UNSIGNED_SHORT,
                bufferObjectPtr( 0 ) );
        if (_drawCap1)
            glDrawRangeElements( GL_TRIANGLE_FAN, _cap1Idx,
                    _cap2Idx, _numCapVerts, GL_UNSIGNED_SHORT,
                    bufferObjectPtr((_cap1Start-_indices)
                    * sizeof(GLushort)) );
        if (_drawCap2)
            glDrawRangeElements( GL_TRIANGLE_FAN, _cap2Idx,
                    _idxEnd, _numCapVerts, GL_UNSIGNED_SHORT,
                    bufferObjectPtr((_cap2Start-_indices)
                    * sizeof(GLushort)) );
    }
    else
    {
        glVertexPointer( 3, GL_FLOAT, 0, _vertices );
        glNormalPointer( GL_FLOAT, 0, _normals );

        if (OGLDif::instance()->getVersion() >= Ver12)
        {
            glDrawRangeElements( GL_QUAD_STRIP, _idxStart,
                    _cap1Idx, _numVerts, GL_UNSIGNED_SHORT,
                    _indices );
            if (_drawCap1)
                glDrawRangeElements( GL_TRIANGLE_FAN, _cap1Idx,
                        _cap2Idx, _numCapVerts, GL_UNSIGNED_SHORT,
                        _cap1Start );
```

```
            if (_drawCap2)
                glDrawRangeElements( GL_TRIANGLE_FAN, _cap2Idx,
                        _idxEnd, _numCapVerts, GL_UNSIGNED_SHORT,
                        _cap2Start );
        }
        else
        {
            glDrawElements( GL_QUAD_STRIP, _numVerts,
                    GL_UNSIGNED_SHORT, _indices );
            if (_drawCap1)
                glDrawElements( GL_TRIANGLE_FAN, _numCapVerts,
                        GL_UNSIGNED_SHORT, _cap1Start );
            if (_drawCap2)
                glDrawElements( GL_TRIANGLE_FAN, _numCapVerts,
                        GL_UNSIGNED_SHORT, _cap2Start );
        }
    }

    glPopClientAttrib();

    OGLDIF_CHECK_ERROR;
}
```

The code first tests to see whether the `Cylinder` object has already been
initialized, and if it hasn't, it calls the `init()` method, which generates
the cylinder vertex and normal data. If the OpenGL version is 1.5 or later,
it also allocates buffer objects and fills them with that data. Download the
example source code to see the `Cylinder::init()` method.

The `draw()` method pushes the client attribute stack with a call to
glPushClientAttrib(). When it calls **glPopClientAttrib**() at the
end of the function, the client states changed by this function—such as the
state of enabled arrays, bound buffer objects, and vertex array pointers—
restore to their previous values.

The `Cylinder` object doesn't specify texture coordinates, so it needs only
to enable the normal and vertex arrays. These arrays must be enabled
regardless of the OpenGL version.

Next, the `draw()` method specifies the vertex data and issues the rendering commands. How `draw()` does this depends on the OpenGL version.

For OpenGL version 1.5, the `Cylinder` object uses three buffer objects: one
for normal data, one for vertex data, and one for the indices into the arrays.
Note that the normal and vertex buffer objects are bound to GL_ARRAY_
BUFFER before calling **glNormalPointer**() and **glVertexPointer**(),
respectively, and that the indices buffer object is bound to GL_ELEMENT_
ARRAY_BUFFER before issuing the drawing commands.

The code draws three primitives—a quad strip and, optionally, two triangle fans—using three **glDrawRangeElements**() commands. The code doesn't use different buffer objects for each primitive. Instead, it passes in different offsets to each **glDrawRangeElements**() call (along with different minimum and maximum index range values) to access the specific data for each primitive.

If the OpenGL version is less than 1.5, the code passes the vertex and normal data directly in its calls to **glNormalPointer**() and **glVertexPointer**().

The code uses **glDrawRangeElements**() if the version is 1.2 or greater, but when less than version 1.5, the code must pass the indices directly to these commands rather than pass offsets.

If the version is less than 1.2, the code assumes version 1.1 and uses **glDrawElements**(). This is the least-desired code path, because OpenGL doesn't know what data to process until after it copies and starts to process each index.

Before returning to the calling application, Cylinder::draw() pops the client attribute stack and tests for OpenGL errors. OGLDIF_CHECK_ERROR is a CPP macro, described in Appendix D, "Troubleshooting and Debugging."

2.3   Drawing Details

When an application submits a primitive to OpenGL for rendering, OpenGL uses the current state to determine what operations to perform on the primitive data.

OpenGL supports a variety of flexible features that affect the appearance of rendered geometry. Some of the more complex operations, such as viewing, lighting, and texture mapping, are covered in their own chapters. This section explains a few of the simpler operations. *OpenGL® Programming Guide* and *OpenGL® Shading Language* present the complete OpenGL feature set.

2.3.1   Clearing the Framebuffer

Before issuing the first rendering command and periodically thereafter (typically, at the start of each frame), applications need to clear the contents of the framebuffer. OpenGL provides the **glClear**() command to perform this operation.

---

void **glClear**(GLbitfield *mask*);

Clears the framebuffer contents. *mask* is one or more bit values combined with the bitwise OR operator that specify the portion of the framebuffer to clear. If GL_COLOR_BUFFER_BIT is present in *mask*, `glClear`() clears the color buffer. If GL_DEPTH_BUFFER_BIT is present in *mask*, `glClear`() clears the depth buffer. If both bit values are present, `glClear`() clears both the color and depth buffers.

`glClear`() can also clear other parts of the framebuffer, such as the stencil and accumulation buffers. For a complete list of bit values accepted by `glClear`(), see "glClear" in *OpenGL® Reference Manual*.

▶ OpenGL version: 1.0 and later.

Typically, applications clear both the color and depth buffers with a single `glClear`() call at the start of each frame.

```
glClear( GL_COLOR_BUFFER_BIT | GL_DEPTH_BUFFER_BIT );
```

Clearing multiple buffers with a single `glClear`() call is more efficient than clearing separate buffers with separate `glClear`() calls. There are rendering techniques that require clearing the depth and color buffer separately, however. Try to clear both buffers at the same time when possible.

Your application controls the color that `glClear`() writes to the color buffer by calling `glClearColor`().

---

void **glClearColor**(GLclampf *red*, GLclampf *green*, GLclampf *blue*, GLclampf *alpha*);

Specifies the clear color used by `glClear`(). *red*, *green*, *blue*, and *alpha* are four values specifying an RGBA color value and should be in the range 0.0 to 1.0. Subsequent calls to `glClear`() use this color value when clearing the color buffer.

▶ OpenGL version: 1.0 and later.

`glClearColor`() sets the current clear color, which is black by default (0.0, 0.0, 0.0, 0.0). This is adequate for some applications. Applications that set the clear color usually do so at program init time.

Note that not all framebuffers contain an alpha channel. If the framebuffer doesn't have an alpha channel, OpenGL effectively ignores the *alpha* parameter when clearing. Specify whether your framebuffer contains an alpha channel with the GLUT command **glutInitDisplayMode**() or platform-specific framebuffer configuration calls.

You can also specify the depth value written into the depth buffer by **glClear**(). By default, **glClear**(GL_DEPTH)BUFFER_BIT) clears the depth buffer to the maximum depth value, which is adequate for many applications. To change this default, see "glDepthValue" in *OpenGL® Reference Manual.*

2.3.2   Modeling Transformations

Complex 3D scenes typically are composed of several objects or models displayed at specific locations within the scene. These objects are routinely modeled in their own modeling-coordinate system and transformed by the application to specific locations and orientations in the world-coordinate system. Consider a scene composed of an aircraft flying over a terrain model. Modelers create the aircraft by using a modeling software package and might use a coordinate system with the origin located in the center of the fuselage, with the aircraft nose oriented toward positive *y* and the top of the aircraft oriented toward positive *z*. To position and orient this aircraft model relative to the terrain model, the application must translate it laterally to the correct position and vertically to the correct altitude, and orient it to the desired pitch, roll, and aircraft heading.

OpenGL transforms all vertices through a geometry pipeline. The first stage of this pipeline is the modeling transformation stage. Your application specifies modeling transformations to position and orient models in the scene. To manage the transformation of your geometry effectively, you need to understand the full OpenGL transformation pipeline. See Chapter 3, "Transformation and Viewing," for details.

2.3.3   Smooth and Flat Shading

To simulate a smooth surface, OpenGL interpolates vertex colors during rasterization. To simulate a flat or faceted surface, change the default shade model from GL_SMOOTH to GL_FLAT by calling **glShadeModel**(GL_FLAT).

---

void **glShadeModel**(GLenum *mode*);

Specifies smooth or flat shading. *mode* is either GL_SMOOTH or GL_FLAT. The default value of GL_SMOOTH causes OpenGL to use Gouraud shading to interpolate vertex color values during rasterization. GL_FLAT causes OpenGL to color subsequent primitives with the color of the vertex that completes the primitive.

▶ OpenGL version: 1.0 and later.

To determine the color of a primitive in flat shade mode, OpenGL uses the color of the vertex that completes the primitive. For GL_POINTS, this is simply the color of the vertex. For all line primitives (GL_LINES, GL_LINE_STRIP, and GL_LINE_LOOP), this is the color of the second vertex in a line segment.

For GL_TRIANGLES, OpenGL colors each triangle with the color of every third vertex. For both GL_TRIANGLE_STRIP and GL_TRIANGLE_FAN, OpenGL colors the first triangle with the color of the third vertex and colors each subsequent triangle with the color of each subsequent vertex.

For GL_QUADS, OpenGL colors each quadrilateral with the color of every fourth vertex. For GL_QUAD_STRIP, OpenGL uses the color of the fourth vertex to color the first quadrilateral in the strip and every other vertex thereafter to color subsequent quadrilaterals.

For GL_POLYGON, OpenGL colors the entire polygon with the color of the final vertex.

2.3.4 Polygon Mode

It shouldn't be a surprise that filled primitives are drawn filled by default. Applications can specify, however, that OpenGL render filled primitives as lines or points with the **glPolygonMode**() command.

---

void **glPolygonMode**(GLenum *face*, GLenum *mode*);

Specifies the rendering style for filled primitives. *mode* is GL_POINT, GL_LINE, or GL_FILL; and *face* must be GL_FRONT, GL_BACK, or GL_FRONT_AND_BACK to specify whether *mode* applies to front- or back-facing primitives, or both.

▶ OpenGL version: 1.0 and later.

Polygon mode is useful for design applications that allow the user to switch between solid and wireframe rendering. Many applications also use it to highlight selected primitives or groups of primitives.

2.3.5   The Depth Test

OpenGL supports the depth test (or *z*-buffer) hidden-surface-removal algorithm (Catmull 1974).

To use the depth test, your application must allocate a depth buffer when creating its display window. In GLUT, use a bitwise OR to include the GLUT_DEPTH bit in the parameter to **glutInitDisplayMode**() before calling **glutCreateWindow**(). Applications typically specify a double-buffered RGB window with a depth buffer by using the following call:

```
glutInitDisplayMode( GLUT_RGB | GLUT_DEPTH | GLUT_DOUBLE );
```

The depth test is disabled by default. Enable it with **glEnable**(GL_DEPTH_TEST).

The depth-test feature discards a fragment if it fails to pass the depth comparison test. Typically, applications use the default comparison test, GL_LESS. In this case, a fragment passes the depth test if its window-space *z* value is less than the stored depth buffer value. Applications can change the default comparison test by calling **glDepthFunc**(). The GL_LEQUAL comparison test, which passes a fragment if its *z* value is less than or equal to the stored depth value, is useful in multipass algorithms. See "glDepthFunc" in *OpenGL® Reference Manual* for a complete description of this function.

OpenGL executes commands in the order in which they are sent by the application. This rule extends to rendering primitives; OpenGL processes vertex array rendering commands in the order in which they are sent by the application and renders primitives within a single vertex array in the order that the array indices specify. This feature allows applications to use the *painter's algorithm* to remove hidden surfaces, rendering a scene in order of decreasing distance. When applications disable the depth test, the first primitives rendered are overwritten by those that are rendered later.

2.3.6   Co-Planar Primitives

You might expect that fragments with the same window-space *x* and *y* values from co-planar primitives would also have identical window-space *z* values. OpenGL guarantees this only under certain circumstances.[4] When co-planar filled primitives have different vertices, floating-point roundoff error usually results in different window-space z values for overlapping pixels. Furthermore, because line primitives don't have plane equations, it's impossible for unextended OpenGL to generate identical window-space z values for co-planar lines and filled primitives. For this reason, setting **glDepthFunc**(GL_LEQUAL) is insufficient to cause co-planar primitives to pass the depth test.

Applications can apply a depth offset to polygonal primitives to resolve co-planarity issues.

---

void **glPolygonOffset**(GLfloat *factor*, GLfloat *units*);

Specifies parameters for altering fragment depth values. OpenGL scales the maximum window-space z slope of the current polygonal primitive by *factor,* scales the minimum resolvable depth buffer unit by *units,* and sums the results to obtain a depth offset value. When enabled, OpenGL adds this value to the window-space z value of each fragment before performing the depth test.

The depth offset feature is also referred to as *polygon offset* because it applies only to polygonal primitives.

▶ OpenGL version: 1.1 and later.

Depth offset applies to polygonal primitives but can be separately enabled and disabled for each of the three polygon modes. To enable depth offset in fill mode, call **glEnable**(GL_POLYGON_OFFSET_FILL). Use GL_POLYGON_OFFSET_POINT and GL_POLYGON_OFFSET_LINE to enable or disable depth offset for point and line mode, respectively.

Typically, applications call **glPolygonOffset**(1.f, 1.f) and **glEnable**(GL_POLYGON_OFFSET_FILL) to render filled primitives that are pushed back slightly into the depth buffer, then disable depth offset and draw co-planar geometry.

Figure 2-4 illustrates rendering co-planar primitives with and without depth offset.

---

4. See Appendix A, "Invariance," in *The OpenGL Graphics System*.

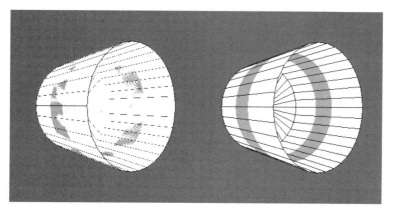

Figure 2-4   This figure illustrates the result of rendering co-planar primitives. When depth offset is disabled (left), differences in rasterization of co-planar primitives results in rendering artifacts known as "z-fighting." Depth offset (right) eliminates these artifacts.

The following code was used to render the cylinders in Figure 2-4:

```
if (enableOffset)
    glEnable( GL_POLYGON_OFFSET_FILL );
else
    glDisable( GL_POLYGON_OFFSET_FILL );

// Draw the large white cylinder
glPolygonOffset( 2.f, 2.f );
glPolygonMode( GL_FRONT_AND_BACK, GL_FILL );
glColor3f( 1.f, 1.f, 1.f );
cylBody.draw();

// Draw the cylinder's center stripe
glPolygonOffset( 1.f, 1.f );
glColor3f( .6f, .6f, 1.f );
cylStripe.draw();

// Draw the cylinder in line mode
glPolygonMode( GL_FRONT_AND_BACK, GL_LINE );
glColor3f( 0.f, 0.f, 0.f );
cylBody.draw();
```

cylBody and cylStripe are instantiations of the Cylinder object defined in the example code. Cylinder::draw() appears in Listing 2-1. The full DepthOffset example source code is available from the book's Web site.

The code either enables or disables depth offset for filled primitives based on a Boolean variable. It draws the white cylinder with **glPolygonOffset** (2.f, 2.f) to push it back in the depth buffer. The cylinder's bluish stripe is drawn with **glPolygonOffset**(1.f, 1.f), which also pushes it back, but not as far as the first cylinder, to prevent *z*-fighting. Finally, the first cylinder draws a second time in line mode. Because depth offset isn't enabled for line mode, it's drawn with no offset.

When drawing 3D scenes with co-planar primitives, applications generally set *factor* and *units* to the same value. This ensures that depth offset resolves the co-planarity regardless of the primitive orientation.

2.3.7 Alpha and Transparency

Internally, OpenGL colors have four components: red, green, blue, and alpha. You can specify each of these components with **glColor4f**(`r`, `g`, `b`, `a`), but even if you specify a color with three components, such as **glColor3f**(`r`, `g`, `b`), OpenGL uses a full-intensity alpha internally.

Applications often store an opacity value in the alpha component, and use the OpenGL blending and alpha test features to render translucent and transparent primitives.

2.3.7.1 Blending

The blending feature combines the incoming (or source) fragment color with the stored (or destination) color in the framebuffer. Commonly used to simulate translucent and transparent surfaces in 3D rendering, blending also has applications in image processing.

This chapter covers simple OpenGL blending. Blending supports many variants that are not covered in this book. For full details on blending, see Section 4.1.8, "Blending," of *The OpenGL Graphics System* and Chapter 6, "Blending, Antialiasing, Fog, and Polygon Offset," of *OpenGL® Programming Guide*.

To use blending, your application must enable it and set an appropriate blending function. Enable and disable blending with GL_BLEND. Call **glEnable**(GL_BLEND) to enable blending, for example. Set the blend function with the **glBlendFunc**() command.

---

void **glBlendFunc**(GLenum *src*, GLenum *dst*);

Sets blending function parameters that control the combination of stored framebuffer colors with fragment colors. *src* and *dst* specify functions that operate on the source and destination colors, respectively. When blending is enabled, OpenGL replaces the fragment color with the sum of the output of these functions.

▶ OpenGL version: 1.0 and later.

When simulating translucent surfaces, applications typically call **glBlendFunc**(GL_SRC_ALPHA, GL_ONE_MINUS_SRC_ALPHA). This multiplies the source fragment color by the source alpha value (typically small to simulate a nearly transparent surface) and multiplies the destination color by 1 minus the source alpha value.

For a complete list of valid *src* and *dst* values, see Table 4.2 in *The OpenGL Graphics System*.

To render translucent surfaces correctly, applications should first render all opaque geometry into the framebuffer. Applications should further sort translucent geometry by distance from the viewer and render it in back-to-front order.

> **Note**   Sorting translucent geometry could negatively affect application performance. Order-independent transparency, currently an area of active research, is outside the scope of this book.

2.3.7.2 Alpha Test

The alpha-test feature discards fragments that have alpha values that fail to pass an application-specified comparison test. Applications use the alpha test to discard partially or completely transparent fragments that, if rendered, would have little or no effect on the color buffer.

To use the alpha test, your application must enable it and specify the comparison test. Enable and disable the alpha test with GL_ALPHA_TEST. Enable it by calling **glEnable**(GL_ALPHA_TEST), for example. To specify the comparison test, use **glAlphaFunc**().

---

void **glAlphaFunc**(GLenum *func*, GLclampf *ref*);

Specifies how the alpha test discards fragments. *func* specifies a comparison function and may be GL_ALWAYS, GL_EQUAL, GL_GEQUAL, GL_GREATER, GL_LEQUAL, GL_LESS, GL_NEVER, or GL_NOTEQUAL. *ref* specifies a constant floating-point reference value used in the comparison.

▶ OpenGL version: 1.0 and later.

Consider setting the following alpha-test state:

```
glEnable( GL_ALPHA_TEST );
glAlphaFunc( GL_NOTEQUAL, 0.f );
```

In this case, OpenGL renders fragments from subsequent geometry only if the fragment alpha value isn't equal to zero.

You might also want to discard fragments with an alpha that doesn't exceed a certain threshold. Setting the alpha function to **glAlphaFunc** (GL_GREATER, 0.1f) passes fragments only if their alpha value is greater than 0.1.

2.4 Performance Issues

Buffer objects and vertex arrays should result in acceptable performance in most rendering situations.

Visit OpenGL vendor Web sites to become informed about the limits of specific OpenGL implementations. If you suspect that your performance is significantly less than typical, add debugging code to obtain an accurate vertex count from your application. Compare your vertex count with vendor specifications, and calculate an expected performance rate. Ensure that you are not specifying more vertices than necessary.

The following sections provide some additional performance tips.

2.4.1 Display Lists

Display lists store a sequence of OpenGL commands in server memory for later execution. Applications execute the entire display list command sequence with a single command, **glCallList**(). Executing commands from display lists is often more efficient than issuing the same sequence of commands individually.

To use display lists, your application must obtain, store, and eventually dispose of display list identifiers. For each display list your application uses, you must store a sequence of OpenGL commands in it. Finally, when you want to execute the stored commands, you'll need to issue the **glCallList**() command.

To obtain unused display list identifiers, use **glGenLists**(). To dispose of display list identifiers when they are no longer needed, call **glDeleteLists**().

GLuint **glGenLists**(GLsizei *s*);
void **glDeleteLists**(GLuint *list*, GLsizei *range*);
GLboolean **glIsList**(GLuint *list*);

Use these commands to manage display list identifiers. **glGenLists**()
creates a sequence of *s* unused display list identifiers and marks them as
used. It returns the first identifier in the sequence. **glDeleteLists**()
deletes the sequence of *range* identifiers starting at *list*. **glIsList**()
returns GL_TRUE if *list* is an existing display list.

▶ OpenGL version: 1.0 and later.

To obtain a single display list identifier, use the following code:

```
GLuint listID;
listID = glGenLists( 1 );
```

Your application can obtain multiple display list identifiers by passing in
an *s* parameter greater than 1. In this case, the returned identifier is the
base, and additional identifiers follow sequentially.

When you call **glDeleteLists**(), OpenGL marks the sequence of identifiers from *list* through *list+range*-1 as unused.

To store OpenGL commands in a display list, issue the **glNewList**() command followed by the sequence of commands you want to store. Stop storing commands in a display list with the **glEndList**() command.

---

void **glNewList**(GLuint *n*, GLenum *mode*);
void **glEndList**(void);

Use these commands to specify OpenGL commands to store in a display
list. *n* is the display list identifier. When *mode* is GL_COMPILE , subsequent OpenGL commands are stored in the display list. Specifying a
mode of GL_COMPILE_AND_EXECUTE also stores commands but additionally executes them. GL_COMPILE_AND_EXECUTE is less efficient
than GL_COMPILE, so avoid GL_COMPILE_AND_EXECUTE.

▶ OpenGL version: 1.0 and later.

As an example, consider the **glBegin**()/**glEnd**() paradigm code for drawing a triangle. Because this method of specifying geometry uses so many

function calls, it's an excellent candidate for storing in a display list. The following code stores in a display list the commands for drawing a triangle:

```
glNewList( listID, GL_COMPILE );

glBegin( GL_TRIANGLES );
  glColor3f( 1.f, 0.f, 0.f );
  glVertex3f( 0.f, 0.f, 0.f );
  glVertex3f( 1.f, 0.f, 0.f );
  glVertex3f( 0.f, 1.f, 0.f );
glEnd();

glEndList();
```

OpenGL doesn't store all commands in a display list. In particular, commands that affect client state aren't stored in display lists, such as **glPush-ClientAttrib**(), **glPopClientAttrib**(), **glEnableClientState**(), **glBindBuffer**(), **glVertexPointer**(), **glNormalPointer**(), and **glTexCoordPointer**(). If these commands are executed between **glNewList**() and **glEndList**(), OpenGL executes them immediately. For a complete list of commands that are not stored in a display list, see Section 5.4, "Display Lists," of *The OpenGL Graphics System.*

Applications can store the vertex array rendering commands **glDraw-Elements**(), **glDrawRangeElements**(), and **glMultiDrawElements**() in display lists. When an application stores a vertex array rendering command in a display list, OpenGL copies the necessary vertex array data into the display list at the same time.

You shouldn't store vertex array rendering commands in display lists if you're using buffer objects, because buffer objects usually store vertex data in high-performance server memory. In this situation, storing the vertex array rendering commands in a display list would cause OpenGL to make a second copy of the data in high-performance server memory. This could adversely affect application performance by unnecessarily consuming additional memory. On the other hand, if your application is running on an OpenGL implementation that doesn't support buffer objects, storing vertex array rendering commands in display lists could boost application performance.

As stated previously, storing a vertex array rendering command in a display list causes OpenGL to copy all necessary vertex array data into the list at the same time. For this reason, your application must enable the appropriate arrays and issue vertex array pointer commands as though it is actually rendering the arrays.

To execute the commands stored in a display list, call **glCallList**().

---

void **glCallList**(GLuint *n*);

Executes stored OpenGL commands from a display list. *n* is the display list identifier to execute.

▶ OpenGL version: 1.0 and later.

An added benefit of display lists is the elimination of application branches and loops. A for loop, for example, at the machine level typically incurs the overhead of an increment, a compare, and a branch per loop iteration. Highly tuned applications often partially unwind loops to minimize this overhead. When creating a display list, the application executes the loop only while creating the list. OpenGL stores only the resulting OpenGL commands, which are executed with a **glCallList**() command as a fully unwound loop.

The drawback to display lists should be obvious. When creating a display list, OpenGL makes a copy of both the commands and their data, possibly creating a burden on memory. If memory is a scarce resource for your application, you should use display lists only for the most performance-critical portions of your code.

2.4.2   Face Culling

The OpenGL face-culling feature discards filled primitives based on the direction they face. Applications typically use face culling to discard faces from the back of models. This boosts performance by not bothering to rasterize primitives that won't be visible in the final image.

To use face culling, your application needs to enable it. You might also need to specify the faces that OpenGL should cull.

OpenGL effectively uses the right-hand rule to determine whether a primitive is front- or back-facing. If the vertices are ordered counterclockwise, the primitive is front facing. Note that a front face can become a back face due to a modeling transformation or change in viewing angle. For this reason, OpenGL performs face culling in window-coordinate space. (Chapter 3, "Transformation and Viewing," describes all OpenGL coordinate spaces. For now, think of window coordinates as pixels onscreen.)

To enable face culling, call **glEnable**(GL_CULL_FACE). By default, this culls back faces, or faces with clockwise-ordered window-coordinate vertices.

You can tell OpenGL to cull front faces instead by calling **glCullFace** (GL_FRONT).

Typically, applications enable face culling when the application renders solid geometry with a complete hull. Many applications create geometry using the right-hand rule so that counterclockwise vertices define front faces. Not all applications behave this way, however, and it's common for 3D model files to store faces with a vertex ordering that doesn't match the OpenGL default. You can change this default with the **glFrontFace**() command. See "glFrontFace" in *OpenGL® Reference Manual*.

For more information on face culling, see Chapter 2, "State Management and Drawing Geometric Objects," of *OpenGL® Programming Guide*.

2.4.3   Vertex Array Size

Most OpenGL implementations can provide maximum performance only if the number of vertices stored in a vertex array is below an implementation-specific threshold. An application can store as many vertices in a vertex array as necessary, but if the number exceeds this threshold, performance could suffer.

Applications can query this implementation-specific threshold with the following code:

```
GLint maxVerts;
glGetIntegerv( GL_MAX_ELEMENTS_VERTICES, &maxVerts );
```

When using **glDrawRangeElements**(), the minimum and maximum index parameters, *start* and *end,* should specify a range smaller than GL_MAX_ELEMENTS_VERTICES to obtain maximum performance.

OpenGL implementations have a similar limit on the number of vertex array indexes. Applications can query this value by calling **glGetIntegerv**() and passing in GL_MAX_ELEMENTS_INDICES. The *count* parameter to both **glDrawElements**() and **glDrawRangeElements**() should be less than GL_MAX_ELEMENTS_INDICES to obtain maximum performance.

Many applications disregard these upper limits and simply specify as many vertices and indices as necessary. If performance is a concern, however, modify your application to respect these limits where feasible.

2.5   More Information

Chapter 2, "State Management and Drawing Geometric Objects," of *OpenGL® Programming Guide* is a much more comprehensive discussion of drawing and state control. It includes discussion of topics outside the scope of *OpenGL® Distilled*, such as line and point state, edge flags, interleaved vertex arrays, and mapping and unmapping buffer objects.

Appendix B, "State Variables," of *OpenGL® Programming Guide* and Chapter 6, "State and State Requests," of *The OpenGL Graphics System* contain thorough reference material on OpenGL state and state queries.

For detailed information regarding any of the vertex array commands discussed in this chapter (**glVertexPointer**(), **glDrawRangeElements**(), etc), see *OpenGL® Reference Manual*. (At this time this book went to press, the fifth edition of that book, which discusses buffer objects, was not yet available.)

The book's Web site contains example source code that demonstrates correct usage of the vertex array and buffer object features, as well as the use of several rendering features, such as polygon mode, depth test, and alpha test. Additional example code is available from the OpenGL Web site at `http://www.opengl.org`.

2.6   References

(Catmull 1974) Catmull, Edwin. "A Subdivision Algorithm for Computer Display of Curved Surfaces." Ph.D. thesis, University of Utah, 1974.

Chapter 3

Transformation and Viewing

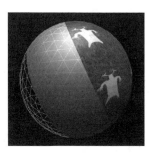

Perhaps the most common problem encountered by programmers who are new to OpenGL is the blank screen; executing an OpenGL program produces an empty window rather than a rendered image. Although several application problems can cause this result, the most common cause is misconfiguring the OpenGL transformation pipeline. To avoid blank screens, you need to be adept at controlling the OpenGL transformation state.

OpenGL provides a powerful, flexible set of routines for controlling transformation and viewing. This programming interface isn't always straightforward, however, especially if it's been a few years since you opened a linear-algebra textbook. OpenGL doesn't provide a "place the camera here" command, for example. To specify a view location and orientation, OpenGL requires the application to compute the inverse of the camera transformation matrix. (Fortunately, GLU somewhat addresses this with **gluLookAt**(), discussed in this chapter.)

Another common source of confusion is the difference between the *view transformation,* which positions and orients the camera, and the *projection transformation,* which determines the field of view, the shape of the view volume, and the projection type (parallel or perspective). Confusing these transformations can cause problems not only with viewing, but also with other OpenGL features, such as lighting and clipping.

This chapter covers the essentials of OpenGL transformation and viewing, and points out areas that are confusing to some programmers.

What You'll Learn

This chapter covers the following topics:

- Characteristics of OpenGL matrices, matrix state, and coordinate systems
- How to control the fixed-function transformation pipeline
- How to create parallel and perspective projection transformations
- How to specify model and view transformations
- Specifying the window area for displaying the final image
- Transforming vertices to and from window coordinates without rendering them
- How to add picking support to your application

What You Won't Learn

The following aspects of the OpenGL transformation system are not covered in this chapter:

- This chapter isn't an introduction to linear algebra.
- OpenGL version 2.0 features a programmable transformation interface. This chapter discusses only the fixed-function method. For more information, see *OpenGL® Shading Language*.
- The chapter doesn't discuss the transpose matrix feature, which allows applications to specify row-order matrices. For more information, see *The OpenGL Graphics System*.
- The chapter doesn't cover the depth-range feature, part of the viewport transformation, which allows applications to control the range of the depth buffer.
- The chapter doesn't cover transforming colors with the color matrix.
- This chapter briefly mentions the **glFrustum**() interface for creating perspective projections but doesn't cover it in detail.

If you need to review linear algebra as applied to the field of computer graphics, see Chapter 5, "Geometrical Transformations," and the appendix, "Mathematics for Computer Graphics," in *Computer Graphics: Principles and Practice*.

3.1 Coordinate Systems and Matrices

This section covers several important aspects of OpenGL transformations and matrix state.

This book assumes that you are familiar with linear algebra. If you need to refresh your knowledge on this subject, refer to Chapter 5, "Geometrical Transformations," of *Computer Graphics: Principles and Practice* or Chapter 1, "Mathematical Fundamentals of Computer Graphics," of *3D Computer Graphics.* In addition to covering the application of linear algebra to 3D computer graphics, both books are excellent computer graphics texts.

Specifically, you should be familiar with the concept of homogeneous coordinates, which are composed of four values: x, y, z, and w. When your application specifies a 3D *xyz* vertex, OpenGL implicitly supplies a w value of 1.0 to create a homogeneous coordinate. Homogeneous coordinates allow graphics systems to implement translation, scale, and rotation as matrix transformations. Also, as part of the transformation pipeline discussed in this chapter, OpenGL uses the w value to effect perspective.

3.1.1 Handedness

Traditionally, graphics systems present a right-handed coordinate system to the application (Core 1979). In a right-handed coordinate system, viewed from the positive end of an axis, positive rotations around that axis proceed counterclockwise.

OpenGL doesn't restrict the application to a right- or left-handed coordinate system, yet many programmers find it easiest to think of OpenGL as exposing a right-handed coordinate system to the application. If your application specifies vertices in a right-handed coordinate system, you'll obtain good results by not using negative scales and by following the typical usage described in this chapter.

To operate in a left-handed system, applications can simply scale by a negative value using the model-view matrix. Applications commonly scale by negative values to create a mirror effect. A scene can be mirrored by rendering it twice with an intervening negative scale, for example. The resulting rendered image will show both a right- and a left-handed scene.

Programmers new to OpenGL should first master the OpenGL transformation pipeline using coordinates in a right-handed system.

3.1.2 **Matrices**

OpenGL transforms vertices using 4 x 4 matrices. Applications typically instantiate an OpenGL matrix in C/C++ as a 1D array of 16 floating-point values (either `GLfloat` or `GLdouble`). The following code declares an array variable *m* suitable for use as an OpenGL matrix:

```
GLfloat m[16];
```

OpenGL® Programming Guide, OpenGL® Reference Manual, and *The OpenGL Graphics System* all follow standard mathematical notation convention and present OpenGL matrices as column major:

$$
\begin{array}{cccc}
m[0] & m[4] & m[8] & m[12] \\
m[1] & m[5] & m[9] & m[13] \\
m[2] & m[6] & m[10] & m[14] \\
m[3] & m[7] & m[11] & m[15]
\end{array}
$$

Correspondingly, OpenGL vectors are displayed as columns:

$$
\begin{array}{c}
x \\
y \\
z \\
w
\end{array}
$$

The OpenGL specification's use of column-major notation is the source of great confusion among some C/C++ programmers who are accustomed to working with row-major 2D arrays. Note that this is a notational convention only. If the convention were changed to transpose matrices and write vectors as rows, OpenGL's interface and internal operation would remain unchanged.[1]

Row- versus column-major ordering is not an issue if applications don't access matrix elements directly but instead restrict themselves to the suite of OpenGL and GLU routines for manipulating matrices. Applications commonly manipulate matrix elements directly, however, especially the view transformation matrix, as described in the section "Setting the Model-View Matrix" later in this chapter. In this case, applications should access

---

1. OpenGL version 1.3 allows applications to specify row-major matrices, which OpenGL internally transposes. See *The OpenGL Graphics System* for details.

the matrix as a 1D array of 16 elements to help prevent confusion between row- and column-major ordering.

An OpenGL matrix should be viewed as the basis for a new coordinate system. Multiplying a vector by a matrix transforms the vector into a new coordinate system defined by the matrix. A C/C++ matrix m with elements $m[0]$ through $m[15]$ defines a new coordinate system as follows:

- The new x axis vector is [$m[0]$ $m[1]$ $m[2]$].

- The new y axis vector is [$m[4]$ $m[5]$ $m[6]$].

- The new z axis vector is [$m[8]$ $m[9]$ $m[10]$].

- The new origin is [$m[12]$ $m[13]$ $m[14]$].

3.1.3 Matrix Stacks and Matrix State

OpenGL uses two matrices in geometry transformation and a texture matrix for each texture unit to transform texture coordinates.[2]

OpenGL stores matrices in matrix stacks, one for each matrix mode and one for each texture unit. All OpenGL matrix operations described in this chapter affect the top of the active matrix stack. Select the active matrix stack by calling **glMatrixMode**().

---

void **glMatrixMode**(GLenum *mode*);

Selects the active matrix stack. Subsequent matrix commands affect the selected stack. *mode* is GL_MODELVIEW, GL_PROJECTION, or GL_TEXTURE to select the model-view, projection, or texture matrix stacks, respectively.

If *mode* is GL_TEXTURE, the selected stack depends on the current texture unit as set by the application with **glActiveTexture**(). See Chapter 6, "Texture Mapping," for further information.

▶ OpenGL version: 1.0 and later.

Like the attribute stacks described in Chapter 1, applications can push the active matrix stack and make changes to it, and then pop it to return to the

---

2. OpenGL also uses a matrix for color transformation, which is not covered in this book. See Chapter 8, "Drawing Pixels, Bitmaps, Fonts, and Images," of *OpenGL® Programming Guide* for information on the color matrix.

original matrix. Issue the commands **glPushMatrix**() and **glPopMatrix**() to push and pop the active matrix stack.

OpenGL initializes all matrix stacks to have the identity matrix as their single entry. Popping a matrix stack with only one entry generates the error GL_STACK_UNDERFLOW. Similarly, pushing a matrix stack that is already full generates the error GL_STACK_OVERFLOW. The size of each matrix stack is at least 2, except for the model-view stack, which must be at least 32.

The section "The Transformation Pipeline" later in this chapter describes how the top of the model-view and projection matrix stacks are used in OpenGL transformations. Chapter 6, "Texture Mapping," describes how the tops of the texture matrix stacks are used to transform texture coordinates.

3.1.4   Matrix Manipulation Commands

OpenGL provides a suite of commands that affect the top of the active matrix stack. Specify the active matrix stack by using **glMatrixMode**() as described previously; then issue matrix manipulation commands to modify the current top of that stack.

---

void **glLoadIdentity**(void);
void **glLoadMatrix**[fd](const *TYPE* m*);
void **glMultMatrix**[fd](const *TYPE* m*);
void **glRotate**[fd](*TYPE theta, TYPE x, TYPE y, TYPE z*);
void **glScale**[fd](*TYPE x, TYPE y, TYPE z*);
void **glTranslate**[fd](*TYPE x, TYPE y, TYPE z*);

Use these commands to modify the top of the active matrix stack.

glLoadIdentity() replaces the top of the active matrix stack with the identity matrix.

glLoadMatrix*() replaces the top of the active matrix stack with *m*.

glMultMatrix*() postmultiplies *m* onto the top of the active matrix stack.

glRotate*() computes a matrix that effects a rotation of *theta* degrees around the axis specified by *x*, *y*, and *z*, and postmultiplies this matrix onto the top of the active matrix stack.

glScale*() creates a matrix that effects a scale in the *x*, *y*, and *z* axes, and postmultiplies this matrix onto the top of the active matrix stack.

glTranslate*() creates a matrix that effects a translation along the *x*, *y*, and *z* axes, and postmultiplies this matrix onto the top of the active matrix stack.

Many OpenGL implementations perform transformations using single precision regardless of the implied precision of the interface. Regardless, applications often specify double-precision matrices to maximize precision during concatenation.

▶ OpenGL version: 1.0 and later.

Note that when using a command that multiplies a matrix onto the top of the active matrix stack, such as **glMultMatrix***(), **glRotate***(), **glScale***(), or **glTranslate***(), OpenGL uses postmultiplication to perform the matrix concatenation. The order in which applications issue matrix commands affects the resulting top of the active matrix stack. As an example, consider the following code:

```
glMatrixMode( GL_MODELVIEW );
glLoadIdentity();
glTranslatef( 2.f, 0.f, 0.f );
glRotatef( -120.f, 0.f, 1.f, 0.f );
```

The above code first selects the model-view matrix stack and sets the top of that stack to the identity matrix. Next, it post-multiplies two matrices: first, a translation along the positive *x* axis, and then a negative 120-degree rotation around the *y* axis. The resulting top of the model-view matrix stack positions geometry at a new origin (2.0, 0.0, 0.0) and then rotates it –120 degrees around the *y* axis at the new origin. In effect, the rotation occurs in the new coordinate system defined by the translation. The results are illustrated in Figure 3-1a.

The following code is identical to the above code, except that it reverses the order of the **glTranslatef**() and **glRotatef**() commands:

```
glMatrixMode( GL_MODELVIEW );
glLoadIdentity();
glRotatef( -120.f, 0.f, 1.f, 0.f );
glTranslatef( 2.f, 0.f, 0.f );
```

The top of the model-view stack that results from this command sequence is quite different. OpenGL rotates subsequent geometry around the *y* axis at its origin, producing a new *x* and *z* axis, and then translates geometry along the new *x* axis. In effect, the translation occurs in the new coordinate system defined by the rotation. The results are illustrated in Figure 3-1b.

Many applications use postmultiplication to their advantage to position geometry relative to other geometry. See the Transformation example

(a)

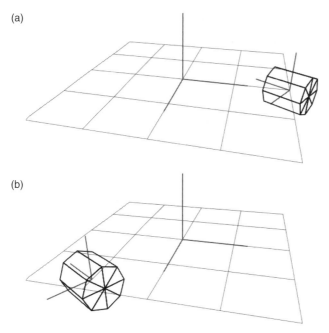

(b)

Figure 3-1   The order of matrix operations affects geometry transformation. In both figures, a cylinder, defined at the origin, is transformed to a new position and orientation. In (a), it is translated first and then rotated. In (b), the rotation occurs first, followed by the translation.

program (downloadable from this book's Web site) for an effective use of nested model transformations.

3.2   The Transformation Pipeline

The OpenGL transformation pipeline (see Figure 3-2) transforms application vertices into window coordinates, where they can be rasterized. Like all 3D graphics systems, OpenGL uses linear algebra; it treats vertices as vectors and transforms them by using vector-matrix multiplication. The transformation process is called a *pipeline* because geometry passes through several coordinate systems on the way to window space. Each coordinate system serves a purpose for one or more OpenGL features.

For each stage of the transformation pipeline, this section describes the characteristics of that coordinate system, what OpenGL operations are performed there, and how to construct and control transformations to the next coordinate system in the pipeline.

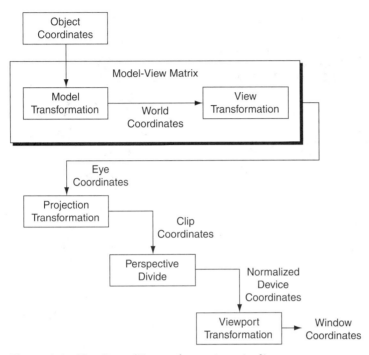

Figure 3-2 The OpenGL transformation pipeline.

Graphics programmers new to OpenGL are often surprised to learn that there is no world-coordinate system in the OpenGL transformation pipeline. This is because there are no OpenGL features that require computation in a world-coordinate system. For this reason, world coordinates are an application construct. Most applications have a concept of world coordinates—setting the view position, for example, is done in terms of world coordinates—and the discussion that follows describes how the OpenGL transformation pipeline accommodates this requirement.

3.2.1   Object Coordinates

Applications specify vertices in object coordinates. The definition of object coordinates is entirely up to the application. Some applications render scenes that are composed of many models, each created and specified in its own individual coordinate system. Consider the Viewing example program (see Figure 3-3), available from this book's Web site.

The Viewing example renders a scene composed of a plane, a sphere, two tori, and four columns. Each of these objects is defined around the same

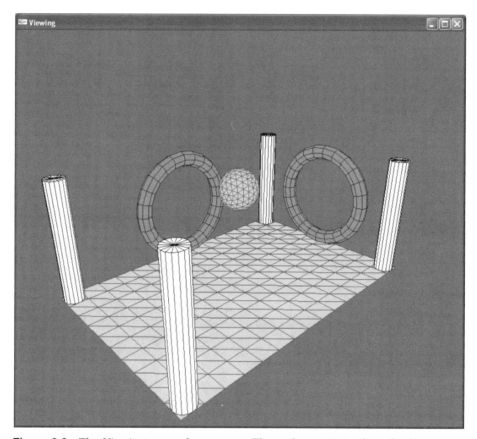

Figure 3-3   The Viewing example program. The code positions the cylinders, tori, sphere, and plane using different model transformations for each object.

object-space origin. The Viewing example, however, uses a model transformation to position and orient the objects in the world-coordinate system.

Without the model transformation, object coordinates wouldn't exist, and all parts of a scene would have to be created in world coordinates, which would prohibit model reuse.

3.2.2   The Model Transformation

The model transformation transforms geometry from object to world coordinates. Applications store both the model and view transformations in the model-view matrix as a single concatenated matrix.

Applications almost always use model transformations to move geometry from a local object-coordinate system to a global world-coordinate system. Typically, applications use the **glRotate***(), **glScale***(), and **glTranslate***() functions to position and orient geometry and models in the world.

In addition to orienting geometry statically, applications use model transformations to create animations by moving objects dynamically from one frame to the next.

Applications often use multiple nested model transformations to transform geometry into a world-coordinate system. Consider how you would create an orrery, or model of the solar system, in which the Moon is located relative to the Earth, and the Earth in turn is located relative to the Sun. The Transformation example program (see Figure 3-4) demonstrates how to use nested model transformations to create and animate this model.

3.2.3 World Coordinates

The world-coordinate system is an application construct that exists between OpenGL's object- and eye-coordinate systems. If the model-view

Figure 3-4 The Transformation example program. The code positions the Earth relative to the Sun with a translation and rotation model transformation; then it uses a nested translation and rotation to position the Moon relative to the Earth. The rotations change from frame to frame to animate the model.

matrix were split into two transformations—the model transformation and the view transformation—multiplying object-space coordinates by the model transformation would produce world coordinates, and multiplying those world coordinates by the view transformation would produce eye coordinates.

Because OpenGL performs no operations in the world-coordinate system, it's not part of the formal OpenGL transformation pipeline.

3.2.4   The View Transformation

In precise terms, the *view transformation* is the inverse of a transformation that positions and orients the camera in the application's world-coordinate system. Methods for setting the view transformation are covered in the section "Setting the Model-View Matrix" later in this chapter.

Applications store both the model transformation and view transformation in the model-view matrix. Load the view transformation into the model-view matrix first; then post-multiply the model transformations.

3.2.5   Eye Coordinates

OpenGL eye coordinates are defined as follows:

- The viewpoint is at the origin.
- The view direction is down the negative *z* axis.
- Positive *y* is up.
- Positive *x* is to the right.

For geometry to be visible in a standard perspective projection, it must lie somewhere along the negative *z* axis in eye coordinates. Geometry along the positive *z* axis is behind the viewpoint and, therefore, is not rendered. To view geometry with coordinates in the positive *z* range, your application needs to translate it into the negative *z* range using the model-view matrix. In this example, your original geometry in the positive *z* range is in object coordinates, and the model-view matrix transforms it into eye coordinates.

Depending on current state, OpenGL computes lighting, fog, certain texture coordinates, user-defined clipping, and point size from eye-coordinate values.

3.2.6 The Projection Transformation

OpenGL multiplies eye coordinates by the projection matrix to produce clip coordinates. The projection matrix defines the size and shape of the view volume and, therefore, determines the portion of eye coordinates that will ultimately be visible. Typically, applications create either perspective or parallel projections. The section "Perspective and Parallel Projections" later in this chapter provides more information on setting the projection transformation.

3.2.7 Clip Coordinates

OpenGL clips primitives that lie outside the view volume in clip-coordinate space. A clip coordinate vertex is within the view volume if its x, y, and z values are all within the $-w$ to w range. Application programmers rarely concern themselves with how this actually works. If your application specifies a well-defined projection matrix using `glOrtho()` or `gluPerspective()`, clipping will happen as expected; OpenGL clips geometry outside the view volume and performs no further processing on it.

3.2.8 Perspective Division

OpenGL divides clip coordinate x, y, and z values by the clip-coordinate w value to produce normalized device coordinates. As with clipping, if your application creates a well-defined projection matrix, you don't need to be concerned with the perspective division. It happens automatically if you specify a perspective projection, and it's effectively a no-op if you specify a parallel projection.

For perspective projections, the perspective division effectively shrinks distant geometry and expands near geometry.

3.2.9 Normalized Device Coordinates

In normalized device coordinates, vertex x, y, and z values lie within the -1.0 to 1.0 range. Whereas previous coordinate systems used homogeneous coordinates, with vertices composed of x, y, z, and w values, normalized device coordinates are 3D Cartesian coordinates.

OpenGL doesn't perform any operations in normalized device coordinates. It is simply a coordinate system that exists between the perspective division and the viewport transformation to window coordinates.

3.2.10 The Viewport Transformation

The viewport transformation is the final stage in the transformation pipeline. It's a scale and translation that maps the –1.0 to 1.0 normalized device-coordinate cube into window coordinates.

Note that this transformation applies not only to x and y values, but also to the z value. The viewport transformation maps normalized device-coordinate z values to the range of acceptable depth buffer values.

Applications usually set the viewport when the window changes size. Set the viewport with a call to **glViewport**(). The section "The Viewport" later in this chapter contains more information.

3.2.11 Window Coordinates

Window coordinates have their xy origin in the bottom-left corner of the window, and window-coordinate z values extend throughout the depth buffer.

Programmers often make the mistake of assuming that window coordinates are integers. OpenGL window coordinates are actually floating-point values; window-coordinate vertices exist at subpixel locations. This is essential for correct rasterization and multisampling.

To understand the concept of floating-point window coordinates, you should imagine the window as being the first quadrant of a Cartesian coordinate system with the origin at the bottom-left corner, positive x extending to the right, and positive y extending up. Pixels cover a square area, with integer gridlines corresponding to pixel boundaries. As a gross oversimplification of the rasterization process, OpenGL rasterizes a pixel based on the intersection of the pixel area and the xy floating-point window-coordinate representation of the primitive.

It's often convenient to think of depth values as normalized, where 0.0 corresponds to the front of the depth buffer and 1.0 corresponds to the back. Actual depth buffer values are device dependent.

3.2.12 Controlling Transformations

Programmers should think of the transformation pipeline as OpenGL state that can be manipulated and controlled through OpenGL commands.

Applications create model and view transformations in the model-view matrix. Routines commonly used to create model transformations, such as

glRotate* (), **glScale*** (), and **glTranslate*** (), are described earlier in this chapter. The section "Setting the Model-View Matrix" later in this chapter covers creating the view transformation.

Applications specify projections in the projection matrix. The section "Perspective and Parallel Projections" later in this chapter discusses how to do this with the **glOrtho** () and **gluPerspective** () commands.

In some application environments, setting the viewport isn't necessary. The default viewport setting maps normalized device coordinates to the entire window. If this is your desired behavior, and your window never changes size, you'll never need to set the viewport. In most modern window systems, however, applications set the viewport whenever the window changes size. Changing the viewport is covered in the section "The Viewport" later in this chapter.

3.2.12.1 Minimal Transformations

Although professional applications always control the transformation pipeline to some extent, a noteworthy fact is that it's possible to render geometry without setting any transformation parameters. The model-view and projection matrices default to the identity matrix, and the viewport transformation defaults to the full window. If your application doesn't change these defaults, object coordinates and normalized device coordinates are identical, and OpenGL renders any geometry your application sends that is between –1.0 and 1.0 in *x*, *y*, and *z*. Professional applications don't do this, but sometimes it's helpful to start with a simplified transformation pipeline when debugging.

3.2.12.2 Obtaining Transformed Values

Applications sometimes need the window coordinate of a vertex without rendering it, or given a window coordinate, applications need the corresponding object-coordinate value. GLU provides two routines that fulfill this need: **gluProject** () and **gluUnProject** ().

GLint **gluProject**(GLdouble *objX*, GLdouble *objY*, GLdouble *objZ*, const GLdouble* *mv*, const GLdouble* *proj*, const GLint* *vp*, GLdouble* *winX*, GLdouble* *winY*, GLdouble* *winZ*);
GLint **gluUnProject**(GLdouble *winX*, GLdouble *winY*, GLdouble *winZ*, const GLdouble* *mv*, const GLdouble* *proj*, const GLint* *vp*, GLdouble* *objX*, GLdouble* *objY*, GLdouble* *objZ*);

Transforms vertices between object coordinates and window coordinates. Given the 16-element model-view and projection matrices *mv* and *proj*, and the 4-element viewport *vp* (as obtained from **glGetIntegerv** (GL_VIEWPORT, vp)), **gluProject** () transforms the given object-coordinate vertex (*objX, objY, objZ*) into window coordinates and returns it as (*winX, winY, winZ*).

gluUnProject () performs the inverse transformation and returns the object-coordinate vertex (*objX, objY, objZ*) computed from the given window-coordinate value (*winX, winY, winZ*).

Both functions return GL_TRUE on success and GL_FALSE on failure.

▶ GLU version: 1.0 and later.

Applications can also use the feedback render mode to transform object coordinates into window coordinates, which can be more efficient than GLU for large numbers of vertices. Feedback is not covered in this book; see Chapter 13, "Selection and Feedback," of *OpenGL® Programming Guide*.

Note   Each time your application calls **gluUnProject** (), GLU inverts the *mv* and *proj* matrix parameters. Although adequate for obtaining a single object-coordinate value, this is extremely inefficient for large numbers of coordinates sharing the same transformation. If your application needs to do this, consider developing your own routine to invert the matrices once; then batch-transform several coordinates.

The Picking example code uses **gluUnProject** () to support dragging selected geometry using the mouse cursor. For each mouse motion event received, the code passes the window-coordinate location of the mouse cursor to **gluUnProject** () to obtain the corresponding object-coordinate value. The code subtracts the previous object-coordinate value to obtain an object-coordinate delta motion vector. The code repositions the selected object by translating it along this vector. The end result is that the mouse cursor appears to drag the object around the scene.

3.3   Setting the Model-View Matrix

As the name *model-view* implies, the model-view matrix stores both model and view transformations. Because OpenGL performs no operations in world coordinates, the model-view matrix transforms directly from object coordinates to eye coordinates. Nearly all applications, however, use a world-coordinate-system paradigm and maintain separate model and view transformations. Typically, applications start each frame by loading a view transformation onto the top of the model-view matrix stack and then post-multiplying model transformations, as in the following example:

```
glMatrixMode( GL_MODELVIEW );
glLoadIdentity();
gluLookAt( ... );

glPushMatrix();
glTranslatef( ... );
// Specify vertices and vertex data
glPopMatrix();
```

The **glMatrixMode**(GL_MODELVIEW) command tells OpenGL that sub-sequent matrix commands operate on the model-view matrix stack. The **glLoadIdentity**() command clears the top of the matrix stack, and **gluLookAt**() creates a matrix that positions and orients the viewer, and multiplies it onto the top of the matrix stack. At this point in the code, the model-view matrix contains only the view transformation.

The **glPushMatrix**() command pushes the stack and places a copy of the view transformation on the new top of the stack. Next, the code postmulti-plies a model transformation onto the top of the matrix stack with a call to **glTranslatef**(). At this point in the code, the model-view matrix con-tains both view and model transformations. OpenGL uses this matrix to transform subsequent vertices and vertex data into eye coordinates.

The final **glPopMatrix**() call effectively erases the model transformation, leaving only the view transformation in the model-view matrix. Applica-tions typically wrap model transformations and their associated geometry with calls to **glPushMatrix**() and **glPopMatrix**() to facilitate changes in model transformation while retaining the same view transformation.

3.3.1   Creating the View Transformation with gluLookAt()

The Picking example code, referred to in the preceding section, uses a GLU routine to position the view.

void **gluLookAt**(GLdouble *eyeX*, GLdouble *eyeY*, GLdouble *eyeZ*, GLdouble *centerX*, GLdouble *centerY*, GLdouble *centerZ*, GLdouble *upX*, GLdouble *upY*, GLdouble *upZ*);

Creates a view transformation and postmultiplies it onto the top of the active matrix stack. When used as the view transformation in the model-view matrix, this function effectively places the viewer at (*eyeX, eyeY, eyeZ*) and orients the viewer to face the point (*centerX, centerY, centerZ*), with the up vector (*upX, upY, upZ*).

The results are undefined if the up vector coincides with a vector from the eye point to the center point.

▶ GLU version: 1.0 and later.

The up direction depends on your application's world-coordinate system. Some applications use positive *y* for up; others use positive *z*. Regardless, you might need to change it from your world-coordinate default if your application emulates, for example, a first-person view from inside a rolling aircraft.

Because OpenGL doesn't provide a viewer-centric interface for creating a view transformation, **gluLookAt** () is very popular and used by several applications. It's suitable only in cases where your application stores both the eye and center locations, however.

In practice, many applications store the eye location and view direction, or they store the view center location, view direction, and distance back to the eye. In these cases, creating a view transformation in application code can be slightly more efficient than using **gluLookAt** ().

3.3.2   Creating the View Transformation Matrix

The view transformation transforms vertices into eye coordinates and is the inverse of a transformation to place and orient the viewer in world coordinates. The view transformation has two components: a 4 x 4 orientation matrix, *O*, and a 4 x 4 translation matrix, *T*. The view transformation matrix, *V*, is the concatenation of the two 4 x 4 matrices:

$$V = OT$$

The orientation matrix *O* is an orthonormal basis derived from the view direction and up vectors. Given an [*x y z*] view direction *d* and an [*x y z*] up vector *u*, compute their cross product *c* as:

$$c = d \times u$$

Discard *u* and compute the actual up vector *u'* as:

$$u' = c \times d$$

Normalize d, c, and u' to unit length, and create the orientation matrix O as follows:

$$\begin{bmatrix} c_x & c_y & c_z & 0 \\ u'_x & u'_y & u'_z & 0 \\ -d_x & -d_y & -d_z & 0 \\ 0 & 0 & 0 & 1 \end{bmatrix}$$

The translation matrix T is simply the inverse translation to the eye location. If you already have the eye location stored in your application, you can use it directly in a call to **glTranslated**(), as shown in the code below. If you don't have the eye location, scale the view direction vector by the distance to the eye, negate it, and add it to the center location. The result is the eye location.

So if an application creates a double-precision orientation matrix called *orientMatrix* using the steps above and has the eye location stored in a double-precision [x y z] array called *eye,* the code to create the view transformation is

```
glMatrixMode( GL_MODELVIEW );
glLoadMatrixd( orientMatrix );
glTranslated( -eye[0], -eye[1], -eye[2] );
```

In fact, **gluLookAt**() does essentially the same thing internally. It computes the view direction by subtracting *eye* from *center* and then follows the above method to create the orientation matrix. For this reason, if your application already stores the *center* location, view direction, and view distance, **gluLookAt**() is slightly less efficient than creating the view transformation in your application code.

3.3.3 View Transformations in the Example Code

The example code manages views with a `View` base class declared in `OGLDView.h` and defined in `OGLDView.cpp`.

The `View` base class manages a view direction vector, up vector, center location, and distance from the center to the eye location. To set the view transformation, the examples call the `View::loadMatrix()` and `View::multMatrix()` methods. These member functions create the two component matrices O and T, and multiply them onto the top of the active matrix stack, as described in the section "Creating the View Transformation Matrix" earlier in this chapter.

To handle mouse interaction, the example code derives two classes from the `View` base class: `AltAzView` and `TrackballView`. These are declared in `OGLDAltAzView.h` and `OGLDTrackballView.h`, and defined in `OGLDAltAzView.cpp` and `OGLDTrackballView.cpp`. These classes provide two different viewing interfaces to the user. Both classes allow the user to view geometry from any viewing angle, but `AltAzView` preserves the initial up vector, whereas `TrackballView` allows arbitrary orientation. Both also let the user change the eye distance by pressing the Shift key while dragging the mouse.

All example view code uses math routines in `OGLDMath.h` and `OGLDMath.cpp` for dot products, normalization, cross products, and so on.

Depending on your application, you might provide an alt-az or trackball view interface, or a completely different view interface. Many simulation applications require a first-person view interface that lets the user move the view position forward and backward, as well as change the view direction.

See the Viewing example (refer to Figure 3-3) to try out both the `AltAzView` and `TrackballView` interfaces.

3.4   Perspective and Parallel Projections

In addition to specifying the position and orientation of the camera, applications need to specify other camera attributes, such as field of view, near and far clip plane distance, and whether to use a perspective or parallel projection. Applications should specify these parameters with the projection matrix.

After performing eye-coordinate operations, such as lighting, OpenGL transforms vertex data into clip-coordinate space by using the projection matrix. This matrix determines the shape and size of the view volume. When the data is in clip-coordinate space, OpenGL clips any geometry outside the view volume and discards it.

The form of the projection matrix determines the clip-coordinate w value. Parallel projection matrices always produce 1.0 for the clip-coordinate w value, whereas perspective matrices produce a range of clip-coordinate w values. OpenGL transforms clip coordinates into normalized device coordinates by dividing the clip-coordinate x, y, and z values by the clip-coordinate w value. For the perspective case, this division causes distant geometry to appear smaller than near geometry.

OpenGL provides two commands that create projection matrices: **glOrtho**`()` and **glFrustum**`()`.

---

void **glOrtho**(GLdouble *left*, GLdouble *right*, GLdouble *bottom*, GLdouble *top*, GLdouble *near*, GLdouble *far*);

Creates a parallel projection matrix and multiplies it onto the top of the active matrix stack. The six parameters define the six sides of a parallel projection view volume. Both *near* and *far* are distances from the eye to the *near* and *far* clip planes. All values have unlimited range.

glOrtho() generates a `GL_INVALID_VALUE` error if *left=right*, *bottom=top*, or *near=far*.

▶ OpenGL version: 1.0 and later.

To create a parallel projection, first set the matrix mode to `GL_PROJECTION`; then load an identity matrix and call **glOrtho**().

Applications use **glOrtho**() to create parallel projections. Several applications also use **glOrtho**() to specify geometry directly in window-coordinate space. Assume, for example, that an application window is 800 pixels wide and 600 pixels high. The following code creates a one-to-one mapping between object coordinates and window coordinates:

```
glMatrixMode( GL_MODELVIEW );
glLoadIdentity();
glMatrixMode( GL_PROJECTION );
glLoadIdentity();
glOrtho( 0., 799., 0., 599., -1., 1. );
```

(This code also requires the correct viewport. See the next section, "The Viewport," for more information.)

To create a perspective projection, OpenGL provides the **glFrustum**() routine. **glFrustum**() allows applications to create a large variety of perspective projection view volumes. In general, applications don't use **glFrustum**(), as GLU provides a simpler interface: **gluPerspective**().

---

void **gluPerspective**(GLdouble *fovy*, GLdouble *aspect*, GLdouble *near*, GLdouble *far*);

Creates a perspective projection matrix and multiples it onto the top of the active matrix stack. *fovy* defines a field-of-view angle in degrees in the *y* direction, with the field of view in *x* defined by (*fovy*aspect*). *near* and *far* are positive distances from the eye to the near and far clipping planes.

▶ GLU version: 1.0 and later.

Compared with **glFrustum**(), **gluPerspective**() allows applications to specify the field of view and aspect ratio directly, and always creates a symmetrical view volume, which satisfies most application rendering requirements.

The example code that comes with this book makes extensive use of **gluPerspective**(). The following code, from the VertexArray example, creates a perspective projection with a 50 degree field of view, and near and far clipping planes at 1.0 and 10.0 coordinate units in front of the eye:

```
glMatrixMode( GL_PROJECTION );
glLoadIdentity();
gluPerspective( 50., (double)w/(double)h, 1., 10. );
```

In the above code, w and h are the window width and height in pixels.

Applications generally set the projection matrix when the program starts and then again every time the user changes the display window size. GLUT applications need only set the projection matrix in the reshape callback function, because GLUT calls the reshape callback when it first opens the window.

The Viewing example code (refer to Figure 3-3) demonstrates how to alternate between parallel and perspective projections.

3.5   The Viewport

In the final stage of the transformation pipeline, OpenGL takes the –1.0 to 1.0 normalized device-coordinate cube and maps it into window coordinates. The x and y window-coordinate values correspond to window subpixel locations with the origin in the bottom-left corner. Window-coordinate z values correspond to depth buffer values in which values increase with distance from the viewpoint.

Applications can control the mapping from normalized device coordinates to window coordinates with the **glViewport**() command.

void **glViewport**(GLint x, GLint y, GLsizei w, GLsizei h);

Determines the xy mapping from normalized device coordinates to window coordinates. Vertices in normalized device coordinates are mapped to an area of the window with the bottom-left corner at (x, y), width w, and height h. x and y can be negative, but w and h must be positive.

▶ OpenGL version: 1.0 and later.

There is a similar function, **glDepthRange**(), for controlling the mapping of normalized device-coordinate z values into window-space depth buffer values. By default, the full range of normalized device-coordinate z values map to the full range of window-space depth buffer values, which is sufficient for most rendering cases. Because **glDepthRange**() is not typically used, it's not covered in this book. See *OpenGL® Reference Manual* for more information.

The default viewport setting maps the entire –1.0 to 1.0 normalized device-coordinate cube to the full window. If the window is resized, by default the viewport values remain unchanged, and OpenGL continues to map normalized device coordinates to the previous window size. As a result, some parts of the new window could be blank, or some of the geometry might be clipped outside the window boundary. To prevent this, call **glViewport**() when the window size changes.

Although OpenGL follows the Cartesian coordinate system first-quadrant standard of placing the origin in the bottom-left corner, many computing platforms place the origin in the top-left corner, with positive *y* pixel values proceeding downward. Applications need to convert mouse *xy* positions before interpreting them as OpenGL window coordinates. Given an operating system window coordinate (*osX*, *osY*), the following code assumes a top-left-corner origin and converts the values to OpenGL window coordinates (*openglWinX*, *openglWinY*):

```
GLint vp[4];
glGetIntegerv( GL_VIEWPORT, vp );
GLfloat openglWinX = osX;
GLfloat openglWinY = vp[3] – osY + vp[1];
```

After OpenGL transforms vertices into window space, transformation is complete, and the next stage of the rendering process is rasterization, as discussed in Chapter 1.

3.6 Selection

Interactive applications typically allow users to pick an object in the scene, which then becomes the focus of further user-directed operations. OpenGL provides this functionality with the selection feature.

To use selection, applications must provide OpenGL a *selection array* for storing *hit records* that correspond to selected objects. Next, the application puts OpenGL in selection mode. While in selection mode, OpenGL doesn't render geometry to the screen; instead, it stores in the selection array hit records that contain information about any visible primitives. Before applications send primitives in selection mode, they typically change the shape of the view volume so that it fits tightly around the area of interest, which typically is the location of a mouse click. When sending geometry in selection mode, applications specify identifiers for geometry or groups of geometry, called *names*. OpenGL stores the names of selected primitives in the hit record for that primitive. After all geometry has been sent, applications examine the hit records in the selection array to determine what primitives were selected by the user.

3.6.1   Performing a Selection Pass

Applications typically use selection in response to user input. Applications usually support a user interface in which a left-mouse-button click indicates that the user is attempting to indicate a model or piece of geometry of interest. An application must perform the operations described below to support the user pick request.

3.6.1.1   Specify the Selection Array

Specify the selection array by allocating enough memory to hold the hit records; then call **glSelectBuffer**().

---

void **glSelectBuffer**(GLsizei *n*, GLuint* *buffer*);

Specifies a block of memory to contain selection results. *buffer* points to the selection array, and *n* specifies its size as a count of GLuints.

▶ OpenGL version: 1.0 and later.

buffer specifies a selection array that OpenGL potentially fills with hit records during a selection pass.

Applications must allocate enough memory for the selection array to hold all hit records that OpenGL might return. The number of hit records that OpenGL writes into the selection array depends on how many primitives are visible during the selection pass and how the application uses the name stack.

Call **glSelectBuffer**() before entering selection mode with a call to **glRenderMode**(GL_SELECT).

3.6.1.2 Change the Render Mode

After your application specifies the selection array with **glSelectBuffer**(), it should change the render mode to enter selection mode. Change the render mode with **glRenderMode**().

By default, the render mode is GL_RENDER, and when you specify geometry, OpenGL renders it to the framebuffer. If you set the render mode to GL_SELECT, instead of rendering geometry, OpenGL returns hit records for each visible primitive in the selection array.

GLint **glRenderMode**(GLenum *mode*);

Selects the current rendering mode. *mode* must be either GL_RENDER or GL_SELECT.[3]

If you are entering selection mode by changing from GL_RENDER to GL_SELECT, **glRenderMode**() returns 0. If you are changing from GL_SELECT back to GL_RENDER, **glRenderMode**() returns the number of hit records written into the selection array.

If the selection array is too small to hold all the hit records, **glRenderMode**() returns –1. Programmers should watch for this during application development and testing, and should allocate more memory for the selection array if necessary.

▶ OpenGL version: 1.0 and later.

Set the selection array with **glSelectBuffer**() before calling **glRenderMode**(GL_SELECT). If you place OpenGL in selection mode without first specifying a selection array, **glRenderMode**() generates the error GL_INVALID_OPERATION.

When OpenGL is in selection mode, it transforms geometry into clip coordinates and performs clipping. OpenGL generates a hit record for any primitives still visible at that point and writes the hit record into the selection array.

3.6.1.3 Narrow the View Volume

In selection mode, OpenGL returns a hit record for each visible primitive. So without changing the model-view or projection matrix, a selection pass

---

3. A third render mode, GL_FEEDBACK, is not covered in this book. See Chapter 14, "Selection and Feedback," of *OpenGL® Programming Guide*.

would return hit records for every primitive visible in the window. This behavior is inadequate to support user picking by clicking the mouse. To support picking, applications narrow the view volume to surround the pick location. GLU provides a routine to help create a view volume suitable for picking: **gluPickMatrix**().

---

void **gluPickMatrix**(GLdouble *x*, GLdouble *y*, GLdouble *width*,
     GLdouble *height*, GLint* *vp*);

Creates a pick matrix and postmultiplies it onto the top of the active matrix stack. Typically, applications call **gluPickMatrix**() as part of the following sequence:

```
glMatrixMode( GL_PROJECTION );
glLoadIdentity();
gluPickMatrix( ... );
gluPerspective( ... );
```

In this case, the resulting projection transform stored in the top of the projection matrix stack has its center at window coordinates *x* and *y*, and has window-coordinate dimensions *width* and *height*. The *vp* parameter is a four-element array containing the current viewport, as obtained by calling **glGetIntegerv**(GL_VIEWPORT, vp).

▶ GLU version: 1.0 and later.

gluPickMatrix() is designed to support user picking with a mouse click. When the application receives a mouse-click event, it obtains the current mouse *xy* position from the operating system. Applications pass this *xy* location to **gluPickMatrix**() as the *x* and *y* parameters. The *width* and *height* parameters are application dependent; some applications allow the user to specify the width and height of a pick box, whereas other applications hard-code the pick-box dimensions.

Most applications restrict the same view volume that was just used for the previous render pass. In this case, typical code for using **gluPickMatrix**() might look like the following:

```
glMatrixMode( GL_PROJECTION );

// Obtain the current projection matrix
GLdouble proj[16];
glGetDoublev( GL_PROJECTION_MATRIX, proj );

// Set the projection matrix for picking
glLoadIdentity();
gluPickMatrix( x, y, width, height, vp );
glMultMatrixd( proj );
```

In this code, the application obtains the current projection matrix with a call to **glGetDoublev**(GL_PROJECTION_MATRIX, proj) and subsequently postmultiplies it onto the matrix created by **gluPickMatrix**() before performing the selection pass.

3.6.1.4 Render Geometry with Name Identifiers

If your application renders a visible primitive during selection mode, OpenGL generates a hit record for it and writes the record into the selection array. The hit record identifies visible primitives using names, which are unsigned integers (GLuints) stored in a name stack. The hit record contains the entire contents of the name stack at the time the primitive was submitted.

Unlike the attribute and matrix stacks, the OpenGL name stack can contain at least 64 entries and must be initialized with a call to **glInitNames**(). After initialization, the name stack is empty. You can simultaneously push the name stack and store a name onto the new top of stack with a call to **glPushName**(), or you can replace the current top of stack with the **glLoadName**() command. The **glPopName**() command pops the stack one level.

---

void **glInitNames**(void);
void **glPushName**(GLuint *name*);
void **glLoadName**(GLuint *name*);
void **glPopName**(void);

Use these commands to manipulate the name stack. **glPushName**() pushes the name stack one level and stores *name* on the new top of stack. **glLoadName**() replaces the current top of stack with *name*. If the name stack is empty, calling **glLoadName**() generates the error GL_INVALID_OPERATION.

▶ OpenGL version: 1.0 and later.

For hit records in the selection array to have any meaning, your application must initialize the name stack with **glInitNames**(), push it at least once, and store a name onto the top of stack before rendering pickable primitives.

In the simplest use of the name stack, an application initializes it, pushes it once, and then repetitively loads a new name and renders a primitive. In this case, OpenGL creates hit records with a single name, because the name stack is only one entry deep for each visible primitive. Many applications use the name stack to encode an object hierarchy, however.

3.6.1.5 Process Hit Records in the Selection Array

After the application submits all pickable geometry, it returns to render mode with the command **glRenderMode**(GL_RENDER). If the selection array is too small to hold all hit records, this command returns –1. If no hit records were generated because all geometry was outside the selection pass view volume, it returns 0. Otherwise, **glRenderMode**(GL_RENDER) returns the number of hit records in the selection array.

Hit records are a sequence of GLuint values. OpenGL places the following information in each hit record:

- The first GLuint in the hit record is the name stack depth at the time the hit record was created.

- The second and third GLuint values are the minimum and maximum depth values of the selected primitive in the range 0 to 2^{32}–1. (If the application enables depth offset during a selection pass, OpenGL doesn't apply it to the returned depth values.)

- If the name stack depth is greater than 0, each name in the name stack, from the bottom to the top, appears last in the hit record.

3.6.2 Selection in the Example Code

The Picking example program (see Figure 3-5), available from this book's Web site, demonstrates the OpenGL selection feature. This program displays a sphere, a cylinder, and a torus. When the user clicks the left mouse button, the code performs a selection pass. If the user drags an empty part of the scene, OpenGL records no hit records, and the code changes the view. If the user clicks on one of the three objects, however, OpenGL records a hit record. The code marks the object as selected and repositions it in the scene as the user drags the mouse.

The code assigns a unique name to each of the three objects in the scene. The name stack never grows more than a single level; the code doesn't employ a name hierarchy. As a result, each hit record contains only a single name.

When multiple primitives overlap, the selection pass could return multiple hit records. If this occurs, the code determines the picked object by finding

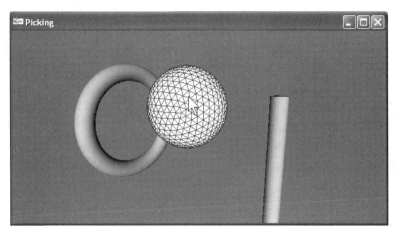

Figure 3-5 The Picking example program. In this image, the user has picked the sphere and is dragging it around the scene.

the hit record with the smallest minimum depth value. This corresponds to the object closest to the viewer.

Sadly, selection is unoptimized in many commodity OpenGL implementations, which perform the selection by using software rather than high-speed graphics hardware. Because selection requires an implementation to transform each vertex into clip coordinates, selection is commonly vertex-limited in unoptimized implementations, creating an unacceptable delay during a selection pass. The example program shows one way to minimize this delay. It displays objects at a relatively high resolution to create acceptable visual quality but uses a low-resolution copy of each object for the selection pass. Reducing the number of vertices during selection results in acceptable performance in implementations with unoptimized selection.

3.7 More Information

OpenGL® Programming Guide provides a comprehensive overview of OpenGL transformations. See Chapter 3, "Viewing"; Appendix E, "Calculating Normal Vectors"; and Appendix F, "Homogeneous Coordinates and Transformation Matrices." Furthermore, in *Computer Graphics: Principles and Practice,* Chapter 5, "Geometrical Transformations," and the appendix, "Mathematics for Computer Graphics," contain an excellent general overview of linear algebra as applied to the field of 3D computer graphics.

For background information on coordinate systems and viewing in particular, see Chapter 6, "Viewing in 3D," of *Computer Graphics: Principles and Practice.*

Chapter 13, "Selection and Feedback," of *OpenGL® Programming Guide* provides additional information on the selection feature to complement this chapter and also discusses the feedback mechanism for obtaining transformed data from OpenGL.

See the book's Web site for example code that demonstrates how to specify modeling, viewing, projection, and selection transformations. Additional example code is available from the OpenGL Web site at `http://www.opengl.org`.

3.8 References

(Core 1979) "Status Report of the Graphics Standards Planning Committee." *ACM SIGGRAPH Computer Graphics* (August 1979).

Chapter 4

Lighting

The earliest lighting algorithms used simple equations to render perfect Lambertian diffuse reflective surfaces and specular highlights. Complex illumination models such as ray tracing and radiosity, and programmable fragment shaders that simulate complex material reflectance properties, employ these simple diffuse and specular lighting equations as building blocks. In fact, simple diffuse and specular lighting suffice for the vast majority of nonphotorealistic interactive computer graphics applications today.

As a low-level graphics API, OpenGL has no direct support for ray tracing and radiosity. It does support ambient, diffuse, and specular lighting, however. This chapter describes how to set OpenGL lighting parameters and coefficients for the typical lighting requirements of most applications. Chapter 6, "Texture Mapping," demonstrates enhanced lighting effects using texture mapping.

If your application requires advanced lighting effects beyond the capabilities of OpenGL lighting and texture mapping, such as per-pixel lighting or bidirectional reflectance distribution functions, you should consider using OpenGL vertex and fragment shaders. Appendix A, "Other Features," discusses this feature briefly. For more in-depth treatment, see *OpenGL® Shading Language*.

What You'll Learn

The following aspects of OpenGL lighting are covered in this chapter:

- Specifying normals—How to keep normals unit length in the presence of uniform and nonuniform scaling. (You already know how to specify normals from Chapter 2, "Drawing Primitives.")

- Configuring light properties—How to enable OpenGL light sources and set their intensity and color.

- Specifying material parameters—How to specify material colors and force material colors to track changes to the primary color.

- Controlling positional and directional lights—How to set the light-source position and direction parameters.

- Debugging—How to resolve common problems you might encounter while adding support for OpenGL lighting to your application.

What You Won't Learn

The following aspects of OpenGL lighting are not covered in this chapter:

- Spotlights—The chapter doesn't cover how to restrict a positional light source to emit a cone or beam of light.

- Attenuation—The chapter doesn't cover how to reduce light intensity as a function of distance.

- Lighting model parameters—This chapter doesn't cover OpenGL's light model parameters, such as global ambient light, local viewer, and color control. The chapter provides some information on two-sided lighting as an explanation for parameters to **glMaterial***(), however.

- Emissive light—The chapter doesn't show how to render geometry that appears to emit light.

- Ambient light—The default ambient light setting is adequate for most rendering. This chapter discusses ambient light but doesn't provide full details on controlling it completely.

- Lighting in color index mode—Color index mode is rarely used in modern OpenGL applications.

- Specific light equations—The exact mathematical equations used by OpenGL to compute light values aren't covered.

Though useful in some rendering circumstances, these features are outside the scope of this book. If your application requires this functionality, see *OpenGL® Programming Guide* and *OpenGL® Reference Manual*.

4.1   Overview

In reality, light is electromagnetic radiation in the visible spectrum. The apparent color of an object is a function of the wavelengths it reflects or absorbs, the wavelengths emitted by light source(s) shining on the object and their intensities, whether the object surface is glossy or dull, the position of the object relative to the light source(s) and viewer, and the presence of other objects that might contribute reflected (indirect) light.

Like most real-time 3D graphics APIs, OpenGL features a simpler lighting model that is powerful enough to approximate real-world lighting adequately.

4.1.1   Ambient, Diffuse, and Specular Light

OpenGL features three types of light, as shown in Figure 4-1:

- *Ambient light* simulates indirect lighting. It illuminates all geometry in your scene at the same intensity.

Figure 4-1   An example of ambient, diffuse, and specular light reflection.

- *Diffuse light* illuminates a surface based on its orientation to a light source. OpenGL diffuse lighting adheres to Lambert's law, in which the amount of illumination is proportional to the cosine of the angle between the surface normal and the light vector, and the diffused light reflects equally in all directions (Blinn 1977).

- *Specular light* approximates the reflection of the light source on a shiny surface. OpenGL specular highlights adhere to the simple Phong illumination model (Phong 1975), in which the specular highlight peaks along the incident light reflection vector,[1] rather than more complex specular highlight models such as Torrance-Sparrow (Torrance 1967).

4.1.2   Controlling OpenGL Lighting

Enable OpenGL lighting by calling **glEnable**(GL_LIGHTING), and disable it by calling **glDisable**(GL_LIGHTING).

By default, lighting is disabled, and OpenGL uses the current primary color, as set by your application with **glColor3f**(), to color rendered primitives.

When lighting is enabled, however, OpenGL doesn't use the current primary color. Instead, it uses the current material colors, as set by your application with calls to **glMaterial***(). Material colors determine the amount of ambient, diffuse, and specular light reflected by geometry. For information on controlling these values, see "Material Parameters" later in this chapter.

OpenGL supports at least eight active light sources at any given time. Each light source can be individually enabled or disabled.

Your application will need to enable individual OpenGL light sources, as well as set light parameters to control the colors and intensities of the ambient, diffuse, and specular light they emit. For information on controlling these values, see "Light Parameters" later in this chapter. To control light-source position and direction, see "Positional and Directional Lights" later in this chapter.

OpenGL computes both diffuse and specular light based on the orientation of the geometry with respect to the light (and to the eye for specular light).

---

1. Phong also outlined a shading method for interpolating surface normals during rasterization to render "perfect" specular highlights. OpenGL lighting is per-vertex unless you use fragment shaders (see *OpenGL® Shading Language*), and uses the Gouraud shading method to interpolate color values during rasterization.

OpenGL uses the current vertex normal to determine orientation. For information on specifying unit length normals, see the section "Normals" later in this chapter.

4.1.3 Minimal Lighting Code

At first glance, controlling OpenGL lighting might appear complex. The amount of code required to obtain simple lighting effects, however, is actually quite small. The minimal code for enabling lighting effects is

```
// Enable OpenGL lighting
glEnable( GL_LIGHTING );

// Enable a single light source
glEnable( GL_LIGHT0 );

// Specify geometry with unit length normals
//   ...
```

This code enables lighting with a single light source, GL_LIGHT0, and otherwise uses default lighting parameters. This results in a white directional light shining directly forward, illuminating a nonglossy white surface. The SimpleLighting code example at the *OpenGL® Distilled* Web site demonstrates this simple technique.

4.1.4 Internal Lighting Computation

When lighting is enabled, OpenGL computes lighting values as part of the vertex processing render stage. For each vertex in your geometry, OpenGL replaces the vertex primary color with the computed lighting value.

OpenGL computes lighting values using the following steps:

1. It multiplies the current ambient material color by the ambient light in the scene.

2. It multiplies the current ambient material color by the ambient light color of each enabled light source.

3. For each enabled light, OpenGL multiplies the current diffuse material color by the diffuse light color and scales the result by the dot product of the current normal and a vector to the light.

4. For each enabled light, OpenGL multiplies the current specular material color by the specular light color. If the dot product of the current

normal and the light's reflection vector is greater than zero, it scales the result by this dot product raised to the specular exponent.

OpenGL sums the color values computed in steps 1 through 4 to arrive at the final lit color for the current vertex. (This is a brief and incomplete summary of the OpenGL lighting equations. For a complete discussion, see Section 2.14.1, "Lighting," of *The OpenGL Graphics System* and Chapter 5, "Lighting," of *OpenGL® Programming Guide*.

4.2 Normals

OpenGL uses the current normal at each vertex to determine the orientation of the surface with respect to the light source and viewer. Lighting calculations occur in eye-coordinate space. OpenGL transforms normals into eye coordinates using a matrix derived from the model-view matrix.

The current normal affects the results of diffuse and specular lighting computation. The OpenGL lighting equations produce realistic results when the current normal is unit length. If you know your model-view matrix doesn't contain a scale transformation, you'll achieve good lighting results by simply sending unit-length normals.

Model-view matrices that contain scale transformations, however, produce distorted eye-coordinate normals that cause abnormal lighting results. This commonly occurs when applications must display models in a non-native unit space (for example, your application uses meter space, but your models were created in feet space—often solved by applying a scale transformation before rendering the model). OpenGL provides two ways to restore distorted normals to unit length: normal rescaling and normalization.

If the model-view scale transformation is uniform in *x*, *y*, and *z,* and if your application specifies unit-length normals (that is, they're unit length in object coordinates before the transformation into eye coordinates), the least expensive method is to enable normal rescaling. This causes OpenGL to scale transformed normals back to unit length, using a scale factor derived from the model-view matrix.

Enable normal rescaling with **glEnable** (GL_RESCALE_NORMAL). Normal rescaling is available in OpenGL version 1.2 and later.

If the model-view scale transformation isn't uniform, or if your object-coordinate normals aren't unit length, OpenGL will make them unit length if you enable normalization. Enable normalization by calling **glEnable**(GL_NORMALIZE). Normalization is available in OpenGL version 1.0 and later.

A simplistic OpenGL implementation effects normalization by computing a square root for each (eye-coordinate) normal and dividing its *x*, *y*, and *z* components by the result. Though less expensive implementations are common, normalization always involves more operations than normal rescaling, which performs better. Of course, the best-performing solution is to scale the vertices of your geometry at init time and ensure that all normals are unit length.

4.3 Light Parameters

OpenGL supports eight or more light sources. Call **glGetIntegerv**() to query the number of supported light sources:

```
GLint maxLights;
glGetIntegerv( GL_MAX_LIGHTS, &maxLights ).
```

Enable and disable individual light sources with **glEnable**(GL_LIGHT*i*) or **glDisable**(GL_LIGHT*i*), respectively, where *i* is zero to (GL_MAX_LIGHTS – 1), inclusive. GL_LIGHT*i* follows the rule GL_LIGHT*i* = GL_LIGHT0 + *i* to simplify setting light parameters with iterative code.

To set the ambient, diffuse, and specular light colors, or the light position, call **glLight*v**().

void **glLight**[fd]**v**(GLenum *light*, GLenum *pname*, const *TYPE* param*)

Controls light-source parameters. *light* is the light to modify, for example, GL_LIGHT0. *pname* is the light parameter, and *param* is the new value for the parameter.

▶ OpenGL version: 1.0 and later.

Valid values for *pname* include GL_AMBIENT, GL_DIFFUSE, GL_SPECULAR, and GL_POSITION. For ambient, diffuse, and specular parameters, *param* should point to an RGBA color value. For the position parameter, *param* should point to an *xyzw* homogenous location vector. For more information on setting the light position, see "Positional and Directional Lights" later in this chapter.

The following code configures `GL_LIGHT1` to emit pale-yellow diffuse light and white specular light:

```
const GLfloat paleYellow[4] = { 1.f, 1.f, .75f, 1.f };
glLightfv( GL_LIGHT1, GL_DIFFUSE, paleYellow );
const GLfloat white[4] = { 1.f, 1.f, 1.f, 1.f };
glLightfv( GL_LIGHT1, GL_SPECULAR, white );
```

By default, all OpenGL lights emit zero-intensity ambient light; their ambient contribution to the primitive color is zero. All lights except `GL_LIGHT0` also default to zero-intensity diffuse and specular light. `GL_LIGHT0` is different; by default, it emits full-intensity (white) diffuse and specular light. This allows an application to obtain simple lighting effects quickly by calling

```
glEnable( GL_LIGHTING );
glEnable( GL_LIGHT0 );
```

4.3.1 Typical Usage

The default ambient color for all lights is zero intensity. OpenGL's light model feature, however, adds a dark-gray ambient light to the entire scene, which is adequate for many applications. For more information, see "glLightModel" in *OpenGL® Reference Manual*. Some applications also set a nonzero ambient intensity for each light, which increases the ambient scene illumination for each enabled light source.

Applications frequently set the diffuse and specular light parameters to full intensity (white). Keep in mind that this is the default value only for `GL_LIGHT0`; other lights default to zero intensity. Note that full-intensity light and material parameters could result in complete saturation. OpenGL handles such cases by clamping the result of light calculations to not exceed full intensity. To avoid clamping artifacts, consider that the sum of the effects from all enabled light sources should not exceed the RGB value (1, 1, 1).

Applications usually set the light position and direction. See "Positional and Directional Lights" later in this chapter for more information.

4.3.2 More Information

Other **glLight***() *pname* parameters let you create spotlights and control attenuation. OpenGL spotlights restrict illumination to a cone of light. They're not commonly used because they tend to exaggerate per-vertex lighting artifacts. Light attenuation diminishes the illumination as a function of distance between geometry and the light source.

For more information, see Chapter 5, "Lighting," of *OpenGL® Programming Guide;* "glLight" in *OpenGL® Reference Manual;* and Section 2.14.1, "Lighting," of *The OpenGL Graphics System.*

4.4   Material Parameters

Material parameters specify how a surface reflects light. Applications change OpenGL material parameters to emulate different colored materials, shiny and flat materials, high-gloss materials such as a pool ball, or broad-gloss materials such as brass. See Plate 1 and the Materials example code at the *OpenGL® Distilled* Web site for examples of different material effects.

As mentioned in Chapter 2, "Drawing Primitives," **glColor3f**() sets the current primary color. It's important to note that OpenGL lighting doesn't use the current primary color; instead, it uses the current material colors. By default, calling **glColor3f**() has no effect when lighting is enabled, but applications often change this default behavior. See "Changing Material Parameters with glColor*()" later in this chapter for more information.

---

void **glMaterial**[fi]**v**(GLenum *face*, GLenum *pname*, const *TYPE** *param*)
void **glMaterial**[fi](GLenum *face*, GLenum *pname*, *TYPE param*)

Use **glMaterial*v**() to specify the ambient, diffuse, and specular material colors, and use **glMaterial***() to specify the specular exponent parameter. *face* specifies a change to front- or back-facing parameters, or both. *pname* is the material parameter, and *param* is the new value for the parameter.

▶ OpenGL version: 1.0 and later.

OpenGL keeps a set of material parameters for both front- and back-facing primitives, and the *face* parameter specifies which set the function call affects. Specify GL_FRONT unless using two-sided lighting. Valid *pname* values for **glMaterial*v**() include GL_AMBIENT, GL_DIFFUSE, and GL_SPECULAR, and for **glMaterial***(), *pname* must be GL_SHININESS.

Note   By default, two-sided lighting is disabled, and OpenGL uses front material parameters to light all primitives. Therefore, using a *face* value of GL_FRONT affects parameters for all primitives.

When two-sided lighting is enabled, OpenGL uses front material parameters to light front faces and back material parameters to light back faces.

OpenGL also reverses normals for back-facing primitives before calculating lighting values. Though uncommon, two-sided lighting is useful in some rendering situations. Consider CAD applications that allow the user to slice into a model with clipping planes. The application could enable two-sided lighting to highlight interior and exterior surfaces.

For more information, see "glLightModel" in *OpenGL® Reference Manual* and Chapter 5, "Lighting," of *OpenGL® Programming Guide*.

To change the ambient, diffuse, or specular material parameters, call **glMaterialfv**() with GL_AMBIENT, GL_DIFFUSE, or GL_SPECULAR, and pass in a four-element array of GLfloats representing the RGBA color value. The following calls create a material that reflects mostly blue diffuse light and white specular light:

```
const GLfloat blue[4] = { .3f, .3f, 1.f, 1.f };
glMaterialfv( GL_FRONT, GL_DIFFUSE, blue );
const GLfloat white[4] = { 1.f, 1.f, 1.f, 1.f };
glMaterialfv( GL_FRONT, GL_SPECULAR, white );
```

Call **glMaterialf**() with a *pname* of GL_SHININESS to set the specular exponent. As in the Phong lighting model (Phong 1975), OpenGL takes the dot product of the reflected light vector and a vector to the eye,[2] and raises the result to the GL_SHININESS exponent. The value must be in the range 0.0 to 128.0. The default value of 0.0 results in a broad specular highlight (anything raised to the 0.0 power is 1.0 or full intensity), whereas increasingly higher values result in tighter highlights. Use values less than 10.0, for example, to simulate broad-gloss surfaces, such as brass or bronze. Use higher values to simulate high-gloss surfaces, such as pool balls.

To create a tight specular highlight on a shiny pool ball, as shown in Figure 4-2, call

```
glMaterialf( GL_FRONT, GL_SHININESS, 128.f );
```

4.4.1 Changing Material Parameters with glColor*()

Earlier in this chapter, you learned that OpenGL uses the current material color (set with **glMaterialfv**()) when lighting is enabled but uses the current primary color (set with **glColor3f**()) when lighting is disabled. This is inconvenient for applications that alternate between displaying models lit and unlit. Also, **glMaterial*v**() is considerably more expensive for OpenGL to process than **glColor3f**().

---

2. By default, OpenGL uses (0,0,1) for a vector to the eye in eye coordinates, which is adequate for most applications.

Figure 4-2 This image demonstrates the effects of different *GL_SPECULAR* material colors and GL_SHININESS specular exponent values. Left: Zero-intensity (0., 0., 0., 1.) specular material color; specular exponent is irrelevant. Center: Low-intensity (.3, .3, .3, 1.) specular material color with a specular exponent of 10.0. Right: Full-intensity (1., 1., 1., 1.) specular material color with a specular exponent of 128.0.

Color material mode addresses these issues. When you enable color material mode, certain current material colors track the current primary color. Enable this mode by calling

```
glEnable( GL_COLOR_MATERIAL );
```

By default, this causes **glColor3f**() calls to change not only the current primary color, but also the current ambient and diffuse material colors. You can change which material parameters track the primary color by calling **glColorMaterial**().

---

void **glColorMaterial**(GLenum *face*, GLenum *mode*);

Specifies which material parameters track the current primary color. *face* determines whether the call affects front- or back-face material parameters, or both. *mode* specifies the material parameters that should track the current primary color.

▶ OpenGL version: 1.0 and later.

Applications typically specify GL_FRONT_AND_BACK for *face* (unless using two-sided lighting). Initially, *mode* is GL_AMBIENT_AND_DIFFUSE. Other valid values include GL_AMBIENT, GL_DIFFUSE, and GL_SPECULAR, which cause the ambient, diffuse, or specular material colors, respectively, to track the current primary color.

For more information on **glColorMaterial**(), see Section 2.14.3, "Color-Material," of *The OpenGL Graphics System* and "glColorMaterial" in *OpenGL® Reference Manual*.

4.4.2   Typical Usage

Applications most often use **glColorMaterial**() with its default mode of GL_AMBIENT_AND_DIFFUSE. This setting allows applications to change the current ambient and diffuse material colors efficiently with a single call to **glColor3f**().

Applications generally either emulate a flat, nonglossy surface with a specular material color near zero intensity, such as (0.1, 0.1, 0.1, 1.), or a shiny surface with a specular material color of (1., 1., 1., 1.). Some applications, however, have a large library of materials such as brass, plastic, and rubber, which require different specular colors.

Applications vary the GL_SHININESS specular exponent to simulate different material reflection properties. Applications rarely use the default GL_SHININESS value of 0.0. Try a value of 10.0 as a good starting value and then tweak it to obtain an appropriate result for the material you're rendering. To simulate some high-gloss surfaces, your application might need to set GL_SHININESS to the maximum value of 128.0.

As an example, to simulate a hard, shiny blue-plastic material, use the following code:

```
// Enable lighting, one light source, and color material
glEnable( GL_LIGHTING );
glEnable( GL_COLOR_MATERIAL );
glEnable( GL_LIGHT0 );

// Specify a white specular highlight
const GLfloat white[4] = { 1.f, 1.f, 1.f, 1.f };
glMaterialfv( GL_FRONT, GL_SPECULAR, white );
glMaterialf( GL_FRONT, GL_SHININESS, 20.f );

// By default, color material modifies ambient and diffuse
//   material colors. Set both ambient and diffuse material
//   colors to blue.
glColor3f( 0.1f, 0.1f, 1.f );

// Specify geometry with unit length normals
//   ...
```

This snippet was taken from the Materials example code at the *OpenGL® Distilled* Web site, which also simulates other material types.

4.4.3   More Information

It's important to remember that your application can only *simulate* real-world materials by using OpenGL lighting. Although OpenGL lighting is adequate for nonphotorealistic rendering, applications that require accurate and realistic rendering of materials should consider using OpenGL vertex and fragment shaders. For further information, see the following sections of *OpenGL® Shading Language:* Section 9.3, "Material Properties and Lighting"; Section 10.5, "Polynomial Texture Mapping with BRDF Data"; Section 11.4, "Bump Mapping"; and Chapter 12, "Noise." In this book, Appendix A, "Other Features," briefly discusses the OpenGL Shading Language.

4.5   Positional and Directional Lights

Positional light sources shine light in all directions. Use a positional light source to simulate local light sources, such as a streetlight or an exposed light bulb. Specify the position as a homogenous *xyzw* coordinate. *x*, *y*, and *z* specify the light position in object coordinates, and the *w* value must be 1.0.

The following code makes GL_LIGHT1 a positional light at (10, 4, –4) in object coordinates:

```
const GLfloat pos[4] = { 10.f, 4.f, -4.f, 1.f };
glLightfv( GL_LIGHT1, GL_POSITION, pos );
```

Directional light sources are always at an infinite distance from your geometry and shine light in a single direction. Use a directional light to simulate nonlocal light sources with effectively parallel light rays, such as the Sun. To specify a directional light, again use a homogenous coordinate, but store a vector pointing toward the light in the *x*, *y*, and *z* values (the light shines in the opposite direction), and set the *w* coordinate to 0.0.

The following code makes GL_LIGHT1 a directional light at positive *x*, with light shining along the negative *x* axis (in object coordinates):

```
const GLfloat pos[4] = { 1.f, 0.f, 0.f, 0.f };
glLightfv( GL_LIGHT1, GL_POSITION, pos );
```

To summarize the above:

- For positional lights, GL_POSITION is an *xyz* location with a *w* value of 1.0.

- For directional lights, GL_POSITION is an *xyz* vector pointing toward the light with a *w* value of 0.0. The light direction is –(*xyz*).

For both positional and directional lights, GL_POSITION is an object-coordinate value. When you call **glLightfv**() to specify the position,

OpenGL multiplies the GL_POSITION value by the current model-view matrix to transform it into eye coordinates, where OpenGL performs lighting calculations. Usually, an application needs to manage only two light-positioning scenarios:

- Headlights—The light position stays fixed relative to the camera, regardless of the camera position. Applications commonly create this effect by specifying the light position in eye coordinates. Because the camera is at the origin in eye coordinates, specifying the light position relative to the camera position is simple. The following code places GL_LIGHT1 directly above the camera:

```
glMatrixModel( GL_MODELVIEW );
glPushMatrix();
glLoadIdentity();
const GLfloat pos[] = { 0., 1., 0., 1. };
glLightfv( GL_LIGHT1, GL_POSITION, pos );
glPopMatrix();
```

- Scene lights—Architectural applications commonly place positional light sources in the scene to simulate a light fixture or table lamp. To create this effect, the model-view matrix must contain the current view transformation, as well as the light modeling transformation (if any), when you specify the light position. You'll need to specify the light position again if the camera changes position or if the light moves (to simulate repositioning a desk lamp, for example).

In either case, always specify the light position before specifying any geometry that the light illuminates.

4.6   Debugging Lights

Several things could cause lighting not to work properly, and there are numerous ways to identify the source of the problem.

4.6.1   Debugging a Blank Window

If OpenGL appears to have rendered nothing, try the following:

- Disable lighting by replacing your call to enable lighting with **glDisable**(GL_LIGHTING). If OpenGL still renders nothing, the problem is elsewhere—possibly an incorrect view transformation or a near/far clipping plane problem. Resolve these issues first before re-enabling lighting.

- If the final rendered color of your geometry happens to be the same color as your clear color, your window will appear blank even though OpenGL rendered the geometry. To make "invisible" geometry appear, try setting a different clear color by calling **glClearColor**() just before you call **glClear**(). If enabling lighting makes your geometry appear black, check to ensure that your application has enabled at least one light source, and set its diffuse and specular colors appropriately.

4.6.2 Normals

When first learning to use OpenGL, many programmers fail to supply correct normals. This type of error causes odd shading artifacts on lit surfaces. As a good rule of thumb, supply a unit-length normal for every vertex.

If the application is specifying unit-length normals, yet odd lighting artifacts persist, it's possible that scale transformations in the model-view matrix are distorting the normals. If necessary, enable GL_RESCALE_NORMAL or GL_NORMALIZE to resolve this issue.

4.6.3 Incorrect Face Culling

If your application enables GL_CULL_FACE but has the vertex winding order reversed, you might be looking at back faces instead of front faces. In addition to causing other visual artifacts, this situation might make the light appear to be on the wrong side of your geometry. Replace your call to enable face culling with a call to **glDisable**(GL_CULL_FACE). If disabling face culling resolves your lighting issue, see "glFrontFace" in *OpenGL® Reference Manual* for information on how to configure face culling properly.

4.6.4 Debugging Position and Direction

If your lights appear in the wrong position or shine from the wrong direction, check to make sure that you're specifying the GL_POSITION each frame with the correct model-view transformation. Specifying the GL_POSITION each frame is required for some light types, and if your light is a headlight or some other type of light that doesn't require a refresh of the GL_POSITION each frame, this is still good debugging technique. You can always optimize specifying the GL_POSITION later, after you've identified and addressed any issues related to light position.

Be sure to specify the `GL_POSITION` before rendering geometry illuminated by that light.

If you use positional lights, first try a directional light instead. This will help verify that you've specified the vertex normals correctly.

4.6.5 Debugging Light Colors

If you're using colored lights and not getting the results you expect, initially use white lights to verify that you've specified the correct material colors. Remember, for example, that a pure-red object lit by a pure-blue light will appear black, because red objects reflect only red light and absorb blue light.

4.6.6 Per-Vertex Lighting Artifacts

The fact that OpenGL calculates lighting at each vertex could create lighting artifacts on low-resolution geometry, as shown in Figure 4-3.

Low-resolution geometry lighting artifacts are especially apparent in specular highlights. Inadequate resolution, however, could also cause visible artifacts in diffuse lighting. These artifacts will appear in the presence of either directional or positional lights, but positional lights often cause them to be more acute. Low-resolution geometry that rotates or moves relative to a light source will often have an unstable specular highlight that appears to crawl or swim over the surface, or to fade in and out.

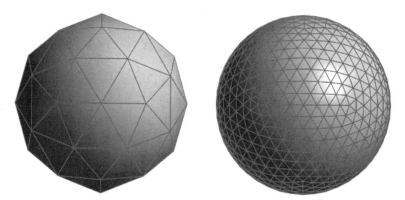

Figure 4-3   The sphere on the left has insufficient resolution for OpenGL to render the specular highlight accurately. This is not an issue for the sphere on the right, due to its higher resolution. Light and material parameters are identical for both spheres.

Geometry must have sufficient vertices for per-vertex lighting and Gouraud shading to produce acceptable results. Increasing geometric resolution could adversely affect performance, however, so try to find a good balance between lighting effects and number of vertices.

You might also try specifying a smaller GL_SHININESS specular exponent to create a larger specular highlight that affects more vertices.

If neither of these methods produces acceptable results, consider other OpenGL features, such as cube maps or per-fragment lighting in a fragment shader. Chapter 6, "Texture Mapping," describes using cube maps to improve specular highlights. You can implement per-fragment lighting in OpenGL version 2.0 by using fragment shaders, but this is beyond the scope of this book. See *OpenGL® Shading Language* for more information.

4.6.7 Missing Specular Highlights

Specular highlights might not appear for several reasons.

Check to ensure that the incident light and viewing angles are correct. The specular highlight won't appear unless the viewing angle coincides with the reflection of the incident light. Incorrect surface normals could cause OpenGL to calculate the reflection vector incorrectly, so check that your application is sending correct unit-length normals.

Check your setting for the specular material color and specular light color. Remember that only GL_LIGHT0 defaults to a full-intensity specular color; other lights default to zero intensity.

Check your GL_SHININESS value. Large values may create specular highlights too small to appear on low-resolution geometry. Temporarily set a much lower value, such as 1.0. If the specular highlight appears, you'll need to increase the resolution of your geometry, as discussed earlier in this chapter, or set GL_SHININESS to a smaller value.

If you're using texture mapping with GL_MODULATE texture environment mode, you'll need to use secondary color or multitexturing to add a specular highlight. See Chapter 6, "Texture Mapping," for more information.

4.6.8 Line and Point Colors

OpenGL is a state machine. When your application enables lighting, OpenGL lights all subsequent primitives, including lines and points. Although lit lines and points can create some interesting effects, often this isn't the desired result. Most applications need to disable lighting before submitting line and point primitives. This causes OpenGL to render the primitives with the current primary color, rather than modify the primary color with lighting results.

4.7   More Information

For information on OpenGL lighting topics not covered in this chapter (such as spotlights, attenuation, lighting model parameters, emissive and ambient light, precise details of OpenGL light equations, and lighting in color index mode), see the following:

- Chapter 5, "Lighting," of *OpenGL® Programming Guide*

- Section 2.14.1, "Lighting," of *The OpenGL Graphics System*

- "glColorMaterial," "glLight," "glLightModel," and "glMaterial" in *OpenGL® Reference Manual*

Because OpenGL applies textures after performing lighting calculations, geometry that is both lit and textured requires special treatment. Chapter 6, "Texture Mapping," discusses techniques for applying textures that preserve OpenGL lighting effects.

OpenGL lighting creates shading effects but doesn't create shadows from one surface on to another. You can implement one of many algorithms in your OpenGL application to create shadows. For information on creating shadow effects, see the following:

- Chapter 6, "Texture Mapping," describes shadow algorithms using OpenGL textures.

- Chapter 14, "Now That You Know," of *OpenGL® Programming Guide* describes the planar projected shadow technique, which renders projected shadow geometry on a plane surface.

The *OpenGL® Distilled* Web site has two examples that demonstrate shadow techniques and other examples that also employ lighting. The OpenGL Web site at http://www.opengl.org also has several coding resources online, including lighting and shadow example code.

4.8 References

(Blinn 1977) Blinn, James F. "Models of Light Reflection for Computer Synthesized Pictures." Proceedings of the 4th Annual Conference on Computer Graphics and Interactive Techniques. 1977.

(Phong 1975) Phong, Bui Tuong. "Illumination for Computer Generated Pictures." *Communications of the ACM* 18:6 (June 1975).

(Torrance 1967) Torrance, K. E., and E. M. Sparrow. "Theory for Off-Specular Reflection from Roughened Surfaces." *Journal of the Optical Society of America* 57:9 (September 1967).

Chapter 5

Pixel Rectangles

The earliest framebuffers were simply mapped into host memory. To render, applications addressed the framebuffer like any normal block of memory and stored final color values at pixel locations within the framebuffer (Sproul 1979). As graphics hardware evolved, providing efficient direct access to the framebuffer became increasingly difficult, and many graphics hardware manufacturers stopped providing memory-mapped framebuffer access altogether. To support hardware that can't be memory mapped, OpenGL allows reading, writing, and copying *pixel rectangles* in the framebuffer.

Chapter 6, "Texture Mapping," describes a much more powerful use for pixel data than simply copying it to the framebuffer. This chapter serves as an introduction to texture mapping, because OpenGL uses the same pixel pipeline to process textures as it does to process pixel rectangles.

What You'll Learn

This chapter covers the basics of drawing, reading, and copying pixel rectangles:

- Drawing pixels—How to send pixel rectangles to OpenGL for display in the framebuffer.

- The raster position—How to specify where pixels should be rendered.

- Reading pixels—How to read framebuffer contents from the framebuffer.

- Copying pixels—How to perform copy (or BLT) operations within the framebuffer.

- Performance issues—Why moving pixel rectangles can stunt performance. The chapter also suggests alternative approaches that provide better performance.

- Debugging—How to resolve some common pitfalls that can cause incorrect behavior in your application.

What You Won't Learn

OpenGL provides a powerful set of commands for processing pixel data. Applications use OpenGL to display and store pixel data in a wide variety of formats, as well as share pixel data between big- and little-endian machines. Most of these commands are outside the scope of this chapter, which focuses on the task of displaying, copying, and reading back pixel data as RGBA unsigned bytes.

The capabilities of OpenGL not covered in this chapter include

- Pixel processing—The chapter does not discuss pixel transfer, pixel map, color table lookup, pixel zoom, the imaging subset, and several other aspects of pixel processing.

- Bitmaps—This chapter discusses bitmaps only in terms of how the **glBitmap**() command affects the current raster position.

For more information on pixel rectangles, bitmaps, and pixel operations, see Chapter 8, "Drawing Pixels, Bitmaps, Fonts, and Images," of *OpenGL® Programming Guide* and Section 4.3, "Drawing, Reading, and Copying Pixels," of *The OpenGL Graphics System*.

5.1   Drawing Pixels

OpenGL allows applications to render pixel rectangles to the framebuffer with the **glDrawPixels**() command. **glDrawPixels**() copies pixel data from an address in application-addressable memory to the framebuffer. OpenGL places the pixel rectangle's bottom-left corner at the current raster position. The next section, "The Current Raster Position," explains how to set the current raster position and how OpenGL transforms it into window space. The section "Drawing Pixel Rectangles with glDrawPixels()" later in this chapter covers the **glDrawPixels**() command in greater detail.

When your application issues a **glDrawPixels**() command, several state values affect how OpenGL interprets and displays the pixel rectangle.

These state values allow applications to specify the byte ordering, row alignment, color table lookup, pixel zoom, and other aspects of OpenGL pixel processing. These state values have several applications in image processing and data sharing. If your application uses RGBA unsigned byte pixel data for simple display and texture mapping, however, the default state is sufficient in most cases. To familiarize yourself with these state values, see Chapter 8, "Drawing Pixels, Bitmaps, Fonts, and Images," of *OpenGL® Programming Guide*.

5.1.1   The Current Raster Position

When your application issues a **glDrawPixels**() command, OpenGL draws the pixels at the current raster position Although **glDrawPixels**() displays a pixel rectangle in window coordinates, applications often specify the raster position in object coordinates, which OpenGL transforms into window coordinates. OpenGL transforms both the raster position and vertices by using the transformation pipeline described in Chapter 3, "Transformation and Viewing."

OpenGL offers several ways to set the raster position. Many applications use the **glRasterPos***() set of commands.

---

void **glRasterPos**[234][sifd](*TYPE x, TYPE y, TYPE z, TYPE w*);

Specifies the object coordinates of the raster position. *x, y, z,* and *w* are the object coordinates of the desired raster position. When using **glRasterPos3***(), the *w* coordinate defaults to 1.0, and when specifying two parameters, *z* defaults to 0.0, and *w* defaults to 1.0.

The **glRasterPos***() command is similar to the **glVertex***() set of commands mentioned briefly in Chapters 1 and 2.

▶ OpenGL version: 1.0 and later.

Just as vertices have vertex states associated with them, the current raster position uses states, such as the current texture coordinate. There are very few applications for applying a single texture coordinate to an entire pixel rectangle, however. For this reason, most applications disable texture mapping when rendering pixel rectangles.

5.1.1.1   Handling Clipped Raster Positions

OpenGL transforms the raster position into clip coordinates and tests it against the clip volume. If the raster position is inside the clip volume,

OpenGL marks it as valid and continues transforming it into window coordinates. When your application issues a **glDrawPixels**() command, OpenGL rasterizes the pixel rectangle with the bottom-left corner at the window-coordinate raster position. Figure 5-1 shows a pixel rectangle rendered with a valid raster position.

If the raster position is outside the clip volume, OpenGL marks it as invalid. When the raster position is invalid, subsequent **glDrawPixels**() commands have no effect; no pixels are rasterized.

OpenGL's treatment of **glDrawPixels**() for invalid raster positions often results in unexpected clipping of the entire pixel rectangle. Figures 5-2 and 5-3 illustrate this behavior.

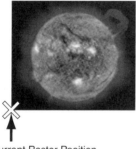

Current Raster Position

Figure 5-1   An image of the Sun rendered at a valid raster position.[1]

Current Raster Position

Figure 5-2   A screenshot from the PixelRectangles example program. The raster position for the image of the Earth is unclipped and valid.

---

1. Astronomical images reproduced in this chapter are owned by NASA. The Earth image was created by the Earth Observatory team (http://earthobservatory.nasa.gov/).

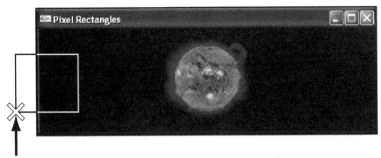

Current Raster Position

Figure 5-3 As the Earth orbits the Sun, its raster position goes outside the left side of the clip volume, and OpenGL marks it as invalid. In this case, OpenGL ignores the **glDrawPixels**() for the Earth, even though part of the image would be visible if OpenGL had rendered it.

As shown in Figure 5-3, the entire image is missing when the raster position is clipped at the left or bottom. To manage this issue, use the **glBitmap**() command.

---

void **glBitmap**(GLsizei *w*, GLsizei *h*, GLfloat *xOrigin*, GLfloat *yOrigin*, GLfloat *xInc*, GLfloat *yInc*, const GLubyte* *data*);

Renders the bitmap (1 bit per pixel) stored in *data* with width *w* and height *h* such that the image origin described by (*xOrigin*, *yOrigin*) corresponds to the current raster position.

After rendering, **glBitmap**() shifts the raster position by (*xInc*, *yInc*) in window coordinates. If *data* is NULL, and *w* and *h* are zero, or if the current raster position is invalid, **glBitmap**() renders nothing but still shifts the raster position.

glBitmap() was intended for rendering raster text, but this use has fallen into disfavor because texture mapped text generally performs better and produces higher-quality results. Modern OpenGL applications typically use **glBitmap**() to shift the raster position.

▶ OpenGL version: 1.0 and later.

To use **glBitmap**() to render pixel rectangles that are clipped on the left or bottom:

1. Set the raster position to a valid (unclipped) position, using **glRasterPos**().

2. Call **glBitmap**() with *xInc* and *yInc* set to shift the raster position in window coordinates to the desired location outside the viewport.

3. Issue the **glDrawPixels**() call. The visible portion of the pixel rectangle will appear inside the viewport.

The PixelRectangles example code uses **glBitmap**() to shift the position of pixel rectangles so that their centers correspond to the current raster position.

5.1.1.2   Pixel Rectangles in 2D

Applications often use **glDrawPixels**() during 2D rendering and, therefore, need to specify the raster position directly in window coordinates.

As described in Chapter 3, "Transformation and Viewing," applications can set the model-view matrix to the identity and use **glOrtho**() to create a projection matrix that allows rendering directly in window coordinates. After this initialization, applications can position pixel rectangles in two dimensions with the **glRasterPos***() command. OpenGL version 1.4, however, provides the **glWindowPos***() command, which allows the application to set the raster position directly in window coordinates. **glWindowPos***() bypasses the transformation and clipping stage of the of the transformation pipeline, and is generally more efficient for setting the raster position in window coordinates than changing the model-view and projection matrices.

---

void **glWindowPos**[23][sifd](*TYPE x, TYPE y, TYPE z*);

Specifies the raster position directly in window coordinates. *x, y,* and *z* specify the window-coordinate location of the current raster position. Unlike **glRasterPos***(), OpenGL doesn't transform or clip **glWindow-Pos***(). When using **glWindowPos2***(), *z* defaults to 0.0.

▶ OpenGL version: 1.4 and later.

Most applications use **glRasterPos3f**() when placing pixel rectangles in three dimensions and use **glWindowPos2i**() when rendering pixel rectangles in 2D window coordinates.

5.1.2   Drawing Pixel Rectangles with glDrawPixels()

You render a pixel rectangle with the **glDrawPixels**() command.

---

void **glDrawPixels**(GLsizei *width*, GLsizei *height*, GLenum *format*,
   GLenum *type*, const GLvoid* *data*);

Renders the *width* x *height* rectangle of color, depth, or stencil pixel data
pointed to by *data*.

The *format* parameter tells OpenGL what the pixel data represents. The
most common *format* values are GL_RGB and GL_RGBA, for sending pixel
data composed of three RGB components per pixel or four RGBA components per pixel. Use GL_STENCIL_INDEX or GL_DEPTH_COMPONENT
to send single-component stencil or depth pixel data.

The *type* parameter describes the pixel data type. Applications usually
specify a *type* parameter of GL_UNSIGNED_BYTE to send RGB and RGBA
color data. OpenGL supports several other useful *type* values, including
GL_UNSIGNED_SHORT, GL_UNSIGNED_INT, and GL_FLOAT.

▶ OpenGL version: 1.0 and later.

glDrawPixels() does nothing if the current raster position is not valid.
Check whether the current raster position is valid or not by calling
glGetBooleanv() as the following code segment shows:

```
GLboolean valid;
glGetBooleanv( GL_CURRENT_RASTER_POSITION_VALID, &valid );
```

If the raster position is valid, **glDrawPixels**() reads the specified pixel
rectangle from client memory and writes it to the framebuffer at the current raster position. The *data* parameter points to the pixel in the bottom-
left corner of the pixel rectangle, and pixels must be in row-major order
proceeding left to right and bottom to top.

Rows of pixels are aligned on 4-byte boundaries by default. To change this
default behavior, see "glPixelTransfer" in *OpenGL® Reference Manual*. If your
application draws only RGBA color unsigned byte pixel data, the default
4-byte alignment will produce correct results.

OpenGL allows applications to render rectangles of color, depth, or stencil
values as specified with the *format* parameter.

OpenGL generates fragments when it rasterizes the pixel rectangle and processes them using the same per-fragment operations as for 3D geometry.
Rasterization state, including texture mapping, affects the appearance of
rendered pixel rectangles. Most applications disable texture mapping with
glDisable(GL_TEXTURE_2D) before calling **glDrawPixels**().

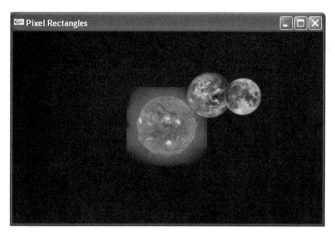

Figure 5-4   Screenshot from the PixelRectangles example program. The code uses **glDrawPixels**() to render images of the Sun, Earth, and Moon. The varying alpha values in the RGBA data allow transparency and translucency.

When drawing a pixel rectangle of color data, each fragment generated during rasterization uses the window-space *z* value from the current raster position. This value is used in the depth test, if enabled.

RGBA pixel data can contain varying alpha values. Applications enable the alpha test and blend operations to draw blocks of pixels that are partially transparent. The PixelRectangles example program from this book's Web site uses these features to render partially transparent solar flares, as well as to anti-alias the outlines of the Earth and Moon, as shown in Figure 5-4 and Plate 2.

5.2   Reading Pixels

Many applications read back pixel data to support printing images and saving images to a 2D image file. To obtain the contents of the framebuffer, use the **glReadPixels**() command.

---

void **glReadPixels**(GLint *x*, GLint *y*, GLsizei *width*, GLsizei *height*,
    GLenum *format*, GLenum *type*, GLvoid* *data*);

Reads the *width* x *height* pixel rectangle with the bottom-left corner at *x* and *y* in window coordinates from the framebuffer and stores it at the address specified by *data*. The *format* and *type* parameters are as for **glDrawPixels**().

▶ OpenGL version: 1.0 and later.

If any part of the read region is not owned by OpenGL (for example, part of the region lies outside the window or is obscured by another window), the read result for that area is undefined.

By default, **glReadPixels**() reads from the back buffer of a double-buffered window. Applications can change this with the **glReadBuffer**() command; see "glReadBuffer" in *OpenGL® Reference Manual* for more information.

If the *format* parameter is GL_RGBA, and the framebuffer doesn't store alpha, OpenGL returns full intensity for the alpha value of each pixel.

OpenGL allows applications to set state values that control how it packs the pixel rectangle into client memory. If your application specifies GL_RGBA for *format* and GL_UNSIGNED_BYTE for *type*, the default settings will tightly pack the pixel rectangle into your client memory area. See Chapter 8, "Drawing Pixels, Bitmaps, Fonts, and Images," in *OpenGL® Programming Guide* for more information on controlling pixel read state.

The PixelRectangles example code available from this book's Web site uses **glReadPixels**() to support saving the rendered image to a TIFF image file.

5.3 Copying Pixels

OpenGL also provides a mechanism to copy pixel data from one framebuffer location to another. The **glCopyPixels**() command behaves as though your application called **glReadPixels**() to obtain a pixel rectangle and then called **glDrawPixels**() to render it back into the framebuffer.

---

void **glCopyPixels**(GLint *x*, GLint *y*, GLsizei *width*, GLsizei *height*, GLenum *type*);

Copies data within the framebuffer. *x*, *y*, *width*, and *height* have the same meaning as for **glReadPixels**(). *type* indicates which portion of the framebuffer to copy and must be GL_COLOR, GL_DEPTH, or GL_STENCIL.

glCopyPixels() copies the *width* x *height* pixel rectangle with the bottom-left corner at *x* and *y* to the current raster position.

▶ OpenGL version: 1.0 and later.

As with **glReadPixels**(), pixel data is undefined if the source region for the copy isn't owned by OpenGL (for example, part of the region lies outside the window or is obscured by another window).

5.4 Performance Issues

Copying pixel rectangles between client (host) memory and server (graphics hardware) memory is often the cause of performance bottlenecks. If your application needs to use **glDrawPixels**() or **glReadPixels**() in performance-critical code, you should read this section and make yourself aware of the performance issues.

5.4.1 Using Alternatives to glDrawPixels()

Applications rarely use **glDrawPixels**() to render pixel rectangles due to poor performance in several implementations. Many implementations fall back to software processing when applications specify uncommon *type* and *format* parameters. For best performance, specify a *format* of GL_RGBA and a *type* of GL_UNSIGNED_BYTE.

Regardless, **glDrawPixels**() still requires OpenGL to copy the entire pixel rectangle to the graphics hardware every time the application issues the **glDrawPixels**() command—typically, every frame. Even if the OpenGL implementation processes **glDrawPixels**() with full hardware acceleration, the performance impact of the data copy could be unacceptable.

The texture mapping feature, described in Chapter 6, "Texture Mapping," provides a more efficient solution. Applications store the pixel rectangle as a texture object, requiring only one data copy over the system bus—typically, at initialization time. To display the pixel rectangle, applications render a texture mapped quadrilateral. Accessing the pixel data from texture memory is extremely efficient on nearly all modern OpenGL implementations.

The GL_ARB_pixel_buffer_object[2] extension allows **glDrawPixels**() commands to source data from buffer objects stored in high-performance server memory. When correctly implemented, this extension allows **glDrawPixels**() to operate with performance comparable to texture

---

2. When this book went to press, GL_ARB_pixel_buffer_object was a candidate for promotion to the OpenGL version 2.1 specification.

mapping. Chapter 7, "Extensions and Versions," discusses the GL_ARB_pixel_buffer_object extension.

5.4.2 Flushing the OpenGL Pipeline

glReadPixels() suffers from the same performance issues as **glDraw-Pixels**()—inherent performance issues related to copying pixel rectangles over the system bus and unoptimized code paths for uncommon *format* and *type* parameters. These issues are minor, however, compared with the fact that **glReadPixels**() completely flushes the OpenGL rendering pipeline.

The **glReadPixels**() command doesn't return to the application until OpenGL has completed the read operation. This completely drains the OpenGL pipeline; the application isn't sending any new commands because it's stalled waiting for **glReadPixels**() to return.

As with **glDrawPixels**(), the GL_ARB_pixel_buffer_object extensions can help boost read performance. Applications read to a buffer object rather than completely back to host memory; then they copy buffer object contents back to the host when a performance delay is acceptable. Again, see Chapter 7, "Extensions and Versions," for a discussion of the GL_ARB_pixel_buffer_object extension.

5.5 Debugging

Several things can cause reading, drawing, and copying of pixels to produce incorrect results.

5.5.1 Incorrect Raster Position

Many problems with **glDrawPixels**() and **glCopyPixels**() stem from a misunderstanding of how OpenGL transforms the raster position. Keep in mind that OpenGL transforms the raster position just as though it were transforming a vertex. To visualize the current raster position, render a single point primitive at the same *xyz* location as passed to **glRasterPos3f**(). OpenGL renders the point at the current raster position. If the point doesn't render, either the raster position is invalid, or the point is obscured in *z*. Keep this in mind to avoid raster position issues in 3D.

For 2D rendering, the best way to avoid problems is to use **glWindowPos2i**()
to specify the raster position. Using **glRasterPos***() means you must
establish a 2D transformation pipeline. If your application mixes 2D and
3D rendering, it must change the transformation pipeline twice each frame.
glWindowPos*() eliminates this issue. If your underlying OpenGL implementation is version 1.4 or later, use the **glWindowPos***() commands.

5.5.2   Clipped Raster Position

OpenGL clips entire pixel rectangles rendered with the **glDrawPixels**()
command when only the raster position is invalid and outside the view
volume. This appears incorrect to new OpenGL programmers when
clipped at the left or bottom of the view volume, because intuitively, some
of the pixel rectangle should still be visible in that case. See Figures 5-2 and
5-3 for an illustration of this behavior.

Check for an invalid raster position by calling **glGetBooleanv**(). If you
know that the raster position will always be valid (or should be valid, if
your code is bug free), use an assert(), as shown in the following code:

```
GLboolean valid;
glGetBooleanv( GL_CURRENT_RASTER_POSITION_VALID, &valid );
assert( valid );
```

If you know the raster position is clipped on the left or bottom, use
glBitmap() to shift the raster position as described in the section "Handling Clipped Raster Positions" earlier in this chapter. As long as your code
sets a valid raster position using **glRasterPos***() or **glWindowPos***(),
you can shift it with **glBitmap**() as much as necessary, and it will still be
valid.

5.5.3   Texture or Fog Enabled

You should disable texture and fog before using the **glDrawPixels**() and
glCopyPixels() commands. The current raster position picks up the current texture coordinates, and if texture mapping is enabled, OpenGL looks
up a texture color value and applies it to your pixel rectangle. This behavior is almost never desired by programmers. In the same way, the raster
position has a distance from the eye that OpenGL uses to determine a fog
color when GL_FOG is enabled. In this case, OpenGL applies the fog color
to your pixel rectangle. Disable texturing and fog with the following
general-purpose code:

```
GLint maxTex;
glGetIntegerv( GL_MAX_TEXTURE_UNITS, &maxTex );
int idx;
for (idx=0; idx<maxTex; idx++)
{
    glActiveTexture( GL_TEXTURE0+idx );
    glDisable( GL_TEXTURE_1D );
    glDisable( GL_TEXTURE_2D );
    glDisable( GL_TEXTURE_3D ); // version 1.2 and higher
    glDisable( GL_TEXTURE_CUBE_MAP ); // version 1.3 and higher
}
glDisable( GL_FOG );
```

You should optimize this code to disable only the states that your application has enabled. Note that the above code assumes that both the development and runtime environments support OpenGL version 1.3 or later; see Chapter 7, "Extensions and Versions," for information on writing version-safe code.

5.5.4 Depth Test

When your application sets the raster position with **glRasterPos*** () or **glWindowPos*** (), OpenGL transforms the raster position into a 3D window coordinate with a depth value. When OpenGL rasterizes the subsequent pixel rectangle, it uses this depth value in the depth test and writes this value into the depth buffer for each pixel in the rectangle. Some applications require this behavior; others don't.

If your application always requires **glDrawPixels** () commands to win the depth test, set the depth function to GL_ALWAYS or simply disable the depth test altogether:

```
glDisable( GL_DEPTH_TEST );
```

5.5.5 Pixel Data Alignment

By default, OpenGL requires that each row in a pixel rectangle start on a 4-byte boundary. Change this with the **glPixelTransfer** () command; see "glPixelTransfer" in *OpenGL® Reference Manual* for details.

Applications commonly send pixel rectangles composed of RGBA unsigned byte data, and in this case, row alignment isn't a problem; each pixel fits into 4 bytes, so each row starts at a 4-byte boundary without padding. If your application sends RGB unsigned byte data, however, and pixel rows aren't a 4-byte multiple in length, you'll need to add padding so that all rows start on a 4-byte boundary.

5.5.6 Obscured Windows

When your application reads pixels from a partially or completely obscured window, OpenGL isn't required to return valid pixel data corresponding to the obscured region. This is true for **glReadPixels**(), as well as for the source regions of **glCopyPixels**() and **glCopyTexImage2D**() (described in the next chapter). This same caveat applies if the source region is outside the window.

The ability of OpenGL to return valid pixel data for obscured windows varies from one window system to the next. For window systems that use backing store or compositing window system technology, obscured regions pose no problem. This issue is still prevalent, however, for many commonly available window systems today. Fortunately, some extensions to OpenGL make this less of an issue:

- *Pbuffers* are nonvisible rendering buffers; because they are usually off-screen, they can never be obscured. Applications access pbuffers by using calls to the window system. Currently, GLUT doesn't provide access to pbuffers, so you need to use a platform-specific API to access them.

- GL_EXT_framebuffer_object is an extension that allows applications to render to destinations other than those provided by the windowing system. Like pbuffers, these render destinations are offscreen and, therefore, can't be obscured.

For more information on pbuffers, refer to platform-specific documentation, as described in Chapter 8, "Platform-Specific Interfaces."

For more information on GL_EXT_framebuffer_object, visit the OpenGL Extension Registry Web site: http://oss.sgi.com/projects/ ogl-sample/registry/. Also see Chapter 7, "Extensions and Versions."

5.5.7 Memory Allocation Issues

Behavior is undefined if the amount of memory pointed to by the *data* parameter to **glDrawPixels**() or **glReadPixels**() is insufficient to hold the pixel rectangle described by the *width*, *height*, *format*, and *type* parameters. This typically causes the application to crash, and the call stack implicates the **glDrawPixels**() or **glReadPixels**() function. Although the crash is inside the OpenGL implementation, the application's failure to allocate sufficient memory is the root cause.

If you have not changed the default state values with **glPixelTransfer**(), you can easily compute the size of your pixel rectangle as follows:

- For *format* set to GL_RGBA and *type* set to GL_UNSIGNED_BYTE, the amount of memory pointed to by *data* must be at least *width* × *height* × 4.

- For *format* set to GL_RGB and *type* set to GL_UNSIGNED_BYTE, if *width* × 3 isn't a multiple of 4, each row must be padded with unused bytes to the next-highest multiple of 4. The total amount of memory pointed to by *data* must be at least this padded row length multiplied by *height*.

These rules for calculating the size of data apply to both **glDrawPixels**() and **glReadPixels**(). For information on calculating the size of *data* for *format* and *type* other than shown above, see Chapter 8, "Drawing Pixels, Bitmaps, Fonts, and Images," of *OpenGL® Programming Guide* and Section 4.3, "Drawing, Reading, and Copying Pixels," of *The OpenGL Graphics System*.

5.6 More Information

OpenGL provides an incredibly rich set of routines for controlling how OpenGL unpacks pixel rectangles submitted by the application, as well as how it packs pixel rectangles to return to the application. Unfortunately, much of this functionality is outside the scope of *OpenGL® Distilled*.

Chapter 8, "Drawing Pixels, Bitmaps, Fonts, and Images," of *OpenGL® Programming Guide* covers this information in depth, including the imaging subset functionality available in the GL_ARB_imaging extension.

See the book's Web site for the PixelRectangle example program source code. The Extensions example program, discussed in Chapter 7, "Extensions and Versions," also demonstrates techniques for rendering pixel rectangles.

5.7 References

(Sproul 1979) Sproul, Robert F. "Raster Graphics for Interactive Programming Environments." Proceedings of the 6th Annual Conference on Computer Graphics and Interactive Techniques, 1979.

Chapter 6

Texture Mapping

Texture mapping is a concept that takes a moment to grasp but a lifetime to master. Complex texture mapping-based algorithms such as environment mapping, depth maps, and light maps had already been developed by the late 1970s. With the recent advent of fully programmable hardware, however, texture mapping and its widespread applications remain a field of active research.

What You'll Learn

The first part of this chapter covers the nuts and bolts of texture mapping. The second part covers how your application can use texture mapping to enhance lighting effects. The chapter concludes with a brief section on debugging texture mapping problems.

Topics covered in this chapter include the following:

- Texture mapping with texture objects—Texture objects were added to OpenGL version 1.1. They provide an efficient encapsulation of texture images and their associated texture state. In this chapter, you'll learn how to create texture objects and use them to store texture images and state.

- Mipmapping (Williams 1983) and filtering—This section shows you how to avoid sampling artifacts by specifying mipmaps and linear filters.

- Multitexturing—OpenGL can apply multiple textures on a single primitive. This chapter shows how to bind texture objects to texture units and set the texture unit state.

- Texture-coordinate generation—Many algorithms require texture coordinates that are too complex for applications to compute on the fly. In this chapter, you'll learn how to configure OpenGL to generate texture coordinates.

- The texture matrix—This section shows you how to specify transformations that modify texture coordinates.

- Cube mapping—OpenGL implements environment mapping with the cube map feature in version 1.3. This chapter focuses specifically on how cube maps support a specific type of environment mapping: producing accurate specular highlights on low-resolution geometry.

- Depth mapping—This chapter discusses three ways to use texture mapping to produce shadows. One of the most powerful methods is depth mapping. The chapter also tells you how to create and use depth maps in your application.

What You Won't Learn

Texture mapping is such a vast subject that entire books are devoted to it alone. Many aspects of texture mapping are not covered in this chapter, such as the following:

- 1D and 3D texture mapping—3D textures are especially useful for volume visualization or playing short video clips as textures.

- Texture tiling—The texture border feature, used primarily for seamlessly tiling several textures together, isn't covered.

- Text—Texture mapping is the de facto standard method for rendering 2D text in a scene. This is just one application of texture mapping not covered in this book, however.

- Full texture state—Several texture parameters, such as texture priority and texture level of detail (LOD) bias, aren't covered.

- Proxy textures—Querying OpenGL for texture supportability isn't covered.

- Texture compression—Compressed texture formats, which reduce the memory footprint of texture maps, isn't covered.

6.1   Using Texture Maps

Texture mapping applies colors from an image to primitives on a per-fragment basis. During rasterization, OpenGL interpolates texture coordinates and assigns them to each generated fragment. OpenGL uses these coordinates as indices to obtain *texels* (texture elements) from a texture image. The texel colors modify the fragment's primary color based on texture state parameters.

OpenGL supports four basic texture map types:

- 1D textures—A 1D texture map is a 1D array of texels. Applications specify a single *s* texture coordinate per vertex.

- 2D textures—A 2D texture map is an image or other 2D array of texel values. This is the most common form of texture mapping. Applications specify both *s* and *t* texture coordinates per vertex.[1]

- 3D textures—3D texture maps commonly used in volume visualization applications are a 3D volume of texels.

- Cube map textures—Cube map textures are a set of six 2D texture maps. Each of the six maps represents a 90-degree field of view of the world from the viewpoint of the geometry using the texture. Cube maps are used for environment mapping and specular highlights.

This chapter covers 2D textures and cube maps. For information on 1D and 3D textures, see Chapter 9, "Texture Mapping," of *OpenGL® Programming Guide*.

OpenGL version 1.1 introduced the concept of texture objects, which encapsulate both texture images and their associated state parameters. This feature allows OpenGL to cache textures in a high-performance working set. Because modern applications almost universally use texture objects, *OpenGL® Distilled* doesn't describe version 1.0-style texture mapping.

If the OpenGL version is 1.3 or later, you can apply multiple textures to a single primitive with the multitexturing feature. Applications frequently use this feature to enhance image realism by storing shadows or other lighting effects in a second texture.

Environment mapping (Blinn 1976) simulates the reflection of an environment on a shiny surface. OpenGL provides two primary mechanisms to support environment mapping. OpenGL version 1.0 allows sphere mapping, but due to its inherent limitations, cube mapping was added to the OpenGL version 1.3 specification. Environment mapping simulates the display of a primitive's surroundings reflected on its surface. Because specular highlights are light-source reflections, applications often use cube

---

1. The depth-mapping feature requires three texture coordinates—*s*, *t*, and *r*—even though the depth map is a 2D texture. See the section "Depth Maps" later in this chapter.

mapping to improve the appearance of specular highlights on low-resolution geometry.

OpenGL version 1.4 contains support for the depth-map shadow algorithm first described by Lance Williams (Williams 1978), refined and popularized in Pixar's short film *Luxo Jr.* (Reeves 1987). Although the original algorithm suffers from aliasing artifacts, it's the simplest mechanism available in OpenGL's fixed-functionality pipeline for producing shadows.

To use texture mapping, perform the following steps in your application:

1. Obtain an unused texture object identifier with **glGenTextures()**, and create a texture object using **glBindTexture()**.

2. Set texture-object state parameters.

3. Specify the texture image using **glTexImage2D()** or **gluBuild2DMipmaps()**.

4. Before rendering geometry that uses the texture object, bind the texture object with **glBindTexture()**.

5. Before rendering geometry, enable texture mapping.

6. Send geometry to OpenGL with appropriate texture coordinates per vertex.

6.1.1 Texture Objects

Texture objects store a texture image and its associated state. Most OpenGL implementations support a limited working set of texture objects, commonly implemented by storing the texture image in dedicated graphics hardware memory. Applications activate texture objects by issuing the **glBindTexture()** command.

Before the introduction of texture objects in OpenGL version 1.1, applications specified the texture image and state before each use, which typically was implemented by transmitting the image over the system bus. OpenGL still supports this usage, but modern OpenGL applications should use texture objects instead.

To use texture objects, your application must obtain, store, and eventually dispose of texture-object identifiers. For each texture object your application uses, you must store a texture image in it, along with the texture state parameters. Finally, when you want to render geometry that uses the texture, you must pass the texture-object identifier to **glBindTexture()**.

To obtain unused texture-object identifiers, use **glGenTextures**(). To dispose of texture-object identifiers when they are no longer needed, call **glDeleteTextures**().

---

void **glGenTextures**(GLsizei *n*, GLuint* *textures*);
void **glDeleteTextures**(GLsizei *n*, const GLuint* *textures*);
GLboolean **glIsTexture**(GLuint *texture*);

Use these functions to obtain or dispose of texture-object identifiers.
glGenTextures() returns *n* unused texture identifiers, marks them as used, and stores them in *textures*.

glDeleteTextures() deletes the texture objects associated with the *n* texture identifiers in *textures* and returns the identifiers to the unused texture identifier pool. If any of the texture identifiers is currently bound (see **glBindTexture**() below), **glDeleteTextures**() unbinds it.

glIsTexture() returns GL_TRUE if *texture* is an existing texture object.

▶ OpenGL version: 1.1 and later.

For example, the following code obtains a single texture-object identifier:

```
GLuint texId;
glGenTextures( 1, &texId );
```

glGenTextures() returns a texture-object identifier, but OpenGL doesn't create the texture object associated with that identifier until you bind the texture object for the first time with **glBindTexture**().

---

void **glBindTexture**(GLenum *target*, GLuint *texture*);

Specifies the active texture object. *target* must be GL_TEXTURE_1D, GL_TEXTURE_2D, GL_TEXTURE_3D, or GL_TEXTURE_CUBE_MAP, depending on whether your texture object stores a 1D, 2D, 3D, or cube map texture, respectively. *texture* specifies the texture-object identifier to bind. If *texture* hasn't been previously bound, **glBindTexture**() initializes it to default values.

▶ OpenGL version: **glBindTexture**() is available in version 1.1 and later.
          GL_TEXTURE_3D is available in version 1.2 and later.
          GL_TEXTURE_CUBE_MAP is available in version 1.3 and later.

The first time your application calls **glBindTexture**() on a given *texture,* OpenGL creates and initializes a 1D, 2D, 3D, or cube map texture object (depending on the *target* parameter) and associates that texture object with the identifier in *texture*. The new texture object has default parameters and a NULL texture image. Applications usually obtain texture-object identifiers and create texture objects during initialization.

Subsequent calls to **glBindTexture**() on a given *texture* activate the texture and texture state stored in the texture object. Applications call **glBindTexture**() at render time just before specifying geometry that uses the texture object.

It's an error to use a different *target* in subsequent calls to bind the same *texture*. **glBindTexture**() generates the error GL_INVALID_OPERATION if you bind a *texture* with a different *target*.

6.1.1.1   Texture Object State

Set texture object state with the **glTexParameteri**() command.

---

void **glTexParameter**[if](GLenum *target*, GLenum *pname*, *TYPE param*);

Sets the texture state parameter specified by *pname* to the value specified by *param* in the texture object currently bound to *target*. Table 6-1 lists valid values for *pname* and *param*. *target* is the same as for **glBindTexture**().

You can use **glTexParameter***() to set other texture parameters not covered in this book. For more information, see "glTexParameter" in *OpenGL® Reference Manual*.

▶ OpenGL version: 1.0 and later. Many *pname* and *param* values, however, are available only in more recent versions. See Table 6-1 for details.

After obtaining a texture-object identifier with **glGenTextures**() and creating its texture object with the first call to **glBindTexture**(), applications usually call **glTexParameteri**() to set texture state parameters for the new texture object.

The texture parameters covered in *OpenGL® Distilled* fall into three categories:

- Mipmap and filter parameters
- Depth-map parameters
- Texture-coordinate wrap parameters

For an explanation of the depth-map parameters GL_DEPTH_TEXTURE_MODE, GL_TEXTURE_COMPARE_FUNC, and GL_TEXTURE_COMPARE_MODE,

Table 6-1   Valid *pname* and *param* Values

pname	Valid *param* Values
GL_DEPTH_TEXTURE_MODE	GL_LUMINANCE, GL_INTENSITY, or GL_ALPHA to format the result of the depth comparison as a luminance, intensity, or alpha texel. For more information, see the section "Depth Maps" later in this chapter. ▶ OpenGL version: 1.4 and later
GL_GENERATE_MIPMAP	GL_TRUE or GL_FALSE to enable or disable mipmap generation. ▶ OpenGL version: 1.4 and later
GL_TEXTURE_COMPARE_FUNC	GL_LEQUAL or GL_GEQUAL[a] to control the depth comparison. For more information, see the section "Depth Maps" later in this chapter. ▶ OpenGL version: 1.4 and later
GL_TEXTURE_COMPARE_MODE	GL_COMPARE_R_TO_TEXTURE or GL_NONE to enable or disable the depth comparison. For more information, see the section "Depth Maps" later in this chapter. ▶ OpenGL version: 1.4 and later
GL_TEXTURE_MAG_FILTER	GL_NEAREST or GL_LINEAR to set the filter method for texture magnification. ▶ OpenGL version: 1.0 and later
GL_TEXTURE_MIN_FILTER	GL_NEAREST, GL_LINEAR, GL_NEAREST_MIPMAP_NEAREST, GL_NEAREST_MIPMAP_LINEAR, GL_LINEAR_MIPMAP_NEAREST, or GL_LINEAR_MIPMAP_LINEAR to set the filter method for texture minification. ▶ OpenGL version: 1.0 and later
GL_TEXTURE_WRAP_S, GL_TEXTURE_WRAP_T, GL_TEXTURE_WRAP_R[b]	GL_CLAMP, GL_REPEAT, or GL_CLAMP_TO_EDGE to set the wrap behavior for texture coordinates outside the range 0.0 to 1.0. ▶ OpenGL version: 1.0 and later[c]

a. OpenGL version 1.5 expands the list of valid *param* values for GL_TEXTURE_COMPARE_FUNC, which this book does not cover. For more information, see Section 3.8.4, "Texture Parameters," of *The OpenGL Graphics System*.

b. GL_TEXTURE_WRAP_S and GL_TEXTURE_WRAP_T are in OpenGL version 1.0, whereas GL_TEXTURE_WRAP_R was not introduced until OpenGL version 1.2.

c. GL_CLAMP_TO_EDGE was added in OpenGL version 1.2. Other wrap modes exist in later versions.

see the section "Depth Maps" later in this chapter. For an explanation
of the texture-coordinate wrap parameters GL_TEXTURE_WRAP_S,
GL_TEXTURE_WRAP_T, and GL_TEXTURE_WRAP_R, see the section "Texture
Coordinates" later in this chapter.

The texture parameters GL_TEXTURE_MIN_FILTER and GL_TEXTURE_
MAG_FILTER control the selection of texels when there isn't a one-to-one
relationship between the generated fragments and the texels.

During rasterization, if a fragment covers less area than a texel, OpenGL
uses the value of GL_TEXTURE_MAG_FILTER to determine the resulting
texture color. When set to GL_NEAREST, OpenGL uses the texel that contains the fragment center. Most applications, however, use the default
value, GL_LINEAR, which causes OpenGL to interpolate between texel
values to arrive at the texture color for the fragment.

If a fragment covers more area than a texel, OpenGL uses the value of
GL_TEXTURE_MIN_FILTER to determine the resulting texture color. In
addition to GL_NEAREST and GL_LINEAR modes, OpenGL supports mipmap modes that cause OpenGL to interpolate between different levels of
detail. The default value is GL_NEAREST_MIPMAP_LINEAR, which instructs
OpenGL to select single texels from the two closest mipmap levels and
then linearly interpolate between them. Most applications use mipmapped
textures but specify a GL_TEXTURE_MIN_FILTER of GL_LINEAR_MIPMAP_
LINEAR instead of the default. This filter mode produces antialiased results
when texels cover less area than fragments.

Do not use mipmapping on depth-map textures. Instead, specify a
GL_TEXTURE_MIN_FILTER of GL_LINEAR. See the section "Depth Maps"
later in this chapter for more information.

If your application uses a mipmapped value for GL_TEXTURE_MIN_FILTER
(for example, GL_LINEAR_MIPMAP_LINEAR), you must specify a complete
set of mipmap levels when you specify the texture image. OpenGL or GLU
can do this for you, however, as described in the next section.

6.1.1.2 Specifying Textures

When you bind your texture object for the first time and set its state, you
should also call **glTexImage2D**() to specify the texture image.

If your application uses a mipmapped value for GL_TEXTURE_MIN_FILTER
(for example, GL_LINEAR_MIPMAP_LINEAR), you must specify all texture
images in the mipmap pyramid. Applications rarely do this manually. If

the OpenGL version is 1.4 or higher, first bind the texture object and then set the GL_GENERATE_MIPMAP texture parameter to GL_TRUE before specifying the texture with **glTexImage2D**(). For example:

```
glTexParameteri( GL_TEXTURE_2D, GL_GENERATE_MIPMAP, GL_TRUE );
glTexImage2D( ... );
```

If your OpenGL version is earlier than 1.4, GL_GENERATE_MIPMAP is unavailable. To create all mipmap levels, use the GLU routine **gluBuild2DMipmaps**() as described later in this section.

---

void **glTexImage2D**(GLenum *target*, GLint *level*, GLint *internalformat*, GLsizei *width*, GLsizei *height*, GLint *border*, GLenum *format*, GLenum *type*, const GLvoid* *data*);

Specifies a 2D texture map or one of the six textures used in a cube map. If your texture object is a 2D texture, specify GL_TEXTURE_2D for *target*. If your texture object is a cube map, see the section "Environment Maps" later in this chapter.

level indicates the mipmap level of this image. For mipmap generation, or if you're not using a mipmap, specify a *level* of 0.

internalformat specifies a base internal format for the image. For backward compatibility with version 1.0, many applications simply specify the number of components per pixel, such as 4 for an RGBA texture, 3 for RGB, or 1 for a depth map or light map. *internalformat* can also be an enumerant indicating the texture format, such as GL_RGBA or GL_DEPTH_COMPONENT. Many such enumerants are available; see "glTexImage" in *OpenGL® Reference Manual* for details.

width and *height* are the texture dimensions. If the OpenGL version is less than 2.0, these must both be powers of 2. If the texture is part of a cube map, *width* and *height* must be equal.

border indicates a texture border width, which is useful for eliminating seams when tiling textures together. Set *border* to 0 if not using texture borders. This book doesn't cover texture borders. See *OpenGL® Programming Guide* for information on using texture borders.

format, *type*, and *data* are the same as for the **glDrawPixels**() command described in Chapter 5, "Pixel Rectangles."

▶ OpenGL version: 1.0 and later.

OpenGL interprets pixel data that is sent as a texture image the same way that it interprets pixel data sent with **glDrawPixels**(). Each row must start on a 4-byte boundary by default.

When GL_GENERATE_MIPMAP is set to GL_TRUE, **glTexImage2D**() filters the texture image into successively lower-detail images to complete the mipmap pyramid. Furthermore, OpenGL recalculates mipmap images if a future change affects the base texture image. Unfortunately, only OpenGL versions 1.4 and later support this functionality. To create mipmap levels in older versions of OpenGL, use the GLU routine **gluBuild2DMipmaps**().

int **gluBuild2DMipmaps**(GLenum *target*, GLint *components*, GLsizei *width*, GLint *height*, GLenum *format*, GLenum *type*, const void* *data*);

Creates mipmapped texture images. *components* is the number of components per image element. All other parameters are the same as for **glTexImage2D**().

▶ GLU version: 1.0 and later.

gluBuild2DMipmaps() creates copies of the texture image specified by *data* at successively lower resolutions to complete a pyramid of mipmapped images. It calls **glTexImage2D**() for each image, passing in a different value for level.

When specifying a mipmapped texture, check the OpenGL version. If the version is 1.4 or greater, use GL_GENERATE_MIPMAP with **glTexImage2D**(); otherwise, use **gluBuild2DMipmaps**(). The following pseudocode illustrates this:

```
if ( version() >= 1.4)
{
    glTexParameteri( GL_TEXTURE_2D, GL_GENERATE_MIPMAP, GL_TRUE );
    glTexImage2D( ... );
}
else
{
    gluBuild2DMipmaps( ... );
}
```

Mipmap generation in OpenGL version 1.4 differs from **gluBuild2D-Mipmaps**() in one very important way: Mipmap generation is state in a texture object. If your application sets GL_GENERATE_MIPMAP to GL_TRUE and then changes the base-level texture image (with a call to **glTexImage2D**()

or **glCopyTexImage2D**(), OpenGL recomputes texture images for each
level of the mipmap pyramid.

6.1.2 Texture Coordinates

Applications assign texture coordinates to each vertex to associate regions
of a texture with a primitive. During rasterization, OpenGL uses a perspective-correct interpolation algorithm to assign appropriate texture coordinates to each generated fragment.

In simple 2D texture mapping, texture coordinates map to texels as though
the texture image were a Cartesian coordinate system consisting of s and t
axes, as shown in Figure 6-1. The (s, t) origin, $(0, 0)$, maps to the bottom-
left corner of the texture image or the first pixel specified in the *data*
parameter to **glTexImage2D**(). Texture-coordinate location $(1, 1)$ maps to
the top-right corner of the image or the last pixel in the data block. Therefore, you can access any texel in a texture image by using normalized 2D

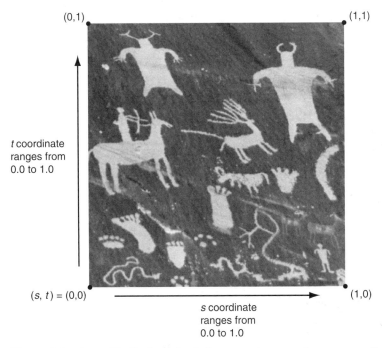

Figure 6-1 OpenGL displays the full texture image using a normalized coordinate
system.

texture coordinates *s* and *t* in the range 0.0 to 1.0, with *s* accessing texels horizontally and *t* accessing texels vertically.

If your application specifies texture coordinates outside the range 0.0 to 1.0, OpenGL uses the GL_TEXTURE_WRAP_S and GL_TEXTURE_WRAP_T state parameters to control texel lookup. The default GL_REPEAT value for these parameters causes the texture map pattern to repeat. In other words, OpenGL performs a modulo function on the texture coordinates, so the effective texture coordinates are always in the range 0.0 to 1.0. Figure 6-2 shows the effect of GL_REPEAT.

GL_REPEAT is inappropriate for many algorithms, especially depth mapping (see the section "Depth Maps" later in this chapter). When performing depth mapping, applications often want *s* and *t* values to clamp when outside the range 0.0 to 1.0. The following code demonstrates how to clamp *s* and *t* to the edge of the texture:

```
glTexParameteri( GL_TEXTURE_2D, GL_TEXTURE_WRAP_S, GL_CLAMP_TO_EDGE );
glTexParameteri( GL_TEXTURE_2D, GL_TEXTURE_WRAP_T, GL_CLAMP_TO_EDGE );
```

Note that GL_CLAMP_TO_EDGE is available in OpenGL version 1.2 and later. Figure 6-3 illustrates the effect of using GL_CLAMP_TO_EDGE.

Figure 6-2   GL_REPEAT texture-coordinate wrap mode. This figure shows a single GL_QUADS primitive. Starting with the vertex at the bottom-left corner and proceeding counterclockwise, the texture coordinates are (–1, –1), (2, –1), (2, 2), and (–1, 2).

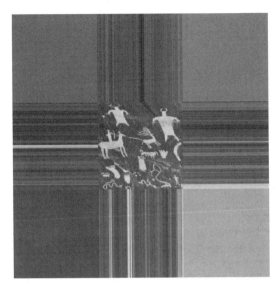

Figure 6-3 `GL_CLAMP_TO_EDGE` texture-coordinate wrap mode.

A third mode, `GL_CLAMP`,[2] is useful if your application tiles textures or uses texture borders. Additional modes, such as `GL_MIRRORED_REPEAT` and `GL_CLAMP_TO_BORDER`, are available in more recent versions of OpenGL. See Chapter 9, "Texture Mapping," of *OpenGL® Programming Guide* for information on texture borders and other wrap modes.

Texture coordinates are actually composed of four values: *s, t, r,* and *q*. When applications specify 2D (*s, t*) texture coordinates, OpenGL implicitly sets *r* to 0.0 and *q* to 1.0. OpenGL transforms each texture-coordinate vector [*s t r q*] by the texture matrix. If `GL_TEXTURE_2D` is enabled, OpenGL uses the transformed coordinate (*s/q, t/q*) to actually look up the texel values. The division by *q* has applications in projective texture mapping. The section "Depth Maps" later in this chapter describes how to use *s/q, t/q,* and *r/q* as perspective-correct coordinates in light space.

6.1.2.1 Specifying Texture Coordinates

Applications commonly specify texture-coordinate data explicitly, as described in the section "Vertex Array Data" in Chapter 2, "Drawing

---

2. Some implementations interpret `GL_CLAMP` as `GL_CLAMP_TO_EDGE` by default, with a device-driver mode switch to change this behavior so that it complies with the OpenGL specification.

Primitives." In summary, applications create an array of texture coordinates, store them in a buffer object, and use **glTexCoordPointer**() to index into the buffer object.

Explicit texture coordinates are inappropriate for some algorithms, however. In environment mapping, for example, texture coordinates derive from surface reflection vectors. Computing these coordinates and dynamically updating the buffer object each frame is inefficient and computationally prohibitive. For this reason, OpenGL features several texture-coordinate-generation modes, as described in the following section.

6.1.2.2   Texture-Coordinate Generation

Enable or disable texture-coordinate generation individually for texture-coordinate values s, t, r, and q with **glEnable**() and **glDisable**(). The following code enables texture-coordinate generation for s, t, r, and q:

```
glEnable( GL_TEXTURE_GEN_S );
glEnable( GL_TEXTURE_GEN_T );
glEnable( GL_TEXTURE_GEN_R );
glEnable( GL_TEXTURE_GEN_Q );
```

Texture-coordinate generation is disabled by default.

OpenGL features a variety of algorithms for generating texture coordinates. You control how OpenGL generates the coordinates with **glTexGeni**() and **glTexGendv**().

---

void **glTexGen**[ifd](GLenum *coord*, GLenum *pname*, *TYPE param*);
void **glTexGen**[ifd]**v**(GLenum *coord*, GLenum *pname*, const *TYPE** *param*);

Specifies how OpenGL generates texture coordinates. In both forms of **glTexGen**(), *coord* must be GL_S, GL_T, GL_R, or GL_Q to specify the relevant texture coordinate.

For **glTexGen***(), pass GL_TEXTURE_GEN_MODE for *pname*, and *params* must be GL_OBJECT_LINEAR, GL_EYE_LINEAR, GL_SPHERE_MAP, GL_REFLECTION_MAP, or GL_NORMAL_MAP.

For **glTexGen*v**(), *pname* can be either GL_OBJECT_PLANE or GL_EYE_PLANE, and *params* points to a four-element array representing a plane equation.

▶ OpenGL version: 1.0 and later. GL_REFLECTION_MAP and GL_NORMAL_MAP are available in version 1.3 and later.

OpenGL® Distilled doesn't cover all texture-coordinate-generation modes. For more information on texture-coordinate generation, see "glTexGen" in *OpenGL® Reference Manual* or Chapter 9, "Texture Mapping," of *OpenGL® Programming Guide.*

As a simple example, consider the following code:

```
glEnable( GL_TEXTURE_GEN_S );
glEnable( GL_TEXTURE_GEN_T );
glTexGeni( GL_S, GL_TEXTURE_GEN_MODE, GL_OBJECT_LINEAR );
glTexGeni( GL_T, GL_TEXTURE_GEN_MODE, GL_OBJECT_LINEAR );
```

The above code enables texture-coordinate generation for both *s* and *t*. The code sets the generation mode to GL_OBJECT_LINEAR. This code causes OpenGL to derive *s* and *t* texture coordinates from the *x* and *y* object coordinates.

That's the short story. What OpenGL does under the hood is somewhat more complex. Both *s* and *t* coordinates have object plane equations, which you can change with the following code:

```
GLdouble sPlaneEq[4] = { ... };
GLdouble tPlaneEq[4] = { ... };
glTexGendv( GL_S, GL_OBJECT_PLANE, sPlaneEq );
glTexGendv( GL_T, GL_OBJECT_PLANE, tPlaneEq );
```

OpenGL computes the *s* texture coordinate by taking the dot product of the four-element *xyzw* object coordinate and the *s* coordinate object plane. OpenGL computes the *t* coordinate similarly. By default, the *s* and *t* object plane equations are (1, 0, 0, 0) and (0, 1, 0, 0), respectively.

Later in this chapter, the section "Depth Maps" describes how to use GL_EYE_LINEAR to generate texture coordinates in the light source's coordinate space for use with depth-map textures. The section "Environment Maps" describes how to use GL_REFLECTION_MAP to produce improved specular highlights.

6.1.2.3 The Texture Matrix

OpenGL transforms all texture coordinates, whether specified explicitly or generated with **glTexGen**(), by the top of the texture matrix stack before using the texture coordinates to index into the texture image.

Chapter 3, "Transformation and Viewing," describes the **glMatrixMode**() function. You can set the current matrix mode to GL_MODELVIEW or GL_PROJECTION to specify matrices that transform vertices and normals. You can also set the matrix mode to GL_TEXTURE, however. This command

configures OpenGL so that subsequent matrix operations (**glPushMatrix**(),
glPopMatrix(), **glLoadMatrixf**(), **glMultMatrixd**(), **glRotatef**(),
and so on) affect the texture-matrix stack. By default, the top of the texture-
matrix stack is an identity matrix. If applications don't use the texture-matrix
stack, OpenGL uses their texture coordinates effectively untransformed.

Applications use the texture matrix for a variety of purposes. Computer
games, for example, often animate clouds moving across the sky by translating sky-geometry texture coordinates.

The examples available on the *OpenGL® Distilled* Web site use texture
matrices in two ways:

- The SecondaryColor example program applies a small translation to the
  texture image so that it appears in the correct location on the torus.

- The CubeMap example program uses the texture matrix to transform
  reflection vectors in response to changes in the eye-coordinate light
  position. For more information, see the section "Environment Maps"
  later in this chapter.

Each texture unit has its own texture-matrix stack. See the next section,
"Multitexturing," for more information.

6.1.3 Multitexturing

If the OpenGL version is 1.3 or later, you can configure OpenGL to apply
multiple textures per primitive by using the multitexturing feature. Many
applications use multitexturing to add complex lighting and shadow
effects to texture mapped objects with one image as a base texture and a
second image as a single-channel luminance texture or depth map. Other
applications for multitexturing include decals and detail textures.

The number of textures you can apply to a single primitive is determined
by the number of supported texture units. Query the number of supported
texture units with **glGetIntegerv**() as follows:

```
GLint maxTextureUnits;
glGetIntegerv( GL_MAX_TEXTURE_UNITS, &maxTextureUnits );
```

Each texture unit is numbered, starting with GL_TEXTURE0. The number of
supported texture units is implementation dependent but must be at least two.

For each fragment produced by rasterization, OpenGL iterates over all
enabled texture units in sequence, starting with GL_TEXTURE0, and applies
the associated texture to the fragment.

To use multitexturing, you need to perform the following steps:

1. Set the active texture unit.

2. Set state specific to that texture unit.

3. Specify geometry with a texture-coordinate set for each texture unit.

6.1.3.1 Setting the Active Texture Unit

Select the active texture unit with the **glActiveTexture**() command.

---

void **glActiveTexture**(GLenum *texture*);

Selects the active texture unit. *texture* must be GL_TEXTURE0,
GL_TEXTURE1, and so on up to GL_TEXTURE*i*, where *i* is the value of
GL_MAX_TEXTURE_UNITS minus 1.

▶ OpenGL version: 1.3 and later.

glActiveTexture() selects the active texture unit in OpenGL. The
default texture unit is GL_TEXTURE0. Applications set the active texture
unit before issuing commands that affect texture unit state, as described in
the next section.

6.1.3.2 Texture Unit State

Several OpenGL commands affect texture unit state, such as:

- **glBindTexture**(), which associates a texture object with the active
  texture unit.

- **glTexGen**(), which sets texture-generation parameters for the active
  texture unit.

- Matrix commands, which affect the active texture-unit matrix stack when
  the current matrix mode (set with **glMatrixMode**()) is GL_TEXTURE.
  There is a separate texture-matrix stack for each texture unit.

- **glTexEnvi**(), which controls how the active texture unit applies the
  texture image.

- **glEnable**()/**glDisable**() for texture-coordinate generation, which
  determines whether the active texture unit generates texture coordinates.

- **glEnable**()/**glDisable**() for GL_TEXTURE_2D or GL_TEXTURE_
  CUBE_MAP, which specifies whether the active texture unit applies a 2D
  or cube map texture.

All these state variables can be used without multitexturing. If your application never calls **glActiveTexture**(), the variables affect the default texture unit, GL_TEXTURE0, and all other texture units remain disabled.

Most of the state items listed above have already been discussed in this chapter. The one remaining state variable is **glTexEnvi**(), which controls how the texture unit combines the texture color with the primary color of the incoming fragment.

---

void **glTexEnv**[if](GLenum *target*, GLenum *pname*, *TYPE param*);

When *target* is GL_TEXTURE_ENV and *pname* is GL_TEXTURE_ENV_MODE, the value of *param* controls how the active texture unit applies texture color values to fragments. Valid values for *param* include GL_MODULATE, GL_REPLACE, GL_DECAL, and GL_ADD.

Although OpenGL supports other values for *target*, *pname*, and *param*, they aren't covered in this book. You can also use similar functions **glTexEnvf**(), **glTexEnviv**(), and **glTexEnvfv**() to set other texture environment parameters. For more information, see "glTexEnv" in *OpenGL® Reference Manual*.

▶ OpenGL version: 1.0 and later.
        GL_ADD is available in version 1.3 and later.

To replace the incoming fragment's color value completely with the texture color, set *param* to GL_REPLACE as follows:

```
glTexEnvi( GL_TEXTURE_ENV, GL_TEXTURE_ENV_MODE, GL_REPLACE );
```

Although GL_REPLACE has some applications, keep in mind that it eliminates nearly all lighting effects computed with **glEnable**(GL_LIGHTING). Because lighting effects are part of the fragment's primary color before OpenGL performs texturing, GL_REPLACE completely replaces the (lit) primary color value with the (unlit) texture color.

The default texture environment mode is GL_MODULATE, which replaces the fragment's primary color with the result of a componentwise multiplication of the texture color and the incoming primary color. Applications often use GL_MODULATE in conjunction with lighting, because it preserves ambient and diffuse lighting effects. GL_MODULATE mutes specular highlights, however. OpenGL provides two mechanisms to improve the appearance of specular highlights on texture mapped surfaces: the separate specular color feature, described in the section "Specular Highlights" later in this chapter, and cube maps, described in the section "Environment Maps" later in this chapter.

To add the texture color to the primary color, use GL_ADD. Applications often use GL_ADD in environment mapping to add specular highlights or other reflections to a surface. GL_ADD is available only in OpenGL in version 1.3 or later.

6.1.3.3 Texture-Coordinate Sets

When using multitexturing, applications typically specify a set of texture coordinates for each enabled texture unit. Texture-coordinate sets can be identical or different for each texture unit, or specified explicitly for one unit and generated for another.

glActiveTexture() selects the active texture unit for server-side texture unit state. To specify vertex arrays with multiple texture-coordinate sets, OpenGL provides the **glClientActiveTexture**() command. When your application issues the **glTexCoordPointer**() command to specify an array of texture coordinates (either explicitly or sourced from a buffer object), OpenGL assigns that texture-coordinate set to the texture unit specified with **glClientActiveTexture**(). **glEnableClientState** (GL_TEXTURE_COORD_ARRAY) and **glDisableClientState**(GL_TEXTURE_COORD_ARRAY) also reference the client active texture unit.

When rendering, applications typically specify several texture-coordinate sets, as Listing 6-1 shows.

Listing 6-1 Code for setting multiple texture-coordinate sets.

```
int tIdx;
for (tIdx=0; tIdx<numTextures; tIdx++)
{
    glClientActiveTexture( GL_TEXTURE0 + tIdx );
    glEnableClientState( GL_TEXTURE_COORD_ARRAY );
    glBindBuffer( GL_ARRAY_BUFFER, texCoordBuffer );
    glTexCoordPointer( 2, GL_FLOAT, 0, bufferObjectPtr( 0 ) );
}
```

In the above code, *numTextures* is a local variable that specifies the number of texture units required by the application. texCoordBuffer is the identifier of a buffer object containing an array of packed floating-point *s* and *t* texture coordinates.

6.1.4 Texture Mapping Example

The SimpleTextureMapping example, available from this book's Web site, renders a simple texture mapped quadrilateral. The goal of this example is

Figure 6-4   A screen shot from the SimpleTextureMapping example program.

to illustrate how to create a minimal texture object and map the texture to a primitive.

Figure 6-4 shows a single texture mapped quadrilateral. The four vertices use texture coordinates (0, 0), (1, 0), (1, 1), and (0, 1) to show the entire texture image.

Listing 6-2 contains the code for this example program.

Listing 6-2   Code for the SimpleTextureMapping example

```
#include <GL/glut.h>
#include <GL/glu.h>
#include <GL/gl.h>
#include "OGLDPixels.h"
#include "OGLDPlane.h"


Static const int QUIT_VALUE( 99 );

ogld::Plane plane;
GLuint texId( 0 );


static void display()
{
    glClear( GL_COLOR_BUFFER_BIT | GL_DEPTH_BUFFER_BIT );

    glLoadIdentity();
    gluLookAt( 0., 0., 2.,
            0., 0., 0.,
            0., 1., 0. );
```

```
    glBindTexture( GL_TEXTURE_2D, texId );

    plane.draw();

    glutSwapBuffers();
}

static void reshape( int w, int h )
{
    glViewport( 0, 0, w, h );
    glMatrixMode( GL_PROJECTION );
    glLoadIdentity();
    gluPerspective( 40., (double)w/(double)h, 1., 10. );

    /* Leave us in modelview mode for our display routine */
    glMatrixMode( GL_MODELVIEW );
}

static void mainMenuCB( int value )
{
    if (value == QUIT_VALUE)
    {
        // Demonstrates how to delete a texture object.
        //    Unnecessary in this simple case, since the following
        //    call to exit() will destroy the rendering context
        //    and all associated texture objects.
        glDeleteTextures( 1, &texId );
        exit( 0 );
    }
}


static void init()
{
    // Use the ogld::Pixels class to load the image and obtain a pointer
    //    to the pixel data.
    ogld::Pixels image;
    image.loadImage( std::string( "NewspaperRock.tif" ) );
    int width, height;
    image.getWidthHeight( width, height );

    // Obtain a texture ID and create/init the texture object
    glGenTextures( 1, &texId );
    glBindTexture( GL_TEXTURE_2D, texId );

    glTexParameteri( GL_TEXTURE_2D, GL_TEXTURE_MIN_FILTER, GL_LINEAR );
    glTexImage2D( GL_TEXTURE_2D, 0, image.getFormat(), width, height,
        0, image.getFormat(), image.getType(), image.getPixels() );

    glEnable( GL_TEXTURE_2D );
```

```
    glClearColor( .9, .9, .9, 0. );
    glDisable( GL_DITHER );


    glutDisplayFunc( display );
    glutReshapeFunc( reshape );

    int mainMenu = glutCreateMenu( mainMenuCB );
    glutAddMenuEntry( "Quit", QUIT_VALUE );
    glutAttachMenu( GLUT_RIGHT_BUTTON );
}

int main( int argc, char** argv )
{
    glutInit( &argc, argv );
    glutInitDisplayMode( GLUT_RGB | GLUT_DEPTH | GLUT_DOUBLE );
    glutInitWindowSize( 300, 300 );
    glutCreateWindow( "Simple Texture Mapping" );

    init ();

    glutMainLoop ();

    return 0;
}
```

The code employs the ogld::Plane class to render the quadrilateral, which hides the texture-coordinate specification. Listing 6-1 earlier in this chapter shows how to specify texture-coordinate sets. You can also download the example code to see how this is done within ogld::Plane.

The code declares a global GLuint variable, *texId*, which holds the texture-object identifier. The display() callback function references this identifier in the call to **glBindTexture**(). After the code binds the texture object, it renders the ogld::Plane.

Later in the code, the init() function is responsible for creating and initializing the texture object. It employs the ogld::Pixels class to load the texture image from a TIFF file. Next, it initializes texId by obtaining an unused texture ID with a call to **glGenTextures**() and immediately calls **glBindTexture**(GL_TEXTURE_2D, texId), which creates a 2D texture object with default state values.

The next three commands set state in the newly created texture object. The **glTexParameteri**() command changes the texture minification filter from the default GL_NEAREST_MIPMAP_LINEAR to GL_LINEAR, because this code doesn't use mipmapping. Next, the code specifies the texture image with the **glTexImage2D**() command. Finally, the code enables texturing.

> **Tip** Because the default minification filter is a mipmap filter, your code must change this to a nonmipmapped filter or specify a mipmapped texture image. Typically, applications use mipmapped images, but not always.
>
> If you use a mipmap filter without a mipmapped image, OpenGL acts as though texture mapping is disabled. As an exercise, download the Simple-TextureMapping example and comment out the **glTexParameteri**() command, which leaves the minification filter set to its default value of GL_NEAREST_MIPMAP_LINEAR. After this change, the code produces a nontextured white quadrilateral.

Although this example doesn't use multitexturing, the ogld::Plane class uses multitexturing if available in OpenGL. By default, it uses one texture unit, GL_TEXTURE0, which is essentially the same as not using multitexturing.

6.2 Lighting and Shadows with Texture

OpenGL's lighting features, described in Chapter 4, "Lighting," provide lighting and shading effects suitable for many applications. OpenGL lighting isn't a complete solution for all applications, however. This section describes some of the many ways you can use texture mapping to improve the appearance of lit geometry.

Perhaps the most noticeable limitation of OpenGL lighting is the absence of shadows. Most graphics programmers are accustomed to this behavior, because it's the 3D graphics industry-standard lighting model. Shadows provide important visual cues, however, and add to scene realism. The sections "Static Lighting," "Light Maps," and "Depth Maps" later in this chapter all discuss how to use texture mapping to add shadows to your scene.

If your application renders a surface with both a specular highlight and a texture map, the texture map will mute the specular highlight. To learn how to compensate for this artifact of the rendering pipeline, see the section "Specular Highlights" later in this chapter.

OpenGL lighting requires high-resolution geometry to produce acceptable specular highlights, which is unacceptable for applications that are geometry limited. The section, "Environment Maps" later in this chapter describes how to use cube map textures to produce accurate specular highlights on low-resolution geometry.

6.2.1   Static Lighting

One way to add shadows to your scene is to encode them in a texture image. You can use any offline process or tool to create the texture image and apply the image as a texture map at runtime. In terms of complexity and performance, application code for applying static lighting textures is identical to any texture mapping code.

The TextureMapping example code demonstrates applying a texture with a precomputed shadow. The example loads a file containing elevation and image data, and renders that data as a section of texture mapped terrain. Figure 6-5 and Plate 3 show output of the example.

The output of the example code exhibits lighting and shading effects, but these are actually part of the texture image itself. In this case, the texture

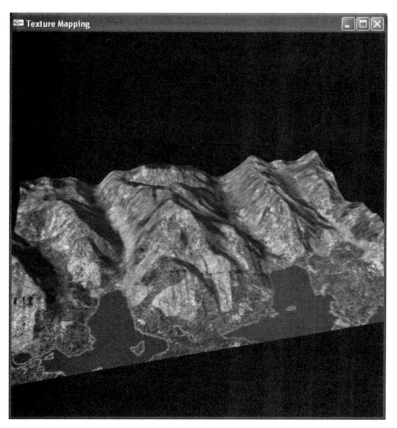

Figure 6-5   A screenshot from the TextureMapping example program, which renders elevation data and imagery for a section of the Teton mountain range in Wyoming. *Source:* SimAuthor.

image shadow effects were generated with an offline tool based on the elevation data. Figure 6-6 and Plate 4 show the texture image used in the TextureMapping example.

Because the texture image already contains lighting effects, the example doesn't use OpenGL lighting as described in Chapter 4, "Lighting." It also uses `GL_REPLACE` for the texture environment mode, because the texture color replaces, rather than modulates, the existing primary color.

The main example code in `TextureMapping.cpp` is self-explanatory. It instantiates a `Terrain` object, described in `Terrain.h` and implemented in `Terrain.cpp`. The `Terrain` class has an `ogld::Texture` member variable to manage the texture map.

Figure 6-6   The texture image used by the TextureMapping example program. Note that the image itself already contains lighting and shading effects. *Source:* SimAuthor.

To render the elevation data, `Terrain` uses a `HeightField` class. Derived from `ogld::Plane`, `HeightField` simply replaces the all-zero *z* values generated by the base class with values derived from the elevation data. The `Terrain` class `draw()` method renders the image by enabling texture mapping with a call to **`glEnable`**(`GL_TEXTURE_2D`), applying the texture, and drawing the `HeightField`.

6.2.2 Light Maps

Modifying an existing texture image with lighting, shading, and shadow effects is suitable only for static scenes in which the light source doesn't move. To handle dynamic scenes, your application needs to keep shadows in a separate texture image and use multitexturing to apply it to textured geometry. This allows your application to update the light map without affecting the color values in underlying textures.

The ProjectedShadows demo, available from this book's Web site, demonstrates one way to do this. The example renders shadows from a cylinder, sphere, and torus onto an underlying plane. It renders the shadows and lighting effects as they would appear on the plane and then uses the rendered image of the shadows as a texture on the plane in the final image. The example uses multitexturing to apply the `GL_LUMINANCE` light-map texture onto a plane textured with another texture image. The example updates the light map when the user changes the light position by rendering the lighting and shadow effects into the back buffer and then copying the contents to the light-map texture object.

Using a simple linear-algebra technique (Savchenko 2005), the Projected-Shadows example renders an orthographic view of shadows projected onto a plane. After reading that image out of the framebuffer, it renders the scene from the camera viewpoint, applying the previously rendered image as a luminance texture on a plane. Figure 6-7 and Plate 5 show the final result.

Figure 6-8 shows just the light map, which contains both lighting and shadow information. To create this image, the ProjectedShadows example sets an orthographic projection that shows the plane from a top-down view. Next, it sets a model transformation to project the geometry onto that plane. It renders a high-resolution plane to capture as much lighting information as possible. Finally, with depth test and the light source disabled, it renders the sphere, cylinder, and torus, which are projected onto the plane.

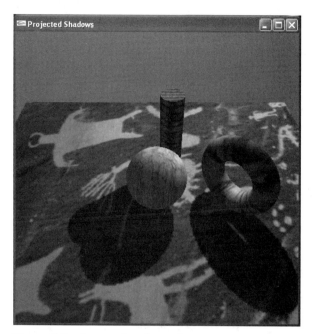

Figure 6-7 Screen shot from the ProjectedShadows example program.

Figure 6-8 The light map with projected shadows from the ProjectedShadows example program.

After rendering, the light map is in the back (undisplayed) buffer. Without swapping buffers, the ProjectedShadows example copies the light map out of the framebuffer and into a texture object using the **glCopyTexImage2D**() command.

---

void **glCopyTexImage2D**(GLenum *target*, GLint *level*, GLenum *internalformat*, GLint *x*, GLint *y*, GLsizei *width*, GLsizei *height*, GLint *border*);

Copies a region of the framebuffer into a texture object. Like **glTexImage2D**(), **glCopyTexImage2D**() defines a texture, but obtains the texture image data from the framebuffer.

target must be GL_TEXTURE_2D or one of the six cube map faces (see "Environment Maps" later in this chapter). *level*, *internalformat*, and *border* are the same as in **glTexImage2D**(). *x*, *y*, *width*, and *height* define the region of the framebuffer to copy.

Just as in **glTexImage2D**(), *width* and *height* must be a power of 2 unless the OpenGL version is 2.0 or later.

▶ OpenGL version: 1.1 and later.

The ProjectedShadows example specifies an *internalformat* of GL_LUMINANCE, which tells OpenGL to copy and store a single luminance value out of the framebuffer.

When the final image is rendered, the plane is the only geometry that requires special treatment. It uses multitexturing to display both a texture image of petroglyphs using texture unit GL_TEXTURE0 and the light map using texture unit GL_TEXTURE1. Because the light map already contains sufficient light information, the plane rendered in the final image is low-resolution—only four vertices. This technique improves performance for geometry-limited applications.

Because the ProjectedShadows example creates shadows only for the ogld::Plane primitive, it doesn't render shadows from the cylinder, sphere, and torus cast onto one another. OpenGL, however, provides a better technique: depth maps, described in the next section.

6.2.3 Depth Maps

The depth-map algorithm (Williams 1978), also known as *shadow mapping,* is a general-purpose shadow solution that elegantly supports self-shadowing.

The algorithm is well suited for nonphotorealistic shadows. In its classic form, however, the depth-map algorithm suffers from aliasing artifacts and, therefore, isn't suitable for photorealistic rendering. Pixar developed the percentage-closer filtering algorithm (Reeves 1987) to eliminate these artifacts and successfully used the depth-map algorithm in films such as *Luxo Jr.*

Depth maps require multiple rendering passes. To use the algorithm, first render the scene as viewed from the light source and copy the resulting depth buffer into a texture object. To prepare for the second rendering pass, configure OpenGL to generate texture coordinates in the same coordinate space as the depth map, and also set depth compare parameters to compare generated texture-coordinate *r* values against stored depth-map values. When you render the scene a second time from the viewer's position, a generated *r* value greater than the corresponding stored depth value indicates that the corresponding fragment is in shadow.

As an example, see the DepthMapShadows program available on this book's Web site. Figure 6-9 and Plate 6 show the final rendered image.

Figure 6-9 A screen shot from the DepthMapShadows example program.

The DepthMapShadows example updates the depth-map texture only if the light source's position has changed since the last frame. To create the depth map, the program clears the depth buffer; the color buffer isn't required to produce a depth map and, therefore, is irrelevant. The code creates a view by using the light position as the viewpoint and then renders the scene. It renders only geometry that actually casts shadows; rendering the plane isn't necessary, because the scene doesn't contain any geometry shadowed by the plane. Also, because the algorithm requires only depth values, the code disables lighting and texture mapping. Finally, the code copies the rendered depth map into the texture object with a call to **glCopyTexImage2D**():

```
glCopyTexImage2D( GL_TEXTURE_2D, 0, GL_DEPTH_COMPONENT, 0, 0, w, h, 0 );
```

The depth map is essentially a normalized coordinate-space representation of the scene as viewed from the light, where *x* and *y* values range horizontally and vertically over the image and look up depth values stored in the depth buffer. Figure 6-10 shows the depth map displayed as a grayscale image.

After creating the depth map, the DepthMapShadows program configures OpenGL to generate texture coordinates in the same coordinate space as the depth map. Generated *s, t,* and *r* values must be in the range 0.0 to 1.0. Visualize this as texture coordinates in normalized device-coordinate space as viewed from the light in the range –1.0 to 1.0 for all axes. Then scale that by 0.5 in all axes, and translate it by 0.5 in all axes. The result is texture coordinates in the range 0.0 to 1.0.

Figure 6-10   The depth map from the DepthMapShadows example program shows light and dark values corresponding to greater and lesser distances from the light source.

Because the depth map is a perspective image, you also need to generate a fourth texture coordinate, q. OpenGL divides s, t, and r values by q, so applications use q to perform perspective division for cases such as depth mapping.

The DepthMapShadows program creates a matrix that transforms OpenGL eye coordinates into depth-map coordinates by concatenating the following matrices:

$$R = TSP_L V_L$$

T translates by 0.5 in x, y, and z, and S scales by 0.5 in x, y, and z. P_L and V_L are the same projection and view matrices used to create the depth map. Each row of the result matrix R is a plane equation for generating s, t, r, and q coordinates. The DepthMapShadows example passes these rows as parameters when configuring texture-coordinate generation, as the following code shows:

```
GLdouble m[16];

// Temporarily use the model-view matrix to create
//   the texture coordinate transform
glMatrixMode( GL_MODELVIEW );
glPushMatrix();
glLoadIdentity();
glTranslatef( .5f, .5f, .5f );
glScalef( .5f, .5f, .5f );
gluPerspective( fov, aspect, 2., 200. );
lightView.multMatrix();
glGetDoublev( GL_MODELVIEW_MATRIX, m );
glPopMatrix();

// m now contains the plane equation values, but separate
//   values in each equation aren't stored in contiguous
//   memory. Transpose the matrix to remedy this.
ogld::matrixTranspose( m );

// Set the active texture unit.
ogld::glActiveTexture( depthMapTexture.getUnit() );
// Specify the texture coordinate plane equations.
glTexGendv( GL_S, GL_EYE_PLANE, &(m[0]) );
glTexGendv( GL_T, GL_EYE_PLANE, &(m[4]) );
glTexGendv( GL_R, GL_EYE_PLANE, &(m[8]) );
glTexGendv( GL_Q, GL_EYE_PLANE, &(m[12]) );
```

Next, you need to configure the depth-map texture object to perform the depth comparison. Do this by setting the parameter GL_TEXTURE_COMPARE_MODE to GL_COMPARE_R_TO_TEXTURE. This tells OpenGL the operands of the comparison. You also need to specify the operator by setting GL_TEXTURE_COMPARE_FUNC to a comparison enumerant such as GL_LEQUAL. After comparing the generated *r* value with the stored depth-map value, OpenGL outputs a Boolean value to indicate the result of the comparison. The following code, for example, tells OpenGL to output TRUE if the *r* value is less than or equal to the stored depth-map value (indicating that the corresponding fragment is lit) and FALSE otherwise (indicating shadow):

```
glTexParameteri( GL_TEXTURE_2D, GL_TEXTURE_COMPARE_MODE,
        GL_COMPARE_R_TO_TEXTURE );
glTexParameteri( GL_TEXTURE_2D, GL_TEXTURE_COMPARE_FUNC, GL_LEQUAL );
```

You also need to tell OpenGL what to do with the Boolean result. As shown earlier in Table 6-1, you can set GL_DEPTH_TEXTURE_MODE to GL_LUMINANCE, GL_INTENSITY, or GL_ALPHA. When GL_DEPTH_TEXTURE_MODE is GL_LUMINANCE, a FALSE *r* compare result produces shadow, whereas a TRUE result produces a lit value. Zero luminance is inadequate for scenes that contain ambient lighting, however, because OpenGL renders shadowed fragments without ambient light in that case.

The DepthMapShadows example preserves ambient lighting in shadows but requires a third rendering pass.[3] After creating the depth map, the code renders the final scene twice: once to produce lit fragments and again to produce shadowed fragments with correct ambient lighting. To do this, the code configures OpenGL to send the Boolean *r* compare result to the fragment's alpha component with the following code:

```
glTexParameteri( GL_TEXTURE_2D, GL_DEPTH_TEXTURE_MODE, GL_ALPHA );
```

It also configures the OpenGL alpha-test feature to discard fragments with zero alpha. The following code shows how DepthMapShadows renders the final scene:

```
// Render unshadowed / lit fragments
depthMapTexture.apply();
glTexParameteri( GL_TEXTURE_2D, GL_TEXTURE_COMPARE_FUNC, GL_LEQUAL );
glTexParameteri( GL_TEXTURE_2D, GL_DEPTH_TEXTURE_MODE, GL_ALPHA );
drawScene( false );

// Disable the light and render shadowed / unlit fragments
depthMapTexture.apply();
glTexParameteri( GL_TEXTURE_2D, GL_TEXTURE_COMPARE_FUNC, GL_GEQUAL );
glDisable( GL_LIGHT0 );
drawScene( false );
```

---

3. The GL_ARB_shadow_ambient extension preserves ambient lighting without requiring a third pass.

In the first pass, OpenGL changes the fragment alpha to 1.0 if the *r* compare indicates a lit fragment. Otherwise, OpenGL sets the alpha to 0.0. Because the alpha test discards fragments with 0.0 alpha, this code renders only lit fragments. The second pass does just the opposite: It sets `GL_TEXTURE_COMPARE_FUNC` to `GL_GEQUAL`, so lit fragments get 0.0 alpha, causing the alpha test to discard them. With the light source disabled, OpenGL renders the shadow fragments using only ambient light.

This algorithm can't produce soft shadows or penumbra effects. The Boolean result of the *r* compare indicates only that the fragment is lit or shadowed. As a result, depth-map shadows suffer from significant aliasing, as visible in Figure 6-9 earlier in this chapter. The DepthMapTextures example tries to minimize this aliasing in two ways:

- The code uses the largest portion of the window possible to produce the depth map. Larger windows increase the resolution of the resulting depth map.

- When setting the projection matrix before rendering the depth map, the code uses a custom field of view based on light distance from the scene. When the light is far away, a narrow field of view uses available screen real estate more efficiently and produces a higher-resolution depth map than a wider field of view would produce.

Finally, your application needs to safeguard against differences between the generated *r* values and the stored depth values in the depth map. The generated *r* value in the final image rarely matches the depth value retrieved from the depth map. Reeves solves this with percentage closer filtering (Reeves 1987).[4] The DepthMapShadows example, however, hides much of the aliasing artifacts with the depth offset feature. When creating the depth map, the example code uses depth offset to push the depth values back into the depth buffer. As a result, the depth map contains depth values that are biased slightly larger than the generated *r* values. The depth offset must balance hiding inherent aliasing artifacts against displacing the shadows; too little bias results in aliasing, whereas too much bias produces incorrect shadow effects.

6.2.4   Specular Highlights

OpenGL uses `GL_TEXTURE_ENV_MODE` to determine how to combine the texture color with the fragment primary color. The result becomes the

---

4. Applications can implement percentage-closer filtering by using fragment shaders (Gerasimov 2004).

new fragment primary color. By default, GL_TEXTURE_ENV_MODE is GL_MODULATE, which means that the colors are combined using componentwise multiplication.

To use both OpenGL lighting and texture mapping, you must use GL_MODULATE. OpenGL computes lighting before performing texture mapping, so the fragment primary color already contains lighting and shading effects. Multiplying these colors by the texture colors produces geometry that is both lit and texture mapped.

Unfortunately, GL_MODULATE adversely affects specular highlights. Consider what happens when the fragment primary color is part of a white specular highlight, but the texture color is very dark or black. Multiplying 1.0 (white) by 0.0 (black) produces 0.0, effectively erasing the specular highlight.

OpenGL version 1.4 provides the separate specular feature to improve the appearance of specular highlights on texture mapped surfaces. This feature introduces a new state variable, GL_LIGHT_MODEL_COLOR_CONTROL, which governs whether OpenGL stores specular lighting effects in the primary or secondary color. It also adds a new per-fragment operation after texture mapping, which adds the secondary color to the fragment primary color. In summary, this feature causes OpenGL to apply the specular highlight after texture mapping.

Figure 6-11 shows the output of the SecondaryColor example program when the separate secondary color feature is enabled.

The SecondaryColor example allows you to disable the separate secondary color feature by using the pop-up menu. Compare Figure 6-11 with Figure 6-12, which has the separate secondary color feature disabled. When this feature is disabled, dark areas of the texture image mute the specular highlight.

Applications that need to render shiny texture mapped surfaces use the separate secondary color feature to produce acceptable specular highlights. To enable this feature, use **glLightModeli**() as follows:

```
glLightModeli( GL_LIGHT_MODEL_COLOR_CONTROL, GL_SEPARATE_SPECULAR_COLOR );
```

By default, GL_LIGHT_MODEL_COLOR_CONTROL is set to GL_SINGLE_COLOR, which instructs OpenGL to apply specular lighting before texture mapping. This is the behavior of OpenGL before the introduction of separate specular color in version 1.4.

In addition to configuring OpenGL to store specular lighting effects in the secondary color, setting GL_LIGHT_MODEL_COLOR_CONTROL to

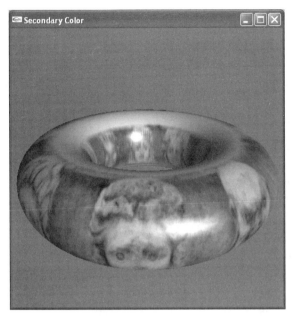

Figure 6-11   A screen shot from the SecondaryColor example program.
Source: Dean Randazzo.

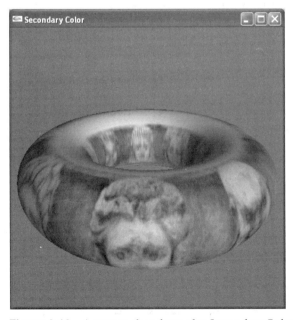

Figure 6-12   A screen shot from the SecondaryColor example program with secondary color disabled. Note the muted specular highlights. *Source:* Dean Randazzo.

GL_SEPARATE_SPECULAR_COLOR turns on the per-fragment operation that adds the secondary color to the fragment primary color after texture mapping. This per-fragment operation can be enabled separately, allowing applications to use secondary color for purposes other than specular highlights. Applications rarely do this, however. For more information, see Chapter 9, "Texture Mapping," of *OpenGL® Programming Guide*.

6.2.5   Environment Maps

Separate secondary color addresses only one problem with specular lighting. As described in Chapter 4, "Lighting," a bigger issue is that OpenGL computes lighting values at each vertex, producing unstable specular highlights on low-resolution geometry. Increasing geometric resolution to improve the appearance of specular highlights reduces performance if your application is geometry limited.

Furthermore, specular highlights produced by traditional graphics hardware are merely an approximation. In reality, specular highlights are reflections of the light source. Shiny surfaces typically reflect more than just a light source; often, they reflect their entire environment (Blinn 1976).

To support environment mapping, OpenGL supports both sphere and cube maps. Cube maps provide superior support for this algorithm and are easier for applications to create than sphere maps. The introduction of cube maps in OpenGL version 1.3 has largely supplanted sphere mapping, which most OpenGL programmers now consider obsolete.

Cube maps are a form of texture mapping that requires six texture images stored in the same texture object. In the classic implementation of environment mapping, each image in the cube map represents a 90-degree field of view of the environment—one image for each major axis direction. At render time, OpenGL uses the *s, t,* and *r* texture coordinates as a direction vector to select one of the six cube map faces and then performs texel lookup with derived *s* and *t* values in the selected face. For environment mapping, applications enable texture-coordinate generation for *s, t,* and *r* with GL_TEXTURE_GEN_MODE set to GL_REFLECTION_MAP. This mode uses the surface normal to produce texture coordinates identical to reflection vectors. As a result, the cube map images appear on rendered geometry as though the surface were highly reflective.

To use cube maps, create a texture object and bind it to GL_TEXTURE_CUBE_MAP, as the following code segment shows:

```
GLuint texId;
glGenTextures( 1, &_texId );
glBindTexture( GL_TEXTURE_CUBE_MAP, _texId );
```

To complete a cube map texture object, your application needs to store six texture images in the object. All six images must be square and have the same dimensions, and all must have the same internal format. Your code will need to make six calls to **glTexImage2D**(), each with a different *target* parameter: GL_TEXTURE_CUBE_MAP_POSITIVE_X, GL_TEXTURE_CUBE_MAP_NEGATIVE_X, GL_TEXTURE_CUBE_MAP_POSITIVE_Y, GL_TEXTURE_CUBE_MAP_NEGATIVE_Y, GL_TEXTURE_CUBE_MAP_POSITIVE_Z, and GL_TEXTURE_CUBE_MAP_NEGATIVE_Z. Note that these target values are sequential C-preprocessor variables, which allow your application to set the six cube map faces with a code loop.

When setting texture-object state for a cube map, use GL_TEXTURE_CUBE_MAP as the target parameter to **glTexParameteri**(). The following code segment sets wrapping and filter parameters in a cube map texture object:

```
glTexParameteri( GL_TEXTURE_CUBE_MAP, GL_TEXTURE_WRAP_S,
    GL_CLAMP_TO_EDGE );
glTexParameteri( GL_TEXTURE_CUBE_MAP, GL_TEXTURE_WRAP_T,
    GL_CLAMP_TO_EDGE );
glTexParameteri( GL_TEXTURE_CUBE_MAP, GL_TEXTURE_WRAP_R,
    GL_CLAMP_TO_EDGE );
glTexParameteri( GL_TEXTURE_CUBE_MAP, GL_TEXTURE_MIN_FILTER,
    GL_LINEAR_MIPMAP_LINEAR );
glTexParameteri( GL_TEXTURE_CUBE_MAP, GL_TEXTURE_MAG_FILTER,
    GL_LINEAR );
```

Another part of texture-object state is whether texture mapping is enabled. For 2D (not cube map) texture objects, you enable texture mapping with **glEnable**(GL_TEXTURE_2D). To enable a cube map texture object, however, you must call **glEnable**(GL_TEXTURE_CUBE_MAP).

To enable texture-coordinate generation, first set the active texture unit for the cube map texture with **glActiveTexture**(). For environment mapping, your application should use GL_REFLECTION_MAP and enable texture-coordinate generation for *s, t,* and *r,* as the following code shows:

```
glEnable( GL_TEXTURE_GEN_S );
glEnable( GL_TEXTURE_GEN_T );
glEnable( GL_TEXTURE_GEN_R );
glTexGeni( GL_S, GL_TEXTURE_GEN_MODE, GL_REFLECTION_MAP );
glTexGeni( GL_T, GL_TEXTURE_GEN_MODE, GL_REFLECTION_MAP );
glTexGeni( GL_R, GL_TEXTURE_GEN_MODE, GL_REFLECTION_MAP );
```

The results produced by environment mapping are only as good as the quality of the individual cube map faces. To environment-map a computer-generated scene, applications simply render the six faces, typically into the back buffer, and use **glCopyTexImage2D**() to load the images into the cube map texture object. Other applications use scanned-in photos of actual environments as cube map images. Creating quality images for environment mapping is often more art than science and depends greatly on your application.

The CubeMap example program, available on this book's Web site, demonstrates a common use for cube maps that features straightforward cube map image generation. The example uses cube maps to apply a stable specular highlight to low-resolution geometry. Figure 6-13 and Plate 7 show a screen shot from this example.

The CubeMap example program uses the `ogld::CubeMap` class to manage the cube map texture object and its images. `ogld::CubeMap` allows an application to load six individual images, but by default, the class creates six images that simulate a specular highlight. To do this, `ogld::CubeMap` creates six `GL_LUMINANCE` format images and clears them to zero intensity (black). For the image corresponding to the positive x axis, however, `ogld::CubeMap` adds a full-intensity (white) circle to the center of the image. As a result, the default images created by `ogld::CubeMap` create a specular highlight for a light source located at positive x in eye coordinates.

Figure 6-13 Screen shot from the CubeMap example program. The geometry lacks sufficient resolution to produce an acceptable specular highlight using OpenGL lighting. Instead, the example uses cube maps to produce the specular highlights.

Most applications don't restrict themselves to lights at positive *x* in eye coordinates, however. Furthermore, applications typically use `GL_REFLECTION_MAP` texture-coordinate generation, which produces eye-coordinate reflection vectors. To use the default `ogld::CubeMap` images in this context, the CubeMap example places a transformation in the texture matrix to transform reflection vectors from eye coordinates to world coordinates and, further, to transform them from the positive *x* axis to the actual light position.

The example code uses transformation *T*, which is the concatenation of two transformations, M^{-1} and V^{-1}:

$$T = M^{-1}V^{-1}$$

M^{-1} is the inverse of a matrix that transforms the positive *x* axis to the light vector. V^{-1} is the inverse of the view transformation. The CubeMap example program takes a shortcut in this computation. Assuming that the light source is located at infinity makes position irrelevant; only direction is important. When a matrix only transforms from one orthonormal orientation basis to another, its inverse is the same as its transpose, which is much simpler to compute. This shortcut produces acceptable results only if the light isn't too close to the geometry. For an example of computing this transformation and storing it in the texture matrix, see the function `setCubeMapTextureMatrix()` in `CubeMap.cpp`.

The CubeMap example uses `GL_ADD` for the texture environment mode. The vast majority of pixels in the cube map images are black, so `GL_ADD` doesn't change the incoming fragment color. For the white pixels in the center of the positive *x* axis image, however, `GL_ADD` adds full-intensity red, green, and blue to the fragment color. OpenGL clamps the result so that the individual components don't overflow. The result is a white specular highlight.

6.3 Debugging

Several things could cause texture mapping not to work properly, and there are numerous ways to identify the source of the problem.

6.3.1 OpenGL Error Code

Check for OpenGL errors after creating texture objects and after rendering each frame. When developing a new application, check for OpenGL errors early in development. This helps isolate the cause of the problem, because new errors are usually generated by new code. Appendix D, "Troubleshooting and Debugging," describes the OGLDIF_CHECK_ERROR CPP macro, defined and used in the example code, which calls **glGetError**() without affecting application performance.

6.3.2   Texture State

New OpenGL programmers frequently confuse texture unit state and texture object state. Some of this confusion stems from OpenGL's history, because many texture state parameters existed in OpenGL version 1.0 before the addition of texture objects in version 1.1 and multitexturing in version 1.3.

For a complete enumeration of texture object and texture unit state, refer to Tables 6.15 and 6.16 in *The OpenGL Graphics System*. The following sections summarize the most essential state items.

6.3.2.1   Texture Object State

OpenGL stores state parameters set by the **glTexParameter***() commands in texture objects. Binding a texture object activates these parameter values. For a complete list of state parameters, see "glTexParameter" in *OpenGL® Reference Manual*. The most common parameters are listed here:

- GL_TEXTURE_MIN_FILTER and GL_TEXTURE_MAG_FILTER

- GL_TEXTURE_WRAP_S, GL_TEXTURE_WRAP_T, and GL_TEXTURE_WRAP_R

- GL_DEPTH_TEXTURE_MODE, GL_TEXTURE_COMPARE_FUNC, and GL_TEXTURE_COMPARE_MODE

- GL_GENERATE_MIPMAP

6.3.2.2   Texture Unit State

OpenGL maintains most other texture state parameters on a per-texture-unit basis to allow each texture unit to operate on texture objects in a unique manner. A few of the most common parameters are listed here:

- The currently bound texture object, set with **glBindTexture**(). Applications can query this (per unit) to retrieve the currently bound texture-object identifier. The following code, for example, shows how to determine which texture object is bound to GL_TEXTURE_2D for texture unit GL_TEXTURE0:

```
glActiveTexture( GL_TEXTURE0 );
GLint texId;
glGetIntegerv( GL_TEXTURE_BINDING_2D, &texId );
```

To query the texture object bound to GL_TEXTURE_CUBE_MAP, use
glGetIntegerv(GL_TEXTURE_BINDING_CUBE_MAP, &texId).

- Enable and disable state for GL_TEXTURE_2D and GL_TEXTURE_CUBE_MAP.

- GL_TEXTURE_ENV_MODE.

- Enable and disable state for GL_TEXTURE_GEN_S, GL_TEXTURE_GEN_T, GL_TEXTURE_GEN_R, and GL_TEXTURE_GEN_Q.

- GL_TEXTURE_GEN_MODE for GL_S, GL_T, GL_R, and GL_Q.

- GL_OBJECT_PLANE and GL_EYE_PLANE for GL_S, GL_T, GL_R, and GL_Q.

- The texture matrix stacks, one for each texture unit. OpenGL transforms each texture coordinate set by the top of the texture-matrix stack for the set's texture unit.

6.3.3 Texture Completeness

If a texture object isn't complete, OpenGL behaves as though the associated active texture unit is disabled. As a result, OpenGL renders your geometry without texture mapping.

A complete texture object meets the following conditions:

- Texture image dimensions must be positive.

- If GL_TEXTURE_MIN_FILTER specifies a mipmap filter, the texture must be mipmap complete.

- If the texture object was first bound to GL_TEXTURE_CUBE_MAP, the texture object must be cube complete. If the cube map uses mipmapping, the texture object must be cube mipmap complete.

6.3.3.1 Mipmap Complete

If your application specified or changed the base texture image while GL_GENERATE_MIPMAP was set to GL_TRUE, or if you used **gluBuild2DMipmaps**() to specify your texture images, OpenGL has already created a mipmap-complete texture object. If you're creating a mipmapped texture object manually, however, with individual calls to

glTexImage2D() for each mipmap level, see Section 3.8.10, "Texture Completeness," of *The OpenGL Graphics System* for the list of mipmap-complete criteria.

The texture-object state parameter GL_TEXTURE_MIN_FILTER defaults to GL_NEAREST_MIPMAP_LINEAR, which is a mipmap filter mode. Beginners commonly fail to change this parameter from its default value and specify a single texture map without a complete mipmap pyramid. In this case, the texture object isn't mipmap complete.

To fix this problem, set the minification filter to a nonmipmapped filter:

```
glTexParameteri( GL_TEXTURE_CUBE_MAP, GL_TEXTURE_MIN_FILTER, GL_LINEAR );
```

If the OpenGL version is 1.4 or later, you can also enable mipmap generation before calling **glTexImage2D**(), so that OpenGL will create a complete mipmap pyramid for you when you specify the base texture image:

```
glTexParameteri( GL_TEXTURE_CUBE_MAP, GL_GENERATE_MIPMAP, GL_TRUE );
```

6.3.3.2 Cube Complete

Your application must create cube map texture objects with six consistent images. A cube-complete texture object must meet the following criteria:

- Each of the six images must have the same positive dimensions, and the width and height must be the same; each image must be square.

- All six faces must have the same internal format.

- All six faces must have the same border width.

- To be cube-mipmap complete, each of the six faces must be mipmap complete when considered individually. (If the texture object's minification filter is a mipmap filter, all texture images must be mipmap complete.)

6.3.4 Missing Textures

There are many ways to misconfigure OpenGL accidentally, resulting in missing textures. The following paragraphs describe a few of the most common mistakes.

Make sure that you've enabled texture mapping. If the texture object bound to the active texture unit is 2D, call **glEnable**(GL_TEXTURE_2D), and if the texture object is a cube map, call **glEnable**(GL_TEXTURE_CUBE_MAP). If you're using multitexturing, make sure you enable each texture unit in use (conversely, be sure to disable texture units that are not in use).

When you enable texture mapping for a certain mode, disable other texture mapping modes. If the bound texture object contains a 2D texture image, for example, your code should ensure that GL_TEXTURE_1D, GL_TEXTURE_3D, and GL_TEXTURE_CUBE_MAP are all disabled. This is more than just good practice; the texture enumerants specify precedence. If GL_TEXTURE_CUBE_MAP is enabled, for example, but the bound texture object is 2D, OpenGL behaves as though texture mapping is completely disabled.

Unfortunately, there's no way to query OpenGL as to whether a texture object meets the texture-completeness criteria described in the section "Texture Completeness" earlier in this chapter. If you've accidentally bound a texture object that isn't texture complete, however, OpenGL will behave as though the active texture unit has texture mapping disabled.

Make sure that you set the appropriate texture environment for each enabled texture unit. Suppose that your application set GL_TEXTURE_ENV_MODE to GL_MODULATE for GL_TEXTURE0 and to GL_REPLACE for GL_TEXTURE1. In this case, the texture bound to GL_TEXTURE1 replaces the result from GL_TEXTURE0, and the final rendered image appears as though texture unit GL_TEXTURE0 is disabled.

6.3.5 Inverted Textures

The OpenGL window-coordinate system follows the Cartesian model of having its origin at the bottom-left corner, with positive x to the right and positive y up. Chapter 3, "Transformation and Viewing," briefly covers how this system clashes with most modern window systems, which have their origin in the top-left corner. This inconsistency causes headaches for most new OpenGL programmers—until they learn how to address this problem.

Similarly, the OpenGL pixel pipeline expects the bottom row of pixels first and the top row last. Many image files, however, store their pixel data inverted from the OpenGL system, with the top row of pixels first and the bottom last. As a result, whether using **glDrawPixels**() or texture mapping, the pixel data appears upside down in the final rendered image.

OpenGL programmers generally use one of two methods to address this issue:

- When designing the code that specifies texture coordinates, plan for this issue, and invert the images (or the texture coordinates).

- Invert the *t* coordinate by using the texture matrix. The best way to do this depends on the *t* coordinate wrap mode. For GL_REPEAT, for example, you can use a simple scale transformation:

```
glMatrixMode( GL_TEXTURE );
glLoadIdentity();
glScalef( 1.f, -1.f, 1.f );
```

  For a quadrilateral rendered with unit-texture coordinates at each vertex, as in the SimpleTextureMapping example, the above transformation produces –1 for *t* at the top of the image and 0 for *t* at the bottom, which inverts the image if the *t* coordinate wrap mode is GL_REPEAT. If the *t* coordinate wrap mode is GL_CLAMP_TO_EDGE, however, scaling *t* by –1 probably is insufficient, and you'd also need to translate in *t*, as shown below:

```
glMatrixMode( GL_TEXTURE );
glLoadIdentity();
glScalef( 1.f, -1.f, 1.f );
glTranslatef( 0.f, 1.f, 0.f );
```

OpenGL implementations typically optimize for an identity texture matrix by eliminating the texture-coordinate transformation. So unless your application already uses the texture matrix, the second option incurs a per-vertex texture-coordinate transformation that could affect application performance.

6.4   More Information

Chapter 9, "Texture Mapping," of *OpenGL® Programming Guide* is a thorough discussion of texture mapping within OpenGL. In *OpenGL® Reference Manual*, see "glTexEnv," "glTexGen," "glTexImage2D," and "glTexParameter." Each function description in *OpenGL® Reference Manual* concludes with a list of related functions; see these as well.

Chapter 8, "Mapping Techniques," of *3D Computer Graphics* provides general discussion of the many application areas for texture mapping, including bump mapping, environment mapping, and billboards. Also, Chapter 9 in that book, "Geometric Shadows," discusses solutions to the special problem of shadow rendering, including solutions that don't use texture mapping.

As an advanced text, much of the book *GPU Gems* (Fernando 2004) concerns the use of textures within vertex and fragment shaders to create various effects. Part II of *GPU Gems,* "Lighting and Shadows," presents shader techniques for rendering shadows. For more OpenGL–specific information along the same lines as *GPU Gems,* see *OpenGL® Shading Language*.

The book's Web site contains several examples that employ texture mapping, including full source for all example programs mentioned in this chapter. Also see the OpenGL Web site at `http://www.opengl.org` for texture mapping examples and programming resources.

6.5 References

(Blinn 1976) Blinn, James F., and Martin E. Newell. "Texture and Reflection in Computer Generated Images." *Communications of the ACM* (October 1976).

(Fernando 2004) Fernando, Randima. *GPU Gems*. Boston: Addison-Wesley, 2004.

(Gerasimov 2004) Gerasimov, Philipp S. "Omnidirectional Shadow Mapping." In *GPU Gems*. Boston: Addison-Wesley, 2004.

(Reeves 1987) Reeves, William T., David H. Salesin, and Robert L. Cook. "Rendering Antialiased Shadows with Depth Maps, ACM SIGGRAPH Computer Graphics." Proceedings of the 14th Annual Conference on Computer Graphics and Interactive Techniques, August 1987.

(Savchenko 2005) Savchenko, Sergei. "Algorithms for Dynamic Shadows." *Dr. Dobb's Journal* (February 2005).

(Williams 1978) Williams, Lance. "Casting Curved Shadows on Curved Surfaces, ACM SIGGRAPH Computer Graphics." Proceedings of the 5th Annual Conference on Computer Graphics and Interactive Techniques, August 1978.

(Williams 1983) Williams, Lance. "Pyramidal Parametrics, Computer Graphics, ACM SIGGRAPH Computer Graphics." Proceedings of the 10th Annual Conference on Computer Graphics and Interactive Techniques, July 1983.

Chapter 7

Extensions and Versions

OpenGL has outlived several generations of computer graphics hardware. This accomplishment would have been unattainable if not for the extension and version system that allowed OpenGL to evolve.

As OpenGL vendors provide new graphics hardware with additional functionality, they create extension specifications that allow developers to access the new functionality using OpenGL. Over time, if these extensions grow in popularity and acceptance, the OpenGL ARB could include the feature in a new version of the OpenGL specification.

You can't count on all your customers to have the same OpenGL version and extension support. As a result, you need to write version- and extension-safe code so that it can run in a wide variety of OpenGL environments. This chapter covers what you need to know to write robust code that uses extension- and version-specific OpenGL features.

What You'll Learn

This chapter covers the essentials of using OpenGL extensions and versions. Topics covered include the following:

- Querying for extension and version support—How to write code that queries the OpenGL implementation at runtime for supported functionality.

- Entry-point addresses—How to obtain addresses for extension- and version-specific command entry points at runtime.

- Development environment issues—How to write code that compiles in a variety of development environments.

What You Won't Learn

Aspects of extensions and versions not covered in this chapter include

- A complete list of available extensions—See the OpenGL Extension Registry Web site for this information: `http://oss.sgi.com/projects/ogl-sample/registry/`

- A complete list of features included in each version—See *The OpenGL Graphics System* for such a list.

7.1 Extensions

OpenGL provides an extension mechanism to expose new graphics features that aren't part of the OpenGL core standard. Each OpenGL extension has a unique name that identifies it at both compile time and runtime. An extension specification defines the extension behavior. Applications usually interact with an extension using a set of new enumerants and commands. It's common for applications to access nonstandard functionality using the extension mechanism.

OpenGL features three types of extensions:

- OpenGL vendors create vendor-specific extensions to expose functionality specific to their OpenGL implementation. Typically, the extension is available only in implementations from a single vendor.

  Vendor-specific extension enumerants and commands are suffixed with a brief sequence of characters, which serve both to identify the vendor and to indicate that they are part of an extension interface. For example, the ATI bump mapping extension, `GL_ATI_envmap_bumpmap`, contains enumerants like `GL_BUMP_ENVMAP_ATI` and `GL_BUMP_TARGET_ATI`, and commands such as **`glTexBumpParameterivATI`**().

- EXT extensions are vendor extensions adopted by more than one vendor. If the EXT extension evolved from a vendor-specific extension, its specification typically is more refined and generalized. EXT extension enumerants and command names are suffixed with EXT.

- Extensions approved by the OpenGL ARB are called ARB extensions. They typically are available in a wide range of OpenGL implementations. A working group of interested ARB members creates ARB extension specifications, which must be approved by a majority vote of ARB voting members. ARB extension enumerants and command names are suffixed with ARB.

Vendor-specific, EXT, and ARB extensions differ only in their implied availability. ARB extensions are expected to be more widely supported than EXT extensions, which are more widely supported than vendor-specific extensions. Applications use the same method to access all extensions, regardless of the extension type.

The OpenGL extension mechanism is intended to be a refinement process for new OpenGL features. Typically, an OpenGL vendor develops a new feature and exposes it as a vendor-specific extension. If the feature is well received by developers, it evolves to EXT status and then to ARB status, and perhaps eventually becomes part of the OpenGL core in a new OpenGL version. After an extension is added to the core, the enumerant and command names are stripped of their extension-specific suffixes.

For backward compatibility, OpenGL implementations often expose the same feature through several different interfaces. It's not uncommon, for example, for an OpenGL implementation to support cube mapping through the core 1.3 interface, the `GL_ARB_texture_cube_map` ARB extension interface, and the `GL_EXT_texture_cube_map` EXT extension interface.

Ideally, you should use the latest available interface for a given feature. The latest interface might not be available on all platforms, however. As an application developer, you need to choose which of several interfaces to use. If your application runs on multiple platforms, and not all platforms support a given OpenGL feature with the latest interface, your application should fall back to an older interface to access the same functionality or fall back to a code path that doesn't use the feature.

Specifications for several OpenGL extensions are available at the OpenGL Extension Registry Web site (`http://oss.sgi.com/projects/ogl-sample/registry/`). Like *The OpenGL Graphics System*, extension specifications are written for OpenGL vendors but also provide valuable information for application developers. Typically, OpenGL vendors provide extension documentation geared to developers as part of their development environment package.

To build an application that uses a specific extension, you need the extension enumerant definitions and command prototypes in your development environment. Typically, OpenGL vendors provide these definitions and declarations in a platform-specific OpenGL development environment package, sometimes referred to as a software development kit (SDK). Optionally, you can create your own development environment using the `glext.h` header file available from the OpenGL Extension Registry.

To access an extension, you need to do the following:

- To determine whether you can use an extension, query the OpenGL implementation at runtime for extension support.

- Obtain and call function pointers for extension-specific commands. Use extension-specific commands and enumerants only if the extension is supported at runtime.

The following sections cover these topics.

7.1.1 Querying for an Extension

Use **glGetString**(GL_EXTENSIONS) to obtain a list of supported extensions. As covered in Chapter 1, "An Introduction to OpenGL," **glGetString**() returns a GLubyte*—a C-style string. When called with the GL_EXTENSIONS parameter, **glGetString**() returns a space-separated list of extension names, one for each extension supported at runtime by the underlying OpenGL implementation. To determine whether a specific extension is supported, search for the extension name in the returned extension string. Because an extension name could be a substring of another extension name, your application should parse the extension string into individual names and look for an exact match.

The following function demonstrates how to parse an OpenGL extension string correctly. The first parameter is the name of an extension to search for; the second parameter is an extension string as obtained with a call to **glGetString**(GL_EXTENSION). The function returns true or false to indicate whether the extension is supported. It uses the C++ Standard Template Library std::string class to facilitate parsing the extension string.

```
bool isExtensionSupported( const std::string& name,
        const GLubyte* extensions )
{
    std::string extStr( extensions );

    while ( !extStr.empty() )
    {
        int idx = extStr.find_first_of( ' ' );
        std::string ext = extStr.substr( 0, idx );
        if (name == ext)
            return true;
        extStr.erase( 0, idx+1 );
    }

    return false;
}
```

Call this function with the extension name as the first parameter and the OpenGL extension string as the second parameter. The following code, for example, shows how to search for the presence of the GL_ARB_pixel_buffer_object extension:

```
const bool usePBO = isExtensionSupported(
        Std::string( "GL_ARB_pixel_buffer_object" ),
        glGetString( GL_EXTENSIONS ) );
```

If an extension is supported in the underlying OpenGL implementation, your application is free to use the extension enumerants and commands. If the extension isn't supported, using an extension enumerant generates an OpenGL error (use **glGetError**() to catch it), and using extension commands could cause an application crash.

> **Note** If your application needs to make a copy of the entire extension string, avoid copying the string to a fixed-size buffer (by using strcpy(), for example). The extension string varies widely in size from one implementation to the next. As a result, the copy operation could succeed on your development platform but overrun the fixed-size buffer when deployed to customers and cause an application crash.

7.1.2 Obtaining and Calling Extension Commands

As discussed in Chapter 1, "An Introduction to OpenGL," an OpenGL implementation typically is a library, and your application interacts with OpenGL by calling library entry points. In an ideal world, the OpenGL version and supported extensions would be identical in all end-user runtime environments, and would match the version and supported extensions in your build environment, but this is rarely the case for professional applications. Consider deploying a single OpenGL application on several end-user systems with OpenGL implementations from a variety of vendors. Because the set of supported extensions varies from one platform to the next, it's impossible to create an executable that resolves all entry points at link time.

Most OpenGL libraries support dynamic rather than static linking, however, and most platforms provide a mechanism to obtain the address of an entry point in a dynamically loaded library. This enables your application to obtain OpenGL function pointers at runtime rather than resolve all symbols at link time.

How you obtain extension entry points depends on your runtime platform. The next few sections describe how to obtain extension entry points for the Linux, Microsoft Windows, and Apple Mac OS X operating systems.

7.1.2.1   Obtaining Entry Points for Linux

Linux operating systems support a set of three functions for opening, obtaining symbols from, and closing a dynamic library. To open a dynamic library and obtain a handle to it, call `dlopen()`. After you have a handle, call `dlsym()` as needed to obtain the address of entry points. When you have obtained all the entry-point addresses required by your application, call `dlclose()`. Some applications use this interface to obtain extension entry points. For documentation on this interface, see the `man` pages for `dlopen`, `dlsym`, and `dlclose`.

Most Linux platforms, however, use Mesa, which provides GLX version 1.4 support. In GLX version 1.4, applications obtain an entry-point address with a single call to **glXGetProcAddress**().

---

typedef void (*GLfunction)(void);
extern GLfunction **glXGetProcAddress**(const GLubyte* *procName*);

Returns the address of an OpenGL entry point. *procName* specifies the name of the desired entry point. If the entry point doesn't exist (for example, the extension isn't supported at runtime), **glXGetProc-Address**() returns NULL.

You should typecast the return value to the appropriate function pointer type before calling through it.

▶ GLX version: 1.4.

Because **glXGetProcAddress**() is available in GLX version 1.4, you should use the C preprocessor symbol `GLX_VERSION_1_4` to ensure that your development environment supports version 1.4 before using this command:

```
#ifdef GLX_VERSION_1_4
    // OK to call glXGetProcAddress()
#endif
```

If your Linux system doesn't support GLX version 1.4, you should download and install the latest version of Mesa. See the section "Extension- and Version-Safe Code" later in this chapter for more information on writing version-safe code.

7.1.2.2   Obtaining Entry Points for Microsoft Windows

Microsoft Windows supports an interface that is nearly identical to the Linux `GLX_ARB_get_proc_address` interface. To obtain an extension entry-point address for Microsoft Windows, call **wglGetProcAddress**().

WINGDIAPI PROC WINAPI **wglGetProcAddress**(LPCSTR *procName*);

Although the function prototype contains many Windows-specific symbols, the function works identically to `glXGetProcAddress`(); it takes a `const char*` entry-point name as a parameter and returns a `void*` function pointer.

`wglGetProcAddress`() returns NULL if the entry point doesn't exist. This usually occurs if the extension isn't supported at runtime, but beware of typographical errors when coding this function call; misspelling the entry-point name could also cause `wglGetProcAddress`() to return NULL.

Unlike `glXGetProcAddress`(), `wglGetProcAddress`() is part of the Windows operating system and has been available since Windows first supported OpenGL. Your application doesn't need to check for the correct WGL version at compile time.

7.1.2.3 Obtaining Entry Points for Apple Mac OS X

Under Mac OS X, if an extension name is listed in the OpenGL extension string at runtime, applications can use the extension entry points without having to obtain entry-point addresses. For any given version of Mac OS X, OpenGL exposes a common set of extensions supported by all underlying graphics hardware vendors. Rather than use a routine such as **wglGetProcAddress**(), applications statically link with extension entry points. For this reason, Mac OS X applications have a greatly reduced need to obtain entry-point addresses dynamically compared with other platforms.

Mac OS X does provide interfaces for obtaining entry-point addresses dynamically, however. Applications will need to use this interface to run in multiple releases of Mac OS X. If your application needs to use this interface, review Apple's documentation on the subject. The following Web site contains general information on querying OpenGL capabilities:

```
http://developer.apple.com/technotes/tn2002/tn2080.html
```

The following Web site is devoted specifically to obtaining entry-point addresses:

```
http://developer.apple.com/qa/qa2001/qa1188.html
```

If your application has no need to obtain entry-point addresses under Mac OS X, you can skip the following section.

7.1.2.4 Declaring and Typecasting Entry Points

As described in the preceding sections, the runtime platform typically returns an extension entry-point address to your application as a void* function pointer. Your application should typecast this return value to a function pointer of the appropriate type. Your development environment contains extension entry-point prototypes. As an example, the following code segment shows how to declare the single extension entry-point function pointer for the GL_ARB_multisample[1] extension, obtain its entry point for Microsoft Windows, and correctly typecast the return value:

```
// Note: PFNGLSAMPLECOVERAGEARBPROC declared in platform-specific
//    dev environment header file (or glext.h).
PFNGLSAMPLECOVERAGEARBPROC glSampleCoverageARB;
const bool useARBmultisample = isExtensionSupported(
        std::string( "GL_ARB_multisample" ),
        glGetString( GL_EXTENSIONS ) );
if (useARBmultisample)
    glSampleCoverageARB = (PFNGLSAMPLECOVERAGEARBPROC)
            wglGetProcAddress( "glSampleCoverageARB" );
```

Perform the same declaration and typecast regardless of your runtime platform.

7.2 Versions

The OpenGL specification has been revised several times since its inception in 1992. The OpenGL ARB assigns a version number to each major revision and publishes its specification. Download current and past OpenGL specifications at the OpenGL Web site: http://www.opengl.org. Appendices C through I of *The OpenGL Graphics System* summarize the changes to each version of the specification.

Unfortunately, there is significant lag time between the approval of a new version of the specification and widespread industry adoption of that new version. As a result, most multiplatform OpenGL applications must support several OpenGL versions at runtime. To accomplish this, employ the tactics described in the section "Extensions" earlier in this chapter. To reiterate:

- Use a development environment that contains definitions and declarations corresponding to the latest OpenGL version that your application requires.

---

1. GL_ARB_multisample was folded into the OpenGL version 1.3 specification. Some applications still use the ARB extension interface for compatibility with older OpenGL implementations.

- Check for the supported version at runtime using **glGetString**
  (GL_VERSION).

- Conditionally obtain version-specific entry points, and execute version-specific code only if the version is supported in the runtime environment.

In concept, version-specific code is essentially the same as extension-specific code.

Your development environment must contain the definitions and declarations for the latest OpenGL version that your application uses. You can't compile code that uses OpenGL version 2.0 features if your development environment doesn't contain the version 2.0 enumerant definitions and command entry-point prototypes. If your OpenGL vendor doesn't provide a development environment for the latest version, obtain glext.h from the OpenGL Extension Registry Web site.

Although glext.h allows you to compile new code, linking is still an issue because the linker can't resolve the latest version-specific entry points if the OpenGL stub library is out of date. Fortunately, the same mechanism available for obtaining extension entry points at runtime also lets your application obtain any entry point in the underlying OpenGL implementation. This allows you to declare function pointers to current OpenGL features and to obtain function addresses by using dlsym(), **glXGetProcAddress**(), or **wglGetProcAddress**() just as though it were an extension entry point.

In fact, if you intend to deploy your application in Microsoft Windows, your application must employ this technique for all OpenGL features after version 1.1.[2] The reason is that Microsoft operating systems include only OpenGL version 1.1 support in opengl32.dll. Correspondingly, the opengl32.lib stub library also contains only version 1.1 symbols.

Chapter 1, "An Introduction to OpenGL," contains example code for checking the OpenGL runtime version using **glGetString**(GL_VERSION). The OGLDif class in the example code cooks the OpenGL version string down to a simple enumerant, such as Ver14 if the OpenGL runtime version is 1.4. This enumerant allows fast runtime version checking. The following code snippet, for example, shows how to execute cube map code conditionally only if the OpenGL runtime version is 1.3 or later:

```
if (ogld::OGLDif::instance()->getVersion() >= ogld::Ver13)
    // Use cube mapping
```

---

2. At the WinHEC 2005 conference, Microsoft announced plans to upgrade base OpenGL support to version 1.4 in a future release of its operating system.

The OGLDif class uses the singleton design pattern. It calls **glGetString**(GL_VERSION) only in its constructor. The getVersion() method simply returns the cooked version enumerant.

Finally, the example code ogld namespace declares function pointers for all OpenGL entry points added after version 1.1, and the OGLDif constructor initializes them if the runtime version supports the entry point.

7.3 Extension- and Version-Safe Code

To create a single application that runs in multiple OpenGL implementations, your application must query OpenGL for version and extension support at runtime using **glGetString**(). If you intend to write code for distribution to others, however, you also need to make sure the code will compile in an uncontrolled development environment where extension- and version-specific definitions and declarations might not exist.

In the C binding for OpenGL, the gl.h and glext.h header files define C preprocessor symbols to indicate extension and version support. This allows your code to compile extension- and version-specific code conditionally only when the development environment supports it.

C preprocessor definitions for extensions are the same as the extension name. If the development environment contains enumerant definitions and entry-point declarations for the GL_ARB_multisample extension, for example, it defines GL_ARB_multisample as a C preprocessor symbol.

To indicate supported versions, the development environment defines possibly multiple symbols of the form GL_VERSION_<major>_<minor>, where <major> and <minor> indicate the major and minor OpenGL version number. If the development environment supports version 2.0, it defines GL_VERSION_2_0 as a C preprocessor symbol. Because each version of OpenGL is backward compatible with previous versions, development environments define a symbol for each supported version—GL_VERSION_1_0, GL_VERSION_1_1, and so on—up to and including a symbol for the latest supported version.

Listing 7-1 shows the PixelBuffer class, part of the example code available from the *OpenGL® Distilled* Web site. PixelBuffer uses an extension feature and requires a specific OpenGL version but compiles in any OpenGL development environment but runs in any OpenGL implementation.

PixelBuffer uses the GL_ARB_pixel_buffer_object[3] extension to speed pixel rectangle rendering using the **glDrawPixels**() command. GL_ARB_pixel_buffer_object is similar to the OpenGL version 1.5 buffer object feature and requires buffer object entry points such as **glGenBuffers**() and **glBufferData**(). Buffer objects allow vertex array commands to source vertex data from high-performance server memory rather than client memory. GL_ARB_pixel_buffer_object extends this functionality to commands that source pixel data, such as **glDrawPixels**(). Because pixel data typically is large, GL_ARB_pixel_buffer_object significantly increases performance of commands such as **glDrawPixels**().

PixelBuffer is derived from Pixels, which uses **glDrawPixels**() without the GL_ARB_pixel_buffer_object extension. So if the development environment doesn't support the GL_ARB_pixel_buffer_object extension or version 1.5, PixelBuffer doesn't compile the extension- and version-specific code; instead, it simply falls back to its base class.

Listing 7-1   Example of extension- and version-safe code

```
#if defined( GL_ARB_pixel_buffer_object ) && defined( GL_VERSION_1_5 )
#  define PIXELBUFFER_BUILD_PBO 1
#endif

class PixelBuffer : public Pixels
{
public:
    PixelBuffer();

private:
    GLuint _pbo;


#ifdef PIXELBUFFER_BUILD_PBO

public:
    virtual ~PixelBuffer();
    virtual void apply();

protected:
    virtual bool init();

#endif // PIXELBUFFER_BUILD_PBO
};
```

---

3. GL_ARB_pixel_buffer_object was promoted from EXT to ARB status in the December 2004 OpenGL ARB meeting. It is a candidate for promotion to the OpenGL version 2.1 specification.

```
PixelBuffer::PixelBuffer()
  : Pixels(),
    _pbo( 0 )
{
}


#ifdef PIXELBUFFER_BUILD_PBO

PixelBuffer::~PixelBuffer()
{
    if ( _valid )
    {
        assert( _pbo != 0 );
        glDeleteBuffers( 1, &_pbo );
    }
}

void
PixelBuffer::apply()
{
    if (!_valid)
    {
        if (!init())
            return;
    }

    assert( _pbo != 0 );
    glBindBuffer( GL_PIXEL_UNPACK_BUFFER_ARB, _pbo );
    glDrawPixels( _width, _height, _format, _type,
            bufferObjectPtr( 0 ) );

    OGLDIF_CHECK_ERROR;
}

bool
PixelBuffer::init()
{
    Pixels::init();

    if (!_valid)
        return false;


    glGenBuffers( 1, &_pbo );
    assert( _pbo != 0 );

    glBindBuffer( GL_PIXEL_UNPACK_BUFFER_ARB, _pbo );
    glBufferData( GL_PIXEL_UNPACK_BUFFER_ARB, size(),
            _pixels, GL_STATIC_DRAW );
```

```
        return _valid;
}

#endif // PIXELBUFFER_BUILD_PBO
```

Because the code that uses pixel buffer objects requires support for both
the `GL_ARB_pixel_buffer_object` extension and version 1.5, the code
defines a C preprocessor symbol, `PIXELBUFFER_BUILD_PBO`, only if the
development environment supports both the required extension and version.

The destructor and the `apply()` and `init()` methods are declared virtual
in the base class. If `PIXELBUFFER_BUILD_PBO` is defined, `PixelBuffer`
overrides them. Otherwise, instantiations of this class use the base-class
member functions.

The `init()` member function is called before any rendering. It allocates a
buffer object using **glGenBuffers**`()` and binds the buffer to an extension-specific target, `GL_PIXEL_UNPACK_BUFFER_ARB`. According to the
`GL_ARB_pixel_buffer_object` specification, when a buffer object is
bound to `GL_PIXEL_UNPACK_BUFFER_ARB`, commands that receive pixel
data from the application, such as **glDrawPixels**`()`, source data from the
bound buffer object rather than client memory. After binding the buffer,
`init()` stores the pixel rectangle in the bound buffer object using the
glBufferData`()` command.

The `apply()` method renders the pixel rectangle. It binds the buffer object
and calls **glDrawPixels**`()` with a pointer to NULL. The class destructor
deletes the buffer object.

The code also needs to handle runtime environments that lack the requi-
site runtime support. Listing 7-1 by itself would fail in a runtime environment that either lacks the `GL_ARB_pixel_buffer` extension or has an
OpenGL version less than 1.5. For this reason, the base `Pixels` class contains a static factory method called `Pixels::create()`, shown in Listing
7-2, that ensures that `PixelBuffer` will be instantiated only if the runtime environment can support it. This simplifies the implementation of
`PixelBuffer` by eliminating redundant runtime checks for the necessary
OpenGL version and presence of the `GL_ARB_pixel_buffer` extension.

Listing 7-2   Factory method for the PixelBuffer class

```
class Pixels
{
public:
    typedef enum {
        NoPBO, UsePBOIfAvailable, ForcePBO
    } PixelsProduct;
```

```
    static Pixels* create( PixelsProduct product=UsePBOIfAvailable );
    ...
};

Pixels*
Pixels::create( PixelsProduct product )
{
    if (product == NoPBO)
        return new Pixels();

    const std::string pboStr( "GL_ARB_pixel_buffer_object" );
    const bool pboAvailable = (
            (OGLDif::instance()->getVersion() >= Ver15) &&
            (OGLDif::instance()->isExtensionSupported(
            pboStr, glGetString( GL_EXTENSIONS ) )) );

    if (pboAvailable)
        return new PixelBuffer();

    if (product == UsePBOIfAvailable)
        // PBO not supported, use Pixels instead
        return new Pixels();

    // product == ForcePBO, but it's not supported
    return NULL;
}
```

`Pixels::create()` implements a parameterized factory design pattern. Calling code can pass in the level of `GL_ARB_pixel_buffer` support desired. If the calling code does not want the `Pixels` object to use `GL_ARB_pixel_buffer`, it passes `NoPBO` as a parameter, and `create()` responds by returning an instantiation of the `Pixels` base class.

Otherwise, `create()` checks for runtime extension support using the `isExtensionSupported()` function. If the OpenGL implementation supports the extension and supports OpenGL version 1.5, it sets the local variable `pboAvailable` to `true`. The code then uses the value of `pboAvailable`, along with the *product* parameter, to determine whether to instantiate `PixelBuffer`, `Pixels` or simply return NULL. The logic in this code ensures that `PixelBuffer` is instantiated only if the runtime environment supports `GL_ARB_pixel_buffer` and OpenGL version 1.5 or later.

7.4 More Information

The definitive resource for OpenGL extensions is the OpenGL Extension Registry Web site, `http://oss.sgi.com/projects/ogl-sample/`

`registry/`, which provides access to vendor-specific, EXT, and ARB extension specifications. Also, the appendix, "ARB Extensions," of *The OpenGL Graphics System*, enumerates all ARB-approved extensions, even those that have already been folded into the core specification.

Due to its scope, *OpenGL® Distilled* doesn't provide an exhaustive list of features added to each OpenGL version. But *The OpenGL Graphics System*, Appendices C through I, provides this information.

The book's Web site contains version-safe example code, as well as full source for the Extensions program, which uses the `PixelBuffer` class in Listing 7-1.

Chapter 8

Platform-Specific Interfaces

As a platform-independent API, OpenGL leaves framebuffer and state management up to the underlying window system.

The window system determines how the final rendered image appears in the presence of overlapping windows. It also provides access to several framebuffer configurations. If the window system is network transparent, it provides local and remote access to OpenGL rendering contexts.

Although GLUT is an excellent tool for developing small platform-independent demos, it has its limitations. Most notably, it limits the application to one rendering context per window. Applications often use multiple rendering contexts, and share OpenGL objects and display lists between them. To access this functionality, you'll need to write platform-specific code.

This chapter leaves GLUT behind and describes the platform-specific interfaces for three popular OpenGL runtime environments.

What You'll Learn

Topics covered in this chapter include the following:

- Apple Mac OS X, Linux, and Microsoft Windows—In addition, you can apply what you learn regarding Linux to any Unix platform that supports the X Window System.

- Configuring the framebuffer—This chapter covers how to request a double-buffered, RGBA window with a depth buffer.

- Onscreen rendering—Most OpenGL applications render to a visible window, and this chapter focuses primarily on window rendering.

- Creating, using, and deleting GL contexts.

- Sharing objects between contexts—The chapter shows how to share display lists, texture objects, and buffer objects between contexts.

- Swapping buffers.

What You Won't Learn

This chapter omits the following information:

- Offscreen rendering—This chapter covers only onscreen rendering.

- Copying rendering contexts, or copying state from one rendering context to another.

- Query routines—The chapter does not cover platform-specific interfaces for querying a platform for state, version, or extension information.

- Commands unrelated to OpenGL—This is not a full platform reference and does not document all platform-specific commands that you might need to use. Creating windows, for example, is discussed but not documented.

Covering interfaces for all platforms is outside the scope of this book. One noteworthy omission is EGL, designed to be implemented on a variety of platforms and currently available in many embedded systems for use with OpenGL ES. Obtain the EGL spec from the OpenGL Web site.

See the platform-specific documentation for information on the topics not covered in this chapter.

8.1 Concepts

Platform-specific OpenGL code, by definition, differs from platform to platform. The concepts and coding tasks involved are very similar, however. On every platform, applications typically perform the following tasks:

- Specify the framebuffer configuration—The interface typically is an array or C struct that the application fills in with constants and values to describe the desired framebuffer configuration.

- Create a rendering context—This generally is done after the application specifies the framebuffer configuration so that the context is initialized accordingly.

- Create a window.

- Associate the context with the window—This is usually done on a per-thread basis.

- After rendering each frame, swap buffers.

- When the application exits, delete the rendering context.

In most of the example source code, GLUT performs these tasks. The example source code also includes a platform-specific example, however, to demonstrate how applications can perform these tasks using interfaces specific to Apple Mac OS X, Linux, and Microsoft Windows.

In addition to window (onscreen) rendering, all platforms provide off-screen rendering capabilities. Because rendering to a buffer in host RAM usually invokes a software rendering path, most OpenGL implementations support the concept of *pbuffers*—offscreen buffers in graphics-card RAM that support hardware-accelerated rendering. Pbuffers are allocated by the operating system, so each platform-specific interface supports a pbuffer extension.

More recently, implementations have moved to support the `GL_EXT_framebuffer_object` extension. Like pbuffers, this extension enables hardware-accelerated rendering to offscreen buffers. `GL_EXT_framebuffer_object` is an extension to OpenGL and not to the platform-specific interface, however. Therefore, applications access its features using (platform-independent) OpenGL extension commands rather than different commands for each platform. `GL_EXT_framebuffer_object` also provides additional capabilities, such as streamlined render-to-texture, that are not available in the pbuffer feature.

Finally, all platforms also provide a mechanism to share all OpenGL objects, including display lists, texture objects, and buffer objects.

8.2 Apple Mac OS X

Besides GLUT, Apple fully supports three OpenGL interfaces specific to Apple platforms: CGL, NSOpenGL, and AGL. A description of supported Apple interfaces is available at the following Web site:

    http://developer.apple.com/qa/qa2001/qa1269.html

CGL, or Core OpenGL, is the lowest-level of the three interfaces. It can't be used for windowed rendering but can be used for full-screen and offscreen rendering. NSOpenGL, available through Cocoa, is the most recent Apple interface. It presents an object-oriented interface using a set of Objective-C classes.

AGL is the primary OpenGL interface for Carbon applications. *OpenGL® Distilled* focuses on this interface because of its widespread use, support for operating systems older than Mac OS X, and similarities to the WGL and GLX interfaces. *AGL Reference* documents the AGL interface. See the OpenGL section of the Apple Developer Connection Web site for this and other Apple-specific OpenGL information:

> `http://developer.apple.com/graphicsimaging/opengl/`

8.2.1   Creating Contexts

In AGL, you must specify a pixel format when creating a context. The pixel format describes the characteristics and capabilities of the renderer and drawing surface(s).

To obtain a list of pixel formats, call **aglChoosePixelFormat**().

AGLPixelFormat **aglChoosePixelFormat**(const AGLDevice* *gdevs*,
   GLint *ndev*, const GLint* *attribs*);

Returns the identifiers of pixel formats that meet the specified requirements. *gdevs* indicates the graphics devices; pass NULL to obtain pixel formats for all devices installed in a system. *ndev* is the number of devices in *gdevs*; pass zero if *gdevs* is NULL.

attribs is an array of constants that specify specific requirements for the pixel format. An element of the array can be a Boolean value, such as AGL_RGBA, or consecutive elements are constant-value pairs, such as AGL_DEPTH_SIZE, 24. You must terminate the array by specifying AGL_NONE as the final element.

aglChoosePixelFormat() returns the first of possibly several pixel formats meeting the requirements specified by the parameters. To obtain the next pixel format, call **aglNextPixelFormat**(). **aglChoosePixel-Format**() returns NULL if no pixel formats match the list of requirements in *attrib*.

Use **aglChoosePixelFormat**() to specify OpenGL rendering requirements such as color, double buffering, depth buffer size, and color buffer size. The following code, for example, requests a double-buffered RGBA pixel format with 24-bit color buffers and a 24-bit depth buffer:

```
const GLint attrib[] = { AGL_RGBA, AGL_DOUBLEBUFFER,
        AGL_BUFFER_SIZE, 24, AGL_DEPTH_SIZE, 24, AGL_NONE };
AGLPixelFormat fmt = aglChoosePixelFormat( NULL, 0, attrib );
```

The attribute array elements shown above specify the drawing-surface characteristics. Other attribute element values control renderer selection. Include the constants AGL_ACCELERATED and AGL_NO_RECOVERY in *attrib* to select only hardware-accelerated pixel formats, for example.

AGLPixelFormat is an opaque type. The pixel formats returned by **aglChoosePixelFormat**() and **aglNextPixelFormat**() match as closely as possible to the attributes specified in *attrib*. To examine the returned pixel formats in detail to ensure that they meet your application's specifications, use **aglDescribePixelFormat**(). See *Apple OpenGL Reference* for information on **aglDescribePixelFormat**().

After you've obtained an appropriate pixel format, pass it to **aglCreate-Context**() to create a context.

AGLContext **aglCreateContext**(AGLPixelFormat *pix*, AGLContext *share*);

Creates an OpenGL rendering context. *pix* is the desired pixel format, as obtained from **aglChoosePixelFormat**().

share specifies a context to share OpenGL objects with, such as display lists, buffer objects, and texture objects. If *share* is NULL, the context stores its own OpenGL objects.

aglCreateContext() returns NULL if it's unable to create a context for any reason.

To share OpenGL objects between contexts, your application must create the contexts according to certain criteria. If two contexts were created with the same pixel format, AGL allows sharing. There are other, less restrictive rules that also allow sharing; see *Apple OpenGL Reference* for more information.

After creating the context, you can free pixel-format resources by calling **aglDestroyPixelFormat**(pix), where *pix* is the pixel format returned by **aglChoosePixelFormat**().

8.2.2 Using Contexts

Before issuing OpenGL commands, your application needs to associate the rendering context with a drawable and make it current.

To associate the rendering context with a drawable, call **aglSetDrawable**().

GLboolean **aglSetDrawable**(AGLContext *ctx*, AGLDrawable *draw*);

Associates the specified context with the specified drawable. *ctx* is a rendering context, and *draw* is an AGL drawable. The AGLDrawable type is equivalent to a CGrafPtr. Drawables may be windows, offscreen buffers, or pixel buffer objects.

To disable rendering for a context, call **aglSetDrawable**(ctx, NULL).

You can associate multiple contexts with a single drawable, but only one context can be current at a time. To set the current context, call **aglSet-CurrentContext**().

GLboolean **aglSetCurrentContext**(AGLContext *ctx*);

Makes *ctx* the current OpenGL context, and makes the previously current context noncurrent.

aglSetCurrentContext() returns GL_FALSE if it fails for any reason and GL_TRUE otherwise.

The following code demonstrates how to associate a context with a window drawable and make the context current:

```
AGLContext ctx;
WindowRef win;
...
aglSetDrawable( ctx, GetWindowPort(win) );
aglSetCurrentContext( ctx );
```

When you have associated a context with a drawable and made it current, subsequent OpenGL commands use state from the current context, and rendering affects its drawable.

To make the current context noncurrent without making a new context current, call **aglSetCurrentContext**(NULL).

8.2.3 Swapping Buffers

If your context is double buffered (that is, if you specified AGL_ DOUBLEBUFFER in the *attrib* parameter to **aglChoosePixelFormat**() and created a context with the returned pixel format), you must swap buffers after rendering a frame to display the contents of the back buffer. To swap buffers, call **aglSwapBuffers**().

---

void **aglSwapBuffers**(AGLContext *ctx*);

Makes the back buffer associated with *ctx* visible. The contents of the new back buffer are undefined after this call.

aglSwapBuffers() implicitly flushes any buffered OpenGL commands (that is, it implicitly calls **glFlush**()).

AGL supports application control over whether the swap buffer command is synchronized to the monitor vertical retrace. See the description of **aglSwapBuffers**() in *Apple OpenGL Reference* for more information.

8.2.4 Deleting Contexts

To delete a context and free its resources, call **aglDestroyContext**().

GLboolean **aglDestroyContext**(AGLContext *ctx*);

Deletes the OpenGL rendering context specified by *ctx*. If *ctx* is the current context, **aglDestroyContext**() implicitly calls **aglSetCurrent-Context**(NULL), making *ctx* noncurrent and leaving no current context.

Carbon applications typically delete contexts upon receiving the kEventWindowClose event.

8.3 Linux

Linux uses GLX, the OpenGL extension to the X Window System, to provide platform-specific support for OpenGL. For documentation on GLX, see *OpenGL Graphics with the X Window System (Version 1.3),* edited by Paula

Womack and Jon Leech, available from the official OpenGL Web site,
`http://www.opengl.org`. Note, however, that most Linux systems use
Mesa, which provides GLX version 1.4 support.[1]

To run an OpenGL program on a Linux system, the X Windows server
must support the GLX extension. If you purchase a Linux system with an
OpenGL graphics card, the system manufacturer preconfigures X to load
GLX. Run the `glxinfo` client to confirm that your X server supports GLX.

GLX allows OpenGL clients to render onscreen using `GLXWindows`. It also
allows two forms of offscreen rendering: `GLXPixmaps` and `GLXPbuffers`.
Collectively, `GLXWindows`, `GLXPixmaps`, and `GLXPbuffers` are known as
`GLXDrawables`.

Typically, `GLXPixmaps` don't use hardware acceleration. For hardware-
accelerated offscreen rendering, use `GLXPbuffers`. This section focuses primarily on rendering to a window, though most of the concepts also apply
to offscreen rendering. For more information on offscreen rendering, refer
to *OpenGL Graphics with the X Window System*.

8.3.1 Creating Contexts

To create a rendering context that renders to a window, perform the following steps:

1. Choose a suitable `GLXFBConfig`, which describes the OpenGL render
   buffer characteristics.

2. Create a rendering context from the `GLXFBConfig`.

3. Create a `GLXWindow`, the GLX equivalent of the X `Window` object.

To obtain a `GLXFBConfig`, call **glXChooseFBConfig**().

GLXFBConfig* **glXChooseFBConfig**(Display* *dpy*, int *screen*, const int*
   attrib_list, int* *nelements*);

Obtains a list of `GLXFBConfigs` that meet the specified criteria. *dpy* and
screen specify the X Windows server display.

---

1. As of this printing, the GLX version 1.4 specification hasn't been formally approved by
   the OpenGL ARB. Because Linux distributions almost universally provide Mesa, however,
   GLX version 1.4 is widely available.

Each pair of elements in the *attrib_list* array specifies a framebuffer attribute and its desired value. The element pair GLX_DOUBLEBUFFER, True, for example, causes **glXChooseFBConfig**() to return only double-buffered GLXFBConfigs. **glXChooseFBConfig**() doesn't always use exact matching, however. For a list of attributes and their matching criteria, see Table 3.4 in *OpenGL Graphics with the X Window System*.

glXChooseFBConfig() returns an array of GLXFBConfigs that match the attributes specified in *attrib_list*. The number of GLXFBConfigs in the array is returned in *nelements*.

glXChooseFBConfig() returns NULL if no GLXFBConfigs match the list of requirements in *attrib_list*.

Use **glXChooseFBConfig**() to obtain available GLXFBConfigs that meet or exceed your application requirements for rendering buffer characteristics. The following code, for example, obtains a list of GLXFBConfigs for use with double-buffered RGBA rendering to a window. The GLXFBConfigs will have at least 24 color buffer bits and at least 24 depth buffer bits.

```
const int attributes[] = {
    GLX_DRAWABLE_TYPE, GLX_WINDOW_BIT,
    GLX_RENDER_TYPE, GLX_RGBA_BIT,
    GLX_DOUBLEBUFFER, True,
    GLX_BUFFER_SIZE, 24,
    GLX_DEPTH_SIZE, 24,
    None };
int nElements;
GLXFBConfig* fbConfigs = glXChooseFBConfig(
        dpy, screen, attributes, &nElements );
```

GLXFBConfig is an opaque data type. To examine all attributes of a GLXFBConfig, use **glXGetFBConfigAttrib**(). For more information, see *OpenGL Graphics with the X Window System*.

Use XFree() to free the GLXFBConfig array returned by **glXChooseFB-Config**().

After identifying a GLXFBConfig that meets your application's requirements, create a rendering context with a call to **glXCreateNewContext**().

GLXContext **glXCreateNewContext**(Display* *dpy*, GLXFBConfig *config*,
   int *render_type*, GLXContext *share_list*, Bool *direct*);

Creates an OpenGL rendering context. *dpy* identifies the X Windows display server. *config* is a GLXFBConfig, as obtained with **glXChoose-FBConfig**(). Pass GLX_RGBA_TYPE for *render_type*.

If *share_list* isn't NULL, it specifies a rendering context to share OpenGL objects with. The *share_list* context will store display lists, buffer objects, and texture objects that the newly created context creates and uses. If *share_list* is NULL, the newly created context stores its own OpenGL objects.

Use *direct* to specify whether **glXCreateNewContext**() should return a direct or indirect rendering context. Passing True for *direct* requests a rendering context that bypasses the X server, allowing the client application to control the graphics hardware directly. If the server can't create a direct rendering context, **glXCreateNewContext**() will return an indirect rendering context, which renders through the X server.

glXCreateNewContext() returns NULL if it fails for any reason.

GLX has the concept of an address space, which determines whether OpenGL objects can be shared between rendering contexts. For more information, see *OpenGL Graphics with the X Window System.*

If the GLXFBConfig supports rendering to a window (that is, its GLX_DRAWABLE_TYPE attribute has the GLX_WINDOW_BIT set), the GLXFBConfig has an associated X visual. Obtain the XVisualInfo struct from the GLXFBConfig with a call to **glXGetVisualFromFBConfig**().

XVisualInfo* **glXGetVisualFromFBConfig**(Display* *dpy*, GLXFBConfig
    config);

Obtains the X visual from a GLXFBConfig. *dpy* specifies the X Window server, and *config* specifies the GLXFBConfig to obtain an XVisualInfo struct from. **glXGetVisualFromFBConfig**() returns NULL if it fails for any reason.

Applications that render to windows use fields from the returned XVisualInfo struct to create a color map and window.

To render to a window, your application needs to create a standard X Window (for example, XCreateWindow()) with the visual info from the GLXFBConfig and then create a GLXWindow. To create a GLXWindow, call **glXCreateWindow**().

GLXWindow **glXCreateWindow**(Display* *dpy*, GLXFBConfig *config*,
   Window *win*, const int* *attrib_list*);

Creates a new `GLXWindow` and returns its XID. *dpy* specifies the X
Windows server, *config* is a suitable `GLXFBConfig`, as returned by
`glXChooseFBConfig()`, and *win* is a `Window` XID.

attrib_list is reserved for future use. Pass NULL for *attrib_list*.

`glXCreateWindow()` returns the XID of a new `GLXWindow` or NULL if it
fails for any reason. Call `glXDestroyWindow()` to destroy a `GLXWindow`.

8.3.2 Using Contexts

Before you can render to a window, you need to bind the rendering context to the `GLXWindow`. To do this, call `glXMakeContextCurrent()`.

Bool **glXMakeContextCurrent**(Display* *dpy*, GLXDrawable *draw*,
   GLXDrawable *read*, GLXContext *ctx*);

Makes the specified *ctx* current to the specified `GLXDrawables` in the
current thread. *dpy* specifies the X Window server display. *draw* and
read specify the `GLXDrawable` for OpenGL render and read operations,
respectively. Typically, applications pass the same drawable for both
parameters. If your application renders to a window, pass the same
`GLXWindow` XID for both *draw* and *read*. *ctx* specifies the rendering
context to bind to *draw* and *read*.

If `glXMakeContextCurrent()` succeeds, it returns `True`. If it fails for
any reason, it returns `False`. There are several reasons why `glXMake-
ContextCurrent()` might fail; see Section 3.3.7, "Rendering Contexts,"
of *OpenGL Graphics with the X Window System*.

After a successful call to `glXMakeContextCurrent()`, subsequent
OpenGL state commands affect state stored in *ctx,* rendering commands
ultimately appear in *draw,* and read commands (such as `glReadPixels()`)
obtain pixel data from *read.*

In GLX, a thread can have only one context current at a time. If the calling
thread already has a current context, calling `glXMakeContextCurrent()`
flushes the previous context and makes it noncurrent.

To make *ctx* noncurrent without binding a new context to *draw* and *read,* issue the following command:

```
glXMakeContextCurrent( dpy, None, None, NULL );
```

8.3.3 Swapping Buffers

If your context is double buffered (that is, if the GLX_DOUBLEBUFFER attribute of the GLXFBConfig is True), you must swap buffers after rendering a frame to display the contents of the back buffer. To swap buffers, call **glXSwapBuffers**().

---

void **glXSwapBuffers**(Display* *dpy*, GLXDrawable *draw*);

Makes the back buffer associated with *draw* visible. *dpy* specifies the X Window server display, and *draw* specifies the GLXDrawable to swap.

After swapping, the GLXDrawable displays the old contents of the back buffer. The contents of the new back buffer are undefined.

If *draw* is current to a rendering context, **glXSwapBuffers**() implicitly flushes any buffered commands in that rendering context.

Typically, GLX implementations synchronize buffer swaps to the monitor vertical retrace. GLX doesn't specify vertical retrace synchronization, however. As a result, this behavior may vary from one implementation to the next.

8.3.4 Deleting Contexts

When your application no longer has a use for a rendering context, destroy the rendering context with a call to **glXDestroyContext**().

---

void **glXDestroyContext**(Display* *dpy*, GLXContext *ctx*);

Destroys *ctx* and its associated resources. *dpy* specifies the X Window server display, and *ctx* specifies the rendering context to be destroyed.

glXDestroyContext() doesn't destroy the rendering context if it's still current. For this reason, applications typically make the context noncurrent and then destroy it, as in the following code:

```
glXMakeContextCurrent( dpy, None, None, NULL );
glXDestroyContext( dpy, ctx );
```

8.4 Microsoft Windows

Microsoft Windows uses an interface called WGL to provide OpenGL support in Windows. The WGL functions connect OpenGL to the Microsoft Windows windowing system.

WGL doesn't have a formal specification. Although the Microsoft Developer Network (`http://msdn.microsoft.com`) has some documentation, many WGL developers obtain information from WGL extension specifications at the OpenGL Extension Registry (`http://oss.sgi.com/projects/ogl-sample/registry/`). Because the WGL interface is very similar to GLX, you can also refer to the GLX specification and reinterpret it as though it were referring to WGL. Finally, OpenGL vendors typically provide additional documentation to describe their Microsoft Windows implementations. Check with your OpenGL vendor for more information.

Microsoft Windows supports rendering OpenGL to onscreen windows (as created with the Win32 `CreateWindow()` function) and to DIBs resident in system memory. Many OpenGL hardware vendors support pbuffers through an extension to WGL called `WGL_ARB_pbuffer`. This section discusses only rendering to a window.

8.4.1 Creating the Window

To create a window for OpenGL rendering, your application should set the `WS_CLIPCHILDREN` and `WS_CLIPSIBLINGS` window style bits in the third parameter (*dwStyle*) to `CreateWindow()`. This prevents OpenGL from rendering into child and sibling windows. Not setting these bits could cause **SetPixelFormat**() to fail. See the next section for information on **SetPixelFormat**().

8.4.2 Creating Contexts

To create a rendering context for rendering to a window, OpenGL applications typically wait for a `WM_CREATE` event on the window and then perform the following steps:

1. Obtain the index of an appropriate pixel format.

2. Set the pixel format in the device context for the window.

3. Create a rendering context from the device context.

The pixel format specifies properties of an OpenGL drawing surface, such as the number of color and depth buffer bits and whether it supports double-buffered rendering. To obtain an appropriate pixel format for your application, fill in a PIXELFORMATDESCRIPTOR struct and then call **ChoosePixelFormat**().

---

int **ChoosePixelFormat**(HDC *hdc*, const PIXELFORMATDESCRIPTOR* *ppfd*);

Returns the 1-based index of a pixel format supported by *hdc* that best matches the specifications in *ppfd*. *hdc* is the device context handle for the window (or other drawing surface) your application will be rendering to, and *ppfd* contains pixel-format specification information.

If **ChoosePixelFormat**() is unable to find a matching pixel format or fails for any other reason, it returns zero. Call GetLastError() for failure information.

Set values in the PIXELFORMATDESCRIPTOR struct to request an appropriate pixel format for your application. The following code segment, for example, shows how to request a pixel format for rendering to a double-buffered RGBA window with 24 color buffer bits and 24 depth buffer bits:

```
PIXELFORMATDESCRIPTOR pfd;
memset( &pfd, 0, sizeof( PIXELFORMATDESCRIPTOR ) );
pfd.nSize = sizeof( PIXELFORMATDESCRIPTOR );
pfd.nVersion = 1;
pfd.dwFlags = PFD_SUPPORT_OPENGL | PFD_DRAW_TO_WINDOW |
        PFD_DOUBLEBUFFER;
pfd.iPixelType = PFD_TYPE_RGBA;
pfd.cColorBits = 24;
pfd.cDepthBits = 24;
pfd.iLayerType = PFD_MAIN_PLANE;
int iPixelFormat = ChoosePixelFormat( hDC, &pfd );
```

For complete details on the PIXELFORMATDESCRIPTOR struct, see the Microsoft Developer Network documentation.

Because the return value is merely an index into the list of pixel formats supported by *hdc*, your application can't examine pixel-format attributes directly. Use **DescribePixelFormat**() to examine a pixel format to ensure that it's suitable for your application. For information on **DescribePixelFormat**(), see the Microsoft Developer Network documentation.

After obtaining the index of an appropriate pixel format, set it as the current pixel format of the device context by using **SetPixelFormat**().

BOOL **SetPixelFormat**(HDC *hdc*, int *iPixelFormat*, const
  PIXELFORMATDESCRIPTOR* *ppfd*);

Sets the specified pixel format on the device context. *hdc* is the device context handle for the window (or other drawing surface) your application will be rendering to. *iPixelFormat* is the 1-based index of a pixel format supported by *hdc*.

ppfd is used by the system metafile component and otherwise doesn't affect the behavior of **SetPixelFormat**(). Pass the same PIXEL-FORMATDESCRIPTOR for *ppfd* as you pass to **ChoosePixelFormat**().

SetPixelFormat() returns TRUE on success and FALSE if it fails. Call GetLastError() for failure information.

After setting the pixel format in the device context, create a rendering context from the device context. The rendering context inherits the pixel format from the device context.

To create a rendering context, call **wglCreateContext**().

HGLRC **wglCreateContext**(HDC *hdc*);

Creates a new rendering context capable of rendering to the window (or other device) referenced by *hdc*. *hdc* is the device context handle for the window (or other drawing surface) your application will be rendering to.

If **wglCreateContext**() succeeds, it returns the handle of the new rendering context; otherwise, it returns NULL. Call GetLastError() for failure information.

After creating the context, make it current, and render OpenGL commands.

8.4.3 Using Contexts

Before issuing OpenGL commands, your application needs to make the rendering context current for the active thread. To make the context current, call **wglMakeCurrent**().

BOOL **wglMakeCurrent**(HDC *hdc*, HGLRC *hglrc*);

Makes *hglrc* current on the specified device context in the current thread. *hdc* is the device context handle for the window (or other drawing surface) your application will be rendering to. *hglrc* is the handle of the rendering context. *hdc* must have the same pixel format as *hglrc*.

If the calling thread already has a current context, **wglMakeCurrent** () flushes its buffered OpenGL commands and then makes it noncurrent. To make the current context noncurrent without setting a new current context, call **wglMakeCurrent** () with NULL for *hglrc*.

wglMakeCurrent () returns TRUE if it succeeds; otherwise, it returns FALSE. Call GetLastError () for failure information.

If **wglMakeCurrent** () returns TRUE, subsequent OpenGL calls affect state in *hglrc* and render to the device specified by *hdc*.

A thread can have only one current rendering context, and a rendering context can be current to only one thread at a time.

Multiple rendering contexts can share the same set of OpenGL display lists, texture objects, and buffer objects. To share display lists and objects between contexts, call **wglShareLists** ().

BOOL **wglShareLists**(HGLRC *hglrc1*, HGLRC *hglrc2*);

Specifies rendering contexts that should share display lists and other OpenGL objects. *hglrc1* is a rendering context that stores display lists, texture objects, and buffer objects. *hglrc1* shares those lists and objects with *hglrc2*, which does not have a display list or object store of its own. If your application has already created display lists or objects using *hglrc2*, **wglShareLists** () implicitly destroys them.

wglShareLists () returns TRUE on success and FALSE if it fails. Call GetLastError () for failure information.

Note   The Microsoft Developer Network documentation states that **wglShareLists** () shares only display lists. This information doesn't reflect the current state of OpenGL implementations in Windows. Current OpenGL implementations share texture objects and buffer objects in the same way that they share display lists.

Not all rendering contexts can share display lists and objects. See **wglShareLists**() in the Microsoft Developer Network documentation for details concerning sharing.

8.4.4 Swapping Buffers

If your pixel format is double buffered (that is, if the dwFlags field of the PIXELFORMATDESCRIPTOR has the PFD_DOUBLEBUFFER bit set), you must swap buffers after rendering a frame to display the contents of the back buffer. To swap buffers, call **SwapBuffers**().

BOOL **SwapBuffers**(HDC *hDC*);

Makes the back buffer associated with *hDC* visible. *hDC* is the device context handle. If the pixel format isn't double buffered, **SwapBuffers**() has no effect.

SwapBuffers() returns TRUE on success and FALSE if it fails. Call GetLastError() for failure information.

After successfully swapping buffers, **SwapBuffers**() leaves the contents of the new back buffer undefined.

8.4.5 Deleting Contexts

To delete a rendering context and free its resources, call **wglDeleteContext**().

BOOL **wglDeleteContext**(HGLRC *hglrc*);

Deletes the specified rendering context. *hglrc* is the rendering context to be deleted.

wglDeleteContext() returns TRUE on success and FALSE if it fails. Call GetLastError() for failure information.

If *hglrc* is current in the calling thread, **wglDeleteContext**() makes it noncurrent first and then deletes it. If *hglrc* is current in another thread, however, **wglDeleteContext**() returns FALSE.

8.5   More Information

Appendix C, "OpenGL and Window Systems," of *OpenGL® Programming Guide* provides further discussion of not just AGL, GLX, and WGL, but also PGL (for the IBM OS/2 Warp platform).

OpenGL Programming for the X Window System (Kilgard 1996) is the definitive reference for both GLUT and GLX. *OpenGL Programming for Windows 95 and Windows NT* (Fosner 1996) is the definitive reference for WGL. Note that both GLX and WGL have evolved via the extension mechanism since these books were published. The current GLX specification, *OpenGL Graphics with the X Window System,* is available for free download from the OpenGL Web site at `http://www.opengl.org`. See the OpenGL Extension Registry Web site at `http://oss.sgi.com/projects/ogl-sample/registry/` for current WGL extension specifications.

See the Platform example program, available from this book's Web site, for a simple demonstration of using platform-specific interfaces.

8.6   References

(Fosner 1996) Fosner, Ron. *OpenGL Programming for Windows 95 and Windows NT.* Reading, MA: Addison-Wesley, 1996.

(Kilgard 1996) Kilgard, Mark J. *OpenGL Programming for the X Window System.* Reading, MA: Addison-Wesley, 1996.

Appendix A

Other Features

After you're comfortable developing software with the functionality described in this book, you'll want to explore OpenGL's other capabilities. To whet your appetite, this appendix contains brief descriptions of a few of those features.

This appendix is not an exhaustive list. For complete details of OpenGL's capabilities, see *OpenGL® Programming Guide* and *The OpenGL Graphics System*.

A.1 Multisample

Multisample, included in OpenGL version 1.3, produces full antialiasing by rasterizing primitives with multiple samples per displayed pixel. Each sample consists of full color, depth, and stencil information, so multisample is order independent (as opposed to traditional antialiasing, which uses alpha and blending).

Just as depth test requires you to allocate a depth buffer for your window, multisample requires you to allocate a sample buffer for your window.

To use the multisample feature:

1. Create a multisample window and rendering context. To do this in GLUT, bitwise-OR the GLUT_MULTISAMPLE bit into the parameter to **glutInitDisplayMode**().

2. At init time, enable multisampling with **glEnable**(GL_MULTISAMPLE).

Once enabled, all primitives will produce antialiased results.

For more information on multisample, see Chapter 6, "Blending, Antialiasing, Fog, and Polygon Offset," of *OpenGL® Programming Guide*.

A.2 Occlusion Queries

Occlusion queries, added in OpenGL version 1.5, allow applications to determine efficiently whether geometry is visible. Applications use occlusion queries to avoid sending complex geometry to OpenGL when the geometry isn't visible.

To use the occlusion query feature:

1. Generate a query object to hold the occlusion query result, typically at application init time.

2. During rendering, initiate an occlusion query, render a simple bounding geometry, and end the occlusion query.

3. Obtain the result from the query object, which is a count of the number of fragments (or samples, if using multisample) that passed the depth test.

4. If the query result indicates that a significant amount of the geometry is visible, render the geometry in full; otherwise, skip it, thereby increasing performance by not rendering occluded geometry.

This overview of occlusion queries might not result in maximum performance. Appendix C, "Performance," describes a more optimal approach.

For more information on occlusion queries, see Sections 4.1.7 and 6.1.12 of *The OpenGL Graphics System*.

A.3 Fog

The fog feature, available since OpenGL version 1.0, blends a fragment color with a fog color based on the fragment distance from the eye. In versions 1.4 and later, applications can explicitly set fog-coordinate values to further control blending between the fragment and fog colors. Applications commonly use the fog feature for depth cueing and atmospheric effects.

To use the fog feature:

1. At init time, enable fog by calling **glEnable**(GL_FOG).

2. The default fog color is black. To set a different fog color, call **glFogfv** (GL_FOG_COLOR, color), where *color* is an array of four GLfloats.

3. You'll probably also want to adjust the default fog density. By default, OpenGL completely fogs a fragment if its eye-coordinate space distance is greater than 1.0. Make the fog less dense by setting a fog density value less than 1.0, such as **glFogf** (GL_FOG_DENSITY, .02f).

For more information on fog, such as changing the fog equation and setting fog coordinates per vertex, see Chapter 6, "Blending, Antialiasing, Fog, and Polygon Offset," of *OpenGL® Programming Guide* and "glFog" in *OpenGL® Reference Manual*.

A.4 Clip Planes

Although OpenGL clips all geometry outside the view volume, you can clip geometry further with application-specified clip planes. Clip planes were introduced in OpenGL version 1.0. Modeling applications commonly use clip planes to render cutaway views of models.

To use clip planes:

1. Enable the plane (for example, **glEnable** (GL_CLIP_PLANE0)).

2. Specify the plane with the four coefficients of the plane equation. For example:

```
GLdouble peq[4] = { ... };
glClipPlane( GL_CLIP_PLANE0, peq );
```

The plane equation defines a half-space. While the plane equation is enabled, OpenGL renders geometry if it falls within the half-space and clips it otherwise.

For further information on clip planes, see Chapter 3, "Viewing," of *OpenGL® Programming Guide* and "glClipPlane" in *OpenGL® Reference Manual*.

A.5 Stencil

Available since OpenGL version 1.0, stencil is a part of the framebuffer that stores an additional value per fragment (or per sample, if using multisample). OpenGL allows applications to store and modify these values, and either passes or discards fragments based on the result of the stencil-test operation.

Stencil is an extremely flexible feature with several applications, including rendering co-planar primitives and concave polygons, shadow volumes, nonrectangular screen space clipping, and computational solid geometry (CSG), just to name a few. Describing its use is outside the scope of this book. For more information on stencil, see Chapter 10, "The Framebuffer," and Chapter 14, "Now That You Know," of *OpenGL® Programming Guide*.

A.6   The Accumulation Buffer

The accumulation buffer is a part of the framebuffer that can't be rendered to directly. Applications can add rendered images from the color buffer into the accumulation buffer, however. By combining several images, applications use the accumulation buffer to create several effects—notably motion blur, soft shadows, and depth of field. Although accumulation-buffer operations can be accelerated in hardware (Haeberli 1990), the accumulation buffer has a reputation for poor performance. The accumulation buffer has been in OpenGL since version 1.0.

For a complete overview of the accumulation buffer, see Chapter 10, "The Framebuffer," of *OpenGL® Programming Guide* and "glAccum" in *OpenGL® Reference Manual*.

A.7   Shading Language

The OpenGL Shading Language (commonly referred to as GLSL), added to OpenGL version 2.0, allows applications to replace portions of the rendering pipeline with vertex and fragment shaders—programs executed on a per-vertex and per-fragment basis that directly control the rendering process. The OpenGL Shading Language is the most revolutionary enhancement to OpenGL since its inception.

Applications replace portions of the OpenGL rendering pipeline with vertex and fragment shaders. Vertex shaders replace texture-coordinate generation; transformation of vertices, normals, and texture coordinates; and lighting operations. Fragment shaders replace texture mapping, fog, and color sum operations.

Applications for shaders are innumerable and still an area of active research. Shaders can be used to create rendering effects such as per-fragment lighting, animated and procedural texturing, geometric and image morphing, soft shadow effects including percentage closer filtering, non-Lambertian surfaces and bidirectional reflectance distribution functions (BRDFs), and bump mapping, not to mention any part of the fixed function OpenGL pipeline they replace, such as texture-coordinate generation, cube mapping, fog, and traditional per-vertex lighting.

To use the OpenGL Shading language, perform the following steps:

1. Write vertex and fragment shader programs using the OpenGL Shading Language. Developers usually keep shader source in separate files, though they can be added as string constants in the application source itself.

2. Load shader source into shader objects, and issue an OpenGL command to compile them.

3. Combine shader objects into program objects, and link them.

4. Set the linked program object shader executable in current state. Subsequent rendering operations are processed by the shader instead of the OpenGL fixed functionality pipeline.

5. At render time, set appropriate values for any uniform variables used by the shader programs.

A.7.1   A Shader Example

Figure A-1 shows an image produced with a simple GLSL fragment shader. The shader reduces the texel color value by one-half if the texture coordinate falls within a circle centered at *st* (0.5, 0.5), producing a dark circle in the center of each face of a cube. The shader also implements the color sum operation to produce specular highlights with the secondary color.

Listing A-1 shows the fragment shader used to produce Figure A-1. Note that a vertex shader isn't required to produce this effect; the fixed function per-vertex operations compute the input values to the fragment shader.

Listing A-1   A simple OpenGL Shading Language fragment shader

```
uniform sampler2D texMap;

void main(void)
{
    vec4 color = texture2D( texMap, gl_TexCoord[0].st );
    const vec2 tc = gl_TexCoord[0].st - .5;
    if (tc.s*tc.s + tc.t*tc.t < .15)
        color *= .5;
    gl_FragColor = color * gl_Color + gl_SecondaryColor;
}
```

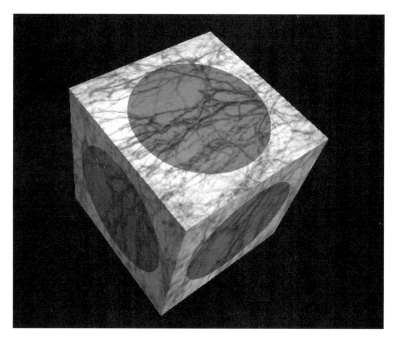

Figure A-1   A cube rendered with a simple fragment shader.

OpenGL produces fragments during rasterization of each face of the cube. To process these fragments with the fragment shader, the application must install a program object containing a fragment shader using the **glUseProgram**() command.

The fragment shader in Listing A-1 contains a single function, main(), which uses a single uniform variable, *texMap*. *texMap* uses the GLSL type sampler2D. Shaders use sampler types such as sampler2D to access textures in texture objects. The application needs to associate a texture object with a sampler2D uniform variable.

The shader uses some predefined variables. gl_TexCoord is an array of four-element vectors (vec4). Each element of gl_TexCoord is the interpolated *strq* texture coordinates for the current fragment. gl_Color and gl_SecondaryColor are the primary and secondary color values for the current fragment. With lighting enabled, the fixed function pipeline calculates lighting values per vertex. The rasterization stage interpolates these values, and effectively stores the results of ambient and diffuse lighting in gl_Color and specular lighting in gl_SecondaryColor. gl_FragColor is a fragment shader output variable and represents the final color of the fragment.

The first line of the shader obtains the texture color value corresponding to the *s* and *t* texture coordinates from the *texMap* sampler and stores the color in a four-element vector variable called *color.*

The next three lines of code check to see whether the *s* and *t* values have a squared distance less than 0.15 from the center (0.5, 0.5). If so, the shader multiplies *color* by 0.5, effectively dimming it by 50 percent.

The final line of code computes the final color value by modulating *color* with the fragment primary color and performing the color-sum operation by adding the secondary color. The code writes the result of this computation to `gl_FragColor`.

A.7.2   More Information

OpenGL® Shading Language (the orange book) is an excellent GLSL programming guide and reference. Note that in its current edition, the book documents the ARB extensions for use with GLSL rather than the OpenGL version 2.0 interface. There are significant differences between the two interfaces. Besides cosmetic command-name changes (**`glCreateShaderObjectARB`**() versus **`glCreateShader`**()), shader and program object identifiers are also different. The ARB extension defines a type `GLhandleARB`, whereas the version 2.0 interface uses the more traditional `GLuint` type for identifiers.

The OpenGL Shading Language (Kessenich 2004) is the formal GLSL specification, and can be downloaded for free as a PDF file from the OpenGL Web site. Finally, Section 2.15, "Vertex Shaders," and Section 3.11, "Fragment Shaders," of *The OpenGL Graphics System* document the OpenGL API for creating and using shaders.

A.8   References

(Haeberli 1990) Haeberli, Paul, and Kurt Akeley. "The Accumulation Buffer: Hardware Support for High-Quality Rendering, ACM SIGGRAPH Computer Graphics." Proceedings of the 17th Annual Conference on Computer Graphics and Interactive Techniques, September 1990.

(Kessenich 2004) Kessenich, John, Dave Baldwin, and Randi Rost. *The OpenGL Shading Language.* 3Dlabs formal OpenGL Shading Language specification, 2004.

Appendix B

Best Practices

This appendix includes OpenGL programming tips designed to improve code reusability and reduce application bugs. Some topics covered will also help improve application performance, but for more performance information, see Appendix C, "Performance."

B.1 State

OpenGL is a state machine, and when your application puts OpenGL in a certain state, OpenGL stays in that state until code changes it to another state. Often, this is the behavior you want. Many applications typically enable depth testing with **glEnable**(GL_DEPTH_TEST) at init time, for example, and leave it enabled for the duration of their program execution.

If state isn't set the way you want it, however, OpenGL probably won't produce the results you want. Consider an application that renders a combination of texture mapped and non–texture mapped primitives. If the code that renders the texture mapped primitives leaves texture mapping enabled with **glEnable**(GL_TEXTURE_2D), the primitives that are supposed to be non–texture mapped probably will render in the wrong color. This happens because the application code for rendering the non–texture mapped primitives probably doesn't bother to send texture coordinates. The primitive is rendered with texture mapping enabled, but OpenGL uses a single texture coordinate to obtain texture colors for the entire primitive. Because the result doesn't look like texture mapping, this type of bug typically stumps many developers.

In this type of situation, you need a mechanism to put OpenGL back into some known state. The best way to do this is to wrap code that changes

OpenGL server state with **glPushAttrib**() and **glPopAttrib**(), and similarly use **glPushClientAttrib**() and **glPopClientAttrib**() to wrap code that changes client state. Applications typically place OpenGL in a known state that the application will most frequently require at init time and then wrap rendering code with calls to push and pop the attribute stacks.

There are several benefits to using the attribute stack:

- It fits well with modularity and object-oriented design, in which code that changes state is responsible for restoring it. As an example, if your application uses alpha test in only a few places, code that doesn't use alpha test shouldn't be responsible for disabling it.

- It removes code assumptions. If your application contains code segments that depend on specific state settings, that code is likely to break when you add new code, rearrange execution order of code segments, or otherwise modify your application.

- It enables code reusability. Code modules and objects that set and restore OpenGL state can easily be incorporated into other applications.

When you push and pop state, consider using GL_ALL_ATTRIB_BITS and GL_CLIENT_ALL_ATTRIB_BITS for the *mask* parameter to increase maintainability. Pushing all state is more expensive than pushing a small subset of state, so use this flag with caution. If you push all state during development, you can revisit the code later during performance tuning.

B.2 Errors

As a general rule, don't place calls to **glGetError**() in production code. OpenGL errors usually are an indication of a bug in your application that should be resolved during development. Furthermore, calls to **glGetError**(), although relatively inexpensive, have a nonzero cost, so they shouldn't appear in production code for performance reasons.

Finally, OpenGL error semantics are subject to change in future revisions of OpenGL. Although *The OpenGL Graphics System* and extension specifications define all the conditions that cause an error, an action that causes an error today might not cause an error in the future. If your application depends on certain errors occurring under certain circumstances, your code will break if those errors go away in a future version of OpenGL.

In summary, you should test for errors, absolutely; see Appendix D, "Troubleshooting and Debugging." But you should not write code that depends on an error for the application to operate correctly.

B.3 Precision

The OpenGL specification requires implementations to provide floating-point accuracy to about 1 part in 10^5. This is slightly less than the accuracy of a single-precision IEEE floating-point number. For details, see Section 2.1.1, "Floating-Point Computation," of *The OpenGL Graphics System*.

B.3.1 Magnitude

Avoid rendering situations that require great precision with large-magnitude vertex coordinates. If your application uses geometry with large-magnitude coordinates, you could encounter the following problems:

- Depth offset with reasonable parameters, such as **glPolygonOffset** (1.f, 1.f), could fail if the object-coordinate vertices lack the precision to make them suitably co-planar. Larger *factor* and *units* parameters might solve some of the issues but aren't a general solution.[1]

- Small translations could fail to produce any results or could produce large apparent jumps in geometry location or viewer position.

B.3.2 Round-Off

Note that OpenGL isn't immune to floating point round-off. Accumulated floating-point operations often reduce the precision of internal OpenGL floating point numbers.

Repeated successive matrix multiplications can dramatically reduce the precision of the resulting matrix, for example. For this reason, you shouldn't structure your code to render multiple frames by accumulating successive matrices. Avoid the following code structure:

```
// DO NOT USE THIS CODE STRUCTURE
const float rotationAngle( 1.f );
For each frame
{
  glRotatef( rotationAngle, x, y, z );
  Render.
}
```

---

1. Stencil might be an alternative to depth offset. See the section "Stencil" in Appendix A, "Other Features," or refer to *OpenGL® Programming Guide* for more information.

Instead, design your application to clear the model-view matrix each frame. Applications that load a new viewing transformation each frame easily avoid this issue. At the start of each frame:

```
glLoadIdentity();
Multiply in a view matrix.
```

To render each primitive or group of primitives with the same modeling transformation:

```
glPushMatrix();
  Multiply in some matrices using glRotatef, glMultMatrix, etc.
  Render.
glPopMatrix();
```

The **glLoadIdentity**() call at the start of the frame effectively cleans the model-view matrix slate. Likewise, wrapping local modeling transformations with **glPushMatrix**() and **glPopMatrix**() restores the model-view matrix to the viewing transformation. This technique minimizes accumulated round-off.

B.3.3   Depth Buffer

In a perspective projection, objects are larger when they're close to the viewer and smaller when they're farther away. In other words, near objects occupy more x and y window-coordinate space, and distant objects occupy less. The perspective divide causes this effect.

Note, however, that OpenGL specifies that the perspective division occur on z as well as x and y. As a result, objects that are close occupy more depth buffer space, and distant objects occupy less depth buffer space. In other words, due to the perspective divide, the depth buffer is exponential rather than linear.

For this reason, applications should always try to place the near clip plane as distant as possible without intersecting geometry in the scene. Keeping the far plane close is also important, but not as important as keeping the near plane distant.

As a general rule of thumb, maintain a far/near ratio of no more than 50 for a 16-bit depth buffer and no more than 10,000 for a 24-bit depth buffer. With a maximized near plane distance, these ratios should provide enough depth buffer precision to resolve at least one world-coordinate unit.

B.4   Objects

Use **glGenLists**(), **glGenBuffers**(), and **glGenTextures**() to obtain unused display list, buffer object, and texture object identifiers.

When creating new display lists, buffer objects, or texture objects, OpenGL doesn't require you to pass in identifiers obtained from **glGenLists**(), **glGenBuffers**(), and **glGenTextures**(). As long as you use an unused identifier, OpenGL will behave as expected. You should resist the urge to assume that an identifier is unused and hard-code it, however, even during the development phase. If you fail to remedy this situation later, the robustness of your code will be compromised. The cost to obtain an unused identifier from **glGenLists**(), **glGenBuffers**(), and **glGenTextures**() is very small and greatly improves the reusability of your code.

Appendix C

Performance

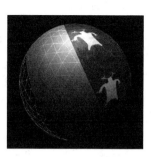

OpenGL® Distilled intentionally doesn't cover inherently inefficient OpenGL techniques. If you've followed the directions in this book, you're already using display lists, vertex arrays, primitives that share vertices, buffer objects, and texture objects, and you're not using the **glBegin**()/**glEnd**() paradigm. As a result, your application should avoid most OpenGL performance pitfalls.

Nonetheless, most professional developers profile their code and optimize it for maximum performance. This is especially important for applications that need to maintain smooth frame rates.

Before tuning, be familiar with the capabilities of your graphics card and computer system so that you'll know what performance to expect.

C.1 Measure Performance

Before you optimize your code, you need a way to measure performance objectively so that you'll know when you've made an improvement.

GLUT provides **glutGet**(GLUT_ELAPSED_TIME), which applications can use to obtain platform-independent timing information. It returns an integer count of milliseconds elapsed since the application started. Many platforms, however, provide platform-specific routines for obtaining time information, which might provide more precision. If you choose to use GLUT_ELAPSED_TIME, you'll need to measure several frames to obtain an accurate measurement on such a coarse timer.

Because OpenGL supports a client-server model, OpenGL often buffers commands internally. As a result, some OpenGL commands return to the application before they execute. This behavior can skew performance measurements if you attempt to time such a command. You can block until OpenGL executes all commands by using **glFinish**(), however. Because **glFinish**() has a nonzero cost, you'll want to measure several rendered frames—possibly hundreds—and then use a single **glFinish**() call before obtaining time information. This amortizes the expense of the **glFinish**() call over all rendered frames, increasing the accuracy of the timing measurement.

---

void **glFinish**(void);

Blocks until all preceding OpenGL commands have been completely executed.

▶ OpenGL version: 1.0 and later.

Although many end-users might not know what it means to synchronize buffer swaps to the monitor refresh rate (or *vertical sync*), as an OpenGL developer, you must disable vertical sync to obtain an accurate performance measurement. Don't measure performance with vertical sync enabled. How you disable it depends on your development platform and graphics card. Some devices control vertical sync with an environment variable; others, with a device-driver control application. Some OpenGL implementations also support an extension to disable vertical sync,[1] which allows your application to disable it programmatically.

To obtain an accurate measurement of frames rendered per second, instrument your application as shown in the following pseudocode:

```
glFinish();
const int start = glutGet( GLUT_ELAPSED_TIME );
Render N frames, where N is large.
glFinish();
const int end = glutGet( GLUT_ELAPSED_TIME );
const float fps = (float)( end - start ) / (float)N;
```

The larger the value of N (the more frames you include in the timing measurement), the more accurate your result will be, as large values of N amortize the cost of the final **glFinish**() call and also compensate for the coarse GLUT timing value.

---

1. GLX_SGI_video_sync is one such extension.

Rather than take timing measurements manually by inserting code to measure the elapsed time, professional software developers often use third-party optimization tools, such as Intel's VTune or the GNU `gprof` profiler. Some OpenGL development tools, such as Apple's OpenGL Profiler, contain both debugging and optimization features.

C.2   Avoid Software Rendering

OpenGL doesn't guarantee hardware acceleration. Even on platforms that allow the application to request hardware-accelerated pixel formats specifically, such as Apple Mac OS X and Microsoft Windows, OpenGL may fall back to software processing if the hardware is incapable of rendering geometry with the current state settings. Furthermore, OpenGL doesn't provide a direct mechanism to query how effectively your application is utilizing graphics hardware.

If your application is using full software rendering, performance will vary depending on the type of rendering operations your application performs but in general will be unacceptably slow. This is usually caused by a system configuration problem or a nonaccelerated pixel format. The following tips will help ensure that your application uses hardware acceleration:

- OpenGL developers are usually on the leading edge of graphics technology and commonly install the very latest graphics-card device drivers on their systems. Many OpenGL vendors—such as 3Dlabs, ATI, and NVIDIA—provide prerelease drivers to registered developers.

  Make sure that your system has the latest available OpenGL device drivers. Work with your OpenGL vendor to obtain them and ensure that they're installed correctly.

- Ensure that your application asks for only the minimum required capabilities when creating a pixel format or rendering context. If you're using GLUT, remove any unnecessary constants from the parameter to **`glutInitDisplayMode`**`()`.

- On systems that allow you to configure the desktop, set the default desktop color depth as high as possible, such as 32-bit. On Linux platforms, use the `glxinfo` client to obtain detailed information about GLX and OpenGL support.

- Check developer documentation and white papers, available from most OpenGL hardware vendor Web sites. Such documentation generally will enumerate performance pitfalls on the latest hardware and device drivers, as well as optimal rendering techniques.

OpenGL implementations can use software, or a combination of hardware and software, if the underlying hardware can't fully support application commands for any reason. Given the maturity of OpenGL, this is much less of a concern when using modern OpenGL hardware than it was with earlier devices but is still a concern for the very latest features. Again, OpenGL provides no direct mechanism to query for this situation.

To identify commands or groups of commands that might not be accelerated, take timing measurements around suspicious blocks of code, or use one of several third-party software performance tools to identify slow blocks of code. When you've identified commands that take exceptionally long to execute, experiment with OpenGL state settings or command parameters. You might try the following:

- If using a command that takes double-precision floats, such as **glMultMatrixd**(), and there is an equivalent command that takes single-precision, such as **glMultMatrixf**(), try the single-precision variant.

- If performance of an equivalent code block is acceptable, determine what state is different between the two blocks of code.

These are just suggestions to get you started. The general idea is to tinker with the code until you find a way to eliminate or minimize the performance hit. Providing general solutions for this type of problem is impossible, because the reasons it can occur are innumerable and vary from one OpenGL implementation to the next.

In conclusion, often, the question of whether application commands are fully hardware accelerated is irrelevant. More important, you must ask, "Is it fast enough?"

C.3   Reduce Pipeline Bottlenecks

As described in Chapter 1, "An Introduction to OpenGL," OpenGL is a pipeline architecture with two main paths: the vertex path and the pixel path (refer to Figure 1-2). Although some applications make extensive use of the pixel path during rendering, most applications tend to load pixel data at init time, and as a result, the rate at which OpenGL processes pixels in the pixel path is rarely a performance issue.

Applications can be bottlenecked in the vertex path in three very broad areas:

- Host computer processing, or *CPU limited*.

- Per-vertex operations, or *geometry limited*.

- Per-fragment operations, or *fill limited*.

To optimize your application, first identify where the application is bottle-necked. Then make modifications to your application to minimize its demand on that portion of the pipeline.

Before attempting to identify the bottleneck, go over your code and ensure that any OpenGL features that your application doesn't need are disabled. Only two OpenGL features are enabled by default—GL_DITHER and GL_MULTISAMPLE—and both could cause your application to be fill limited. Disable both unless your application specifically requires them. Likewise, check for and disable any state left enabled that is unneeded, such as GL_ALPHA_TEST.

C.3.1 CPU Limited

CPU-limited applications are bottlenecked by the processing power of the host computer. To determine whether your application is CPU limited, try the following tests:

- Run the application on less-powerful or more-powerful host comput-ers. For this test to be valid, the graphics hardware and device-driver version should be identical between the two systems. In a classic CPU-limited application, performance scales with processor speed. If you measure a one-third drop in performance running on a system with a 2GHz processor compared with a similar system with a 3GHz proces-sor, your application almost certainly is CPU limited.

- Change the graphics card in your system. If you measure the same application performance regardless of the class of graphics hardware you're using, your application probably is CPU limited. CPU-limited applications can't take advantage of increased graphics hardware horsepower, so performance will not increase if you run on a higher-end device. Likewise, lower-end devices are often capable of handling the load from CPU-limited applications, so swapping in a less-powerful graphics card won't decrease performance.

| Note | If changing systems or graphics cards is impractical, you might be able to change the clock speed of either the CPU or graphics hardware. Visit the hardware vendor's Web site for information on availability of such vendor-specific utilities. |

CPU-limited applications can be bottlenecked in the host computer for many reasons, including inefficient code, memory or bus bandwidth, and excessive cache misses or paging. Use platform-specific resource monitors or third-party optimization software to determine the nature of your bottleneck; then tune accordingly. Tuning a CPU-limited OpenGL application is no different from tuning any nongraphics application. Such optimization tips are beyond the scope of this book.

C.3.2   Geometry Limited

Geometry-limited applications are bottlenecked by how fast OpenGL performs per-vertex operations. To determine whether your application is geometry limited, disable OpenGL per-vertex operations, such as lighting and fog, and see whether performance increases.

Reducing the number of vertices is also a good test, as long as you still render a comparable number of pixels. Consider rendering a simple cylinder by approximating it with 1,024 quadrilaterals, or 2,050 vertices. If you reduce the approximation to 128 quadrilaterals (258 vertices) and maintain the same overall cylinder dimensions, OpenGL will still render approximately the same number of pixels. If this results in a significant boost in performance, rendering the cylinder is geometry limited.

To improve the performance of geometry-limited applications, modify your application to send fewer vertices. Consider some of the following suggestions:

- Implement frustum culling in your application, and use the occlusion query feature to avoid sending geometry to OpenGL that won't be visible in the final rendered scene.

- If your geometry consists of enclosed hulls, enable face culling with **glEnable**(GL_CULL_FACE). Face culling is described in Chapter 2, "Drawing Primitives." Many OpenGL implementations perform face culling earlier in the pipeline than required by the OpenGL specification to reduce per-vertex operations.

- Don't send more vertices than necessary. To use the cylinder example again, it doesn't make much sense to approximate a cylinder with 1,024 quadrilaterals if your application always renders it so small that it will never occupy morc than 100 pixels of screen real estate. Consider implementing a LOD algorithm so that your application sends less-complex geometry for models when their final rendered size is small.

- Along the same line as the previous bullet point, improve detail with texture mapping, and use fewer vertices. Applications sometimes increase the vertex count to obtain acceptable specular highlights, for example. Geometry-limited applications should send fewer vertices, however, and use cube mapping to generate the specular highlight.

Note that this technique effectively pushes processing from one part of the pipeline (per-vertex operations) to another part (per-fragment operations). After making a modification like this, remeasure performance to ensure that you haven't created a new bottleneck in a different part of the pipeline.

- If your application uses lighting, avoid scaling your geometry with **glScale***(). Because this also scales your normals, your application must use either normalization or normal rescaling to restore unit-length normals. Although normal rescaling is less expensive than normalization, both have a nonzero per-vertex expense. You can avoid using **glScale***() by manually scaling your geometry at initialization time. The example code uses this strategy to size its cylinder, torus, sphere, and plane primitives.

- If your application doesn't use the texture matrix to transform texture coordinates, don't use **glLoadMatrix***() to set the texture matrix to the identity. Instead, explicitly set the matrix to the identity with a call to **glLoadIdentity**(). Most OpenGL implementations will optimize for this case and eliminate the texture-coordinate transformation.

Note that using buffer objects doesn't guarantee maximum performance. Specifically, the OpenGL **glDrawRangeElements**() command could perform less optimally if the buffer data is too large. Fortunately, applications can query these implementation-dependent size thresholds with **glGetIntegerv**(), as shown below:

```
GLint maxVertices, maxIndices;
glGetIntegerv( GL_MAX_ELEMENTS_VERTICES, &maxVertices );
glGetIntegerv( GL_MAX_ELEMENTS_INDICES, &maxIndices );
```

Implementations should use these size thresholds to limit the amount of vertex and index data sent to OpenGL via **glDrawRangeElements**(). For large amounts of vertex data, multiple small **glDrawRangeElements**() commands could perform better than a single large command.

C.3.3   Fill Limited

Fill-limited applications are bottlenecked by how fast OpenGL performs per-fragment operations. To determine whether your application is fill limited, try the following tests:

- Make the window smaller. Reducing the window width and height by one-half will reduce the number of pixels filled by one-fourth. If performance improves accordingly, your application certainly is fill limited.

  Note that some LOD-based algorithms could send less geometry when rendering to a smaller window. For this test to be valid, make sure that your application continues to send the same amount of geometry.

- Disable texture mapping and other per-fragment operation used by your application. If performance increases when you reduce per-fragment operations, your application is fill limited.

  Modern OpenGL hardware is optimized to render texture mapped primitives with the depth test enabled, but it's still common for primitives to render faster when texture mapping and depth testing are disabled.

To optimize a fill-limited application, consider the following suggestions:

- Minimize texture size. It doesn't make sense to use a 1,024 × 1,024 texture on a primitive that will never occupy more than a few hundred pixels of screen real estate. Reducing texture size increases texture cache coherency in the graphics hardware and also allows more textures to fit in graphics-card RAM.

- Use `GL_NEAREST_MIPMAP_LINEAR` instead of `GL_LINEAR_MIPMAP_LINEAR`. This change reduces the number of texel fetches per fragment at the expense of some visual quality.

- Measure the *depth complexity* of your scene, and take steps to reduce it if it's too high. The scene depth complexity is the average number of times a pixel was overdrawn to produce the final scene. The higher the depth complexity, the slower the rendering for fill-limited applications.

  The optimal depth complexity of 1.0 is rarely realized in professional OpenGL applications. Typical scenes produce a depth complexity of around 1.5. To reduce depth complexity, organize your geometry to render front to back. In extreme cases, you should render a depth-only pass first, followed by a color pass, which produces a maximum depth complexity of 2.0.

- Reduce or eliminate other per-fragment operations when possible, such as multisample, alpha test, stencil test, depth test, and blending.

C.3.4 Closing Thoughts on Pipeline Bottlenecks

Rendering style often indicates whether applications are geometry limited or fill limited. Applications that send relatively few vertices and draw relatively large primitives, for example, tend to be fill limited. Conversely, applications that send many vertices but draw comparatively few pixels tend to be geometry limited.

It's entirely possible for your application to have several bottlenecks throughout the pipeline in the course of rendering a single frame. Consider a simulation application that renders a scene with a robot walking on terrain under a sky. The terrain uses a LOD algorithm and is CPU limited. The sky dome contains very few vertices but covers a large area; therefore, it is fill limited. The robot is extremely complex and detailed; therefore, it is geometry limited. To optimize such scenes effectively, first identify the part of the scene that consumes the most rendering time, and focus your efforts there. Optimize other parts of the scene later.

C.4   Cull Unseen Geometry

If your application is geometry limited, a good way to avoid bottlenecks, or at least reduce their effects, is to send less geometry to OpenGL in the first place.

Performance-conscious applications commonly perform frustum culling to avoid sending geometry outside the view volume to OpenGL. The six view volume planes can be derived trivially from the projection and model-view matrices whenever the view changes. To cull, simply test a bounding sphere against those planes.

In some instances, geometry is inside the view volume but still not visible. Imagine an automobile design application rendering a model of a car, in which the engine is modeled with complex geometry. The car body occludes the engine, so the application can gain performance by not rendering it. Because it's within the view volume, however, frustum culling alone is insufficient.

OpenGL provides the occlusion query feature for this situation, which Appendix A, "Other Features," describes in brief. Note that occlusion queries return data to the application. This in itself can be the cause of performance problems. To avoid stalling the rendering pipe, issue occlusion queries during rendering, but obtain occlusion query results only at the end of the frame. Use the results when you render the next frame. This technique works well for frame-coherent applications, but for initial frames or sudden changes in views, your application will need to assume that everything is visible and issue a new set of queries for use in successive frames.

Another popular technique for optimizing occlusion queries is to arrange your geometry so that frames are rendered in front-to-back (or outside-to-inside) order. This maximizes the chance for occlusion to occur.

C.5 State Changes and Queries

In general, modern OpenGL graphics hardware performs optimally when processing an uninterrupted stream of geometry data. State changes interrupt this stream and cause delays in processing. In a worst-case scenario, applications make extensive state changes after every triangle, dramatically inhibiting performance.

Avoid unnecessary state changes with the following tips:

- Group geometry that share a state. Group textured primitives when they share a texture to avoid redundant calls to **glBindTexture**().

- To restore several changed states efficiently, use **glPushAttrib**() and **glPopAttrib**(), and their client-side equivalents, **glPushClientAttrib**() and **glPopClientAttrib**(). OpenGL implementations typically optimize these routines so that they're extremely lightweight.

- To restore only a small number of changed-state items efficiently, make explicit calls to change and restore the states. Restoring state explicitly requires that your application track current state or query OpenGL before changing state. Nonetheless, this can be more efficient than using the attribute stacks on some implementations.

- Avoid setting state redundantly. Although most OpenGL implementations are optimized to do nothing in this case, it still costs at least a branch and usually a call through a function pointer.

- Avoid switching between multiple rendering contexts. If your application uses multiple contexts, limit the number of context switches to as few as possible per frame.

Obviously, OpenGL implementations set state in the underlying graphics hardware, but they also keep a shadow copy of many state values in host RAM. Querying a state item stored in shadow state requires only a data copy and, therefore, is relatively inexpensive.

glIsEnabled() is generally lightweight, because enable state is almost always shadowed in host RAM. Some OpenGL implementations keep a shadow copy of the top of the matrix stacks, so getting the matrix usually is as cheap as copying 16 GLfloats (or GLdoubles). Implementations don't—and shouldn't—shadow all state, however. For example, implementations optimally store texture maps generated from framebuffer data (using **glCopyTexImage2D**()) only in graphics hardware RAM. Querying OpenGL to retrieve such a texture map (using **glGetTexImage**()) requires a large data copy over the system bus.

Troubleshooting and Debugging

As a normal part of development, occasionally your application will not render what you intend. This will be less of a problem as you become more proficient with OpenGL but will never go away completely.

This section contains some tips to help you resolve some of the more common OpenGL-related issues in your application.

D.1 Debugging Tools

Several tools exist to aid developers in debugging and tuning their applications. Developers can use these tools to capture sequences of OpenGL commands issued by an application, set breakpoints at OpenGL commands, and examine OpenGL state. Some also provide performance information.

At the time this book went to press, popular OpenGL debugging tools included Apple's OpenGL Profiler, Graphic Remedy's gDEBugger, GLIntercept, and SGI's ogldebug. Linux and Unix systems also feature `glxinfo`. `glxinfo` isn't a debugger but nonetheless is useful as a diagnostic tool.

Information on OpenGL tools is subject to change over time. To stay abreast of current tools, visit the OpenGL Web site regularly, or use an Internet search engine to search for "OpenGL debugger" or "OpenGL tools."

D.2   OpenGL Errors

Examining the OpenGL error code and identifying the OpenGL command that caused it is the single most effective debugging technique for OpenGL applications.

D.2.1   Check the OpenGL Error Code

Get in the habit of using **glGetError**(). To call this routine without impeding performance, use the C preprocessor. Define a macro to check for errors in development builds and act as a no-op in production builds. The *OpenGL® Distilled* example code uses this strategy to define the OGLDIF_ CHECK_ERROR CPP macro. If _DEBUG is defined at compile time, indicating a development build, the OGLDIF_CHECK_ERROR macro expands to a call to the checkError() function:

```
void checkError()
{
    const GLenum error = glGetError();
    if (error != GL_NO_ERROR)
    {
        const GLubyte* errorStr = gluErrorString( error );
        std::cerr << "Error: " << std::string( (char*)errorStr )
            << std::endl;
    }
    assert( error == GL_NO_ERROR );
}

#ifdef _DEBUG
    // Development build: check for errors
#  define OGLDIF_CHECK_ERROR checkError()
#else
    // Release build: no-op
#  define OGLDIF_CHECK_ERROR
#endif
```

A good rule of thumb is to place this call once after your OpenGL initialization code and then again after every frame. If the assertion fails, look in the preceding code for errors. Add calls to **glGetError**() (or to your error-checking CPP macro) throughout the suspect code to help isolate and identify the OpenGL call(s) generating the error.

D.2.2   Specific Errors

Chapter 1, "An Introduction to OpenGL," briefly discusses OpenGL errors and their causes. This section covers errors in greater detail and lists likely causes for the errors.

Note that there are numerous ways to generate errors in OpenGL. Each command description in *OpenGL® Reference Manual* enumerates the errors a command can generate, and under what circumstances. *The OpenGL Graphics System,* along with extension specifications, are the definitive resources for the errors OpenGL commands can generate.

Common causes of OpenGL errors include the following:

- GL_INVALID_ENUM—Your application passed an unacceptable enumerant to an OpenGL command that takes a GLenum as an argument.

  A common cause of GL_INVALID_ENUM is accidentally passing a similarly-named enumerant. OpenGL generates a GL_INVALID_ENUM error, for example, if your application calls **glDrawElements**() with GL_POINT as the *mode* parameter instead of GL_POINTS. (GL_POINT is a valid enumerant for the **glPolygonMode**() command.)

- GL_INVALID_OPERATION—Your application issued a command that wasn't allowed in the current state.

  Code that performs selection generates this error if the application places OpenGL in selection mode with **glRenderMode**(GL_SELECT) before first specifying a selection buffer using the **glSelectBuffer**() command.

  OpenGL returns this error if your application attempts to read the depth buffer using **glReadPixels**(), but there is no depth buffer. The same is true if using **glCopyTexImage2D**() to copy depth buffer data to a depth texture. Check your init code to ensure that it creates a depth buffer.

  OpenGL also returns this error if you attempt to bind a texture object to the wrong target. Bind 2D textures to GL_TEXTURE_2D and cube map textures to GL_TEXTURE_CUBE_MAP to avoid this error.

  Applications that use the (obsolete) **glBegin**()/**glEnd**() paradigm commonly encounter this problem by issuing any one of several commands not allowed between **glBegin**() and **glEnd**() or by failing to call either **glBegin**() or **glEnd**().

  It's an error to call **glGetError**() between **glBegin**() and **glEnd**()—GL_INVALID_OPERATION. Calls that generate errors are required by the OpenGL specification to behave as a no-op, however. For this reason, **glGetError**() doesn't actually return an error code when called between **glBegin**() and **glEnd**(); in fact, it returns GL_NO_ERROR. Your application must retrieve the GL_INVALID_OPERATION error later by calling **glGetError**() outside the **glBegin**()/**glEnd**() pair. You should avoid this somewhat quirky aspect of OpenGL errors by using vertex arrays and buffer objects instead of the **glBegin**()/**glEnd**() paradigm.

- GL_INVALID_VALUE—Your application called an OpenGL command, but at least one of the numerical parameters was out of range.

  Calling **glDrawRangeElements**() with the *end* parameter less than the *start* parameter will generate this error.

  When using OpenGL lighting, the specular exponent (GL_SHININESS value, set with **glMaterialf**()) must be in the range 0 through 128, inclusive; otherwise, OpenGL generates the GL_INVALID_VALUE error. (The GL_NV_light_max_exponent extension allows an implementation to support larger specular exponent values.)

  OpenGL also generates this error if your application specifies a cube map face that isn't square. The *width* and *height* parameters to **glTexImage2D**() must be equal when the *target* parameter indicates a cube map face.

  Accidentally passing the wrong parameter to **glClear**() will generate this error. **glClear**(GL_DEPTH) generates this error, for example, because GL_DEPTH isn't an acceptable enumerant for the **glClear**() command. Instead, call **glClear**(GL_DEPTH_BUFFER_BIT).

- GL_OUT_OF_MEMORY—There was insufficient memory for OpenGL to execute a command.

  Obviously, one way to generate this error is if your application has consumed too much memory. If you receive this error during development, check your process size and available total system RAM.

  OpenGL generates this error in response to a **glBufferData**() command if it's unable to create a data store of the required size. Check to make sure you're passing in a reasonable value for *size*.

  When your application creates a display list, OpenGL makes copies of all the parameters, including copies of data pointed to by address parameters. For this reason, display lists can consume large amounts of memory. The **glEndList**() command will generate GL_OUT_OF_ MEMORY if OpenGL is unable to store all the commands and parameters between **glNewList**() and **glEndList**().

  If the OpenGL version is 1.1 or later, and **glEndList**() generated the GL_OUT_OF_MEMORY error, OpenGL continues to operate in a defined state. Otherwise, OpenGL behavior is undefined.

- GL_STACK_OVERFLOW and GL_STACK_UNDERFLOW—Your application pushed or popped an OpenGL stack beyond its limits.

These errors can occur when your application manipulates one of the matrix stacks, such as the texture, model-view, or projection matrix stacks (**glPushMatrix**()/**glPopMatrix**()), either of the attribute stacks (**glPushAttrib**()/**glPopAttrib**() or **glPushClientAttrib**()/**glPopClientAttrib**()), or the name stack (**glPushName**()/**glPopName**()).

OpenGL generates GL_STACK_UNDERFLOW when your application issues more pop commands than corresponding push commands.

Conversely, GL_STACK_OVERFLOW occurs if you push a stack beyond its maximum number of entries. The OpenGL specification dictates a minimum stack size, but implementations may support larger stacks. Note that the projection and texture stacks can be as small as two entries.

Applications commonly encounter this error by pushing or popping the wrong stack. Note that **glPushMatrix**() and **glPopMatrix**() affect different stacks depending on the current matrix mode, set with **glMatrixMode**(). Furthermore, if the matrix mode is GL_TEXTURE, the affected stack depends on the value of **glActiveTexture**(), because each texture unit has its own stack. As you develop your application, carefully code push and pop calls to ensure that you manipulate the intended stack.

D.3   Debugging a Blank Window

Bugs in your application occasionally cause OpenGL to render nothing, rather than the intended scene. There are many possible causes for a blank window, and enumerating all of them is impossible. This section discusses a few of the more common causes.

D.3.1   Use Good Code Development Practices

To avoid having to consider all the possible causes for a blank window or to examine every line of your application, start simple, and verify correct rendering incrementally as you develop your application. Developers who encounter a blank window while using this strategy know that the bug was introduced in a recent code change, which speeds locating and resolving the issue.

D.3.2   Use glGetError()

If you issue an OpenGL command that generates an error other than GL_OUT_OF_MEMORY, OpenGL ignores the offending command so that it has no effect on framebuffer contents or OpenGL state. As an example of how this could result in a blank window, consider what would happen if your application passed incorrect enumerants to vertex array drawing commands. Each command would generate a `GL_INVALID_ENUM` error; therefore, OpenGL would ignore them. The final rendered image would contain no primitives at all.

See the section "OpenGL Errors" earlier in this appendix for additional information.

D.3.3   Enable Vertex Arrays

If your application issues a vertex array rendering command, OpenGL uses only vertex array data from enabled vertex arrays. To render with vertex, texture coordinate, and normal data, for example, use the following code:

```
glEnableClientState( GL_VERTEX_ARRAY );
glEnableClientState( GL_TEXTURE_COORD_ARRAY );
glEnableClientState( GL_NORMAL_ARRAY );
```

If you issue a vertex array rendering command while `GL_VERTEX_ARRAY` is disabled, OpenGL will render nothing.

D.3.4   Set Appropriate Clip Planes

If your application sets the near and far clip planes incorrectly, OpenGL could clip part or all of your geometry, resulting in a blank or partially rendered image. To avoid this problem, start with liberal values for the near and far clip planes, and tighten their range later to maximize depth buffer precision. Using too tight a range could clip geometry that is more distant than the far plane or closer than the near plane.

Note that if your application uses an orthographic projection, the *near* and *far* parameters to **glOrtho**() are distances from the eye-coordinate origin to the near and far clip planes. Because the viewer is at infinity, *near* and *far* can be negative. If *near=far*, however, **glOrtho**() generates `GL_INVALID_ VALUE`.

Typically, **gluPerspective**() is implemented as a wrapper around **glMultMatrixd**() and doesn't generate an error,[1] even when passed absurd values for *near* or *far*. You should always pass positive (nonzero

---

1. Because **gluPerspective**() calls **glMultMatrixd**(), it generates `GL_INVALID_OPERATION` if called between **glBegin**() and **glEnd**().

and non-negative) values for *near* and *far*. Negative or zero value could cause a blank window or other incorrect rendering.

D.3.5 Use Correct Transformations

If your application sets incorrect model or view transformations, the resulting model-view matrix could translate your geometry outside the view volume. There are multiple ways that model and view transformations could go wrong.

Typical frame-based applications set the model-view matrix to identity at the start of each frame, then multiply a view transformation, then push and pop the matrix stack around local model transformations. New OpenGL developers sometimes fail to set the model-view matrix to identity with **glLoadIdentity**(). As a result, the first frame might render correctly, but subsequent frames would erroneously accumulate transformations on the model-view matrix, resulting in a blank window or other incorrect rendering.

The fact that OpenGL postmultiplies matrices on the current top of matrix stack can confuse new developers. If you write code that assumes your translate will occur before your scale, for example, but OpenGL actually performs the concatenation in the opposite order, your geometry will not render in the expected location.

Because OpenGL provides no facilities for positioning the viewer, setting the correct view transformation is often problematic for new developers. Use the **gluLookAt**() function to establish the view transformation initially, because it has an intuitive interface. Develop code for managing more-complex view transformations later.

When developing transformation code, start simply, and test incrementally. This will help you isolate transformation bugs to the most recently added code.

Review Chapter 3, "Transformation and Viewing," for information on this topic.

D.3.6 Swap Buffers

In a double-buffered application, OpenGL renders all your geometry, but the final image is stored in the back buffer and invisible until you swap buffers. If your application uses GLUT, call **glutSwapBuffers**() at the end of each frame; otherwise, call the platform-specific routine for swapping buffers.

D.3.7 Call `glClear()`

If your application fails to call **`glClear`**(), the initial contents of the color and depth buffers are undefined. This usually results in incorrect rendering for frame-based, double-buffered applications.

Failing to clear the color buffer could cause successive frames to accumulate, as shown in Figure D-1. Because the contents of the color buffer are undefined after a swap, however, OpenGL doesn't guarantee that previously rendered frames remain intact. For this reason, applications shouldn't count on this behavior to accumulate multiple frames.

If your application actually needs to accumulate multiple frames, you should draw into the front buffer; see "glDrawBuffer" in *OpenGL® Reference Manual*.

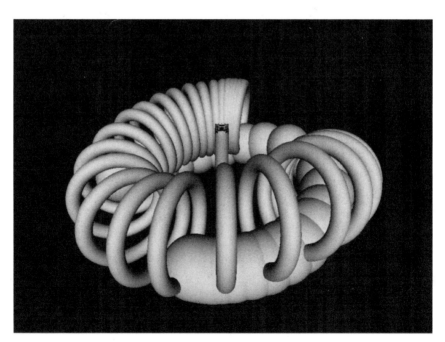

Figure D-1   Failing to clear the color buffer with **`glClear`**(GL_COLOR_BUFFER_ BIT) could cause multiple frames to accumulate.

Failing to clear the depth buffer with **glClear**(GL_DEPTH_BUFFER_BIT) could cause a blank window. Each frame of a depth-buffered application usually requires the depth buffer initialized to the maximum depth value, allowing fragments with smaller depth values to pass the default depth test. If the application fails to clear the depth buffer, OpenGL leaves the contents undefined. The depth buffer might contain depth values left over from the previous frame, or it could contain random values. The result is that part or all of your current frame rendering could be missing.

Bibliography

Akeley, Kurt. "Reality Engine Graphics." Proceedings of the 20th Annual Conference on Computer Graphics and Interactive Techniques. New York, NY, September 1993.

Akin, Allen. "Analysis of PEX 5.1 and OpenGL 1.0." SGI technical white paper, August 1992.

Blinn, James F. "Models of Light Reflection for Computer Synthesized Pictures." Proceedings of the 4th Annual Conference on Computer Graphics and Interactive Techniques. New York, NY, 1977.

Blinn, James F., and Martin E. Newell. "Texture and Reflection in Computer Generated Images." *Communications of the ACM* 19:10 (October 1976).

Carson, George S. "Standards Pipeline: The OpenGL Specification." *ACM SIGGRAPH Computer Graphics* 31:2 (May 1997).

Catmull, Edwin. "A Subdivision Algorithm for Computer Display of Curved Surfaces." Ph.D. thesis, University of Utah, 1974.

Cojot, Vincent S. "OpenGL Programming on Linux." *Linux Journal* (November 1996).

Fernando, Randima. *GPU Gems*. Boston: Addison-Wesley, 2004.

Foley, James D., Andries van Dam, Steven K. Feiner, and John F. Hughes. *Computer Graphics: Principles and Practice, Second Edition.* Reading, MA: Addison-Wesley, 1990.

Fosner, Ron. *OpenGL Programming for Windows 95 and Windows NT.* Reading, MA: Addison-Wesley, 1996.

Geist, Robert and James Westall. "Bringing the High End to the Low End: High Performance Device Drivers of the Linux PC." ACM Southeast Regional Conference Proceedings. New York, NY, April 1998.

Gerasimov, Philipp S. "Omnidirectional Shadow Mapping." In *GPU Gems*. Boston: Addison-Wesley, 2004.

Haeberli, Paul, and Kurt Akeley. "The Accumulation Buffer: Hardware Support for High-Quality Rendering." Proceedings of the 17th Annual Conference on Computer Graphics and Interactive Techniques. New York, NY, September 1990.

Kessenich, John, Dave Baldwin, and Randi Rost. *The OpenGL Shading Language.* 3Dlabs formal OpenGL Shading Language specification, 2004.

Kilgard, Mark J. *OpenGL Programming for the X Window System*. Reading, MA: Addison-Wesley, 1996.

Kilgard, Mark J. "Realizing OpenGL: Two Implementations of One Architecture." Proceedings of the ACM SIGGRAPH/EUROGRAPHICS Workshop on Graphics Hardware. New York, NY, August 1997.

Lichtenbelt, Barthold. "Design of a High Performance Volume Visualization System." Proceedings of the ACM SIGGRAPH/EUROGRAPHICS Workshop on Graphics Hardware. New York, NY, August 1997.

Macintosh OpenGL Programming Guide, `http://developer.apple.com/graphicsimaging/opengl/`.

McCormack, Joel, et al. "Neon: A Single-Chip 3D Workstation Graphics Accelerator." Proceedings of the ACM SIGGRAPH/EUROGRAPHICS Workshop on Graphics Hardware. New York, NY, and Lisbon, Portugal, August 1998.

Microsoft Developer Network, `http://msdn.microsoft.com`.

Open GL ARB and Dave Shreiner. *OpenGL® Reference Manual, Fourth Edition.* Boston: Addison-Wesley, 2004.

Open GL ARB, Dave Shreiner, Mason Woo, Jackie Neider, and Tom Davis. *OpenGL® Programming Guide Fifth Edition.* Boston: Addison-Wesley, 2006.

OpenGL® Distilled Web site, `http://www.opengldistilled.com`.

OpenGL Extension Registry Web site, `http://oss.sgi.com/projects/ogl-sample/registry/`.

The OpenGL Graphics System Utility Library, `http://www.opengl.org/resources/libraries/index.html`.

OpenGL Graphics with the X Window System (Version 1.3). Edited by Paula Womack and Jon Leech. On OpenGL Web site, `www.opengl.org`.

OpenGL Web site, `http://www.opengl.org`.

Phong, Bui Tuong. "Illumination for Computer Generated Pictures." *Communications of the ACM* 18:6 (June 1975).

Reeves, William T., David H. Salesin, and Robert L. Cook. "Rendering Antialiased Shadows with Depth Maps." Proceedings of the 14th Annual Conference on Computer Graphics and Interactive Techniques. New York, NY, August 1987.

Rost, Randi. *OpenGL® Shading Language, Second Edition.* Boston: Addison-Wesley, 2006.

Rost, Randi J., Jeffrey D. Friedberg, and Peter L. Nishimoto. "PEX: A Network-Transparent 3D Graphics System." *IEEE Computer Graphics and Applications* 9:4 (1989).

Savchenko, Sergei. "Algorithms for Dynamic Shadows." *Dr. Dobb's Journal* (February 2005).

Scheifler, Robert W., and Jim Gettys. "The X Window System." *ACM Transactions on Graphics* (April 1986).

Segal, Mark, and Kurt Akeley. *The OpenGL Graphics System: A Specification.* Edited by Jon Leech (September 2004). On OpenGL Web site, `http://www.opengl.org`.

Sproul, Robert F. "Raster Graphics for Interactive Programming Environments." Proceedings of the 6th Annual Conference on Computer Graphics and Interactive Techniques. New York, NY, 1979.

"Status Report of the Graphics Standards Planning Committee." *ACM SIGGRAPH Computer Graphics* 13:3 (August 1979).

Torrance, K. E., and E. M. Sparrow. "Theory for Off-Specular Reflection from Roughened Surfaces." *Journal of the Optical Society of America* 57:9 (September 1967).

Watt, Alan. *3D Computer Graphics.* Reading, MA: Addison-Wesley, 1999.

Williams, Lance. "Casting Curved Shadows on Curved Surfaces." Proceedings of the 5th Annual Conference on Computer Graphics and Interactive Techniques. New York, NY, August 1978.

Williams, Lance. "Pyramidal Parametrics, Computer Graphics." Proceedings of the 10th Annual Conference on Computer Graphics and Interactive Techniques. New York, NY, July 1983.

Index

OpenGL® Titles Available from Addison-Wesley

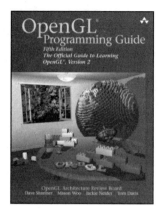

OpenGL® Programming Guide, Fifth Edition

OpenGL Architecture Review Board, Dave Shreiner, Mason Woo, Jackie Neider, and Tom Davis

The *OpenGL® Programming Guide, Fifth Edition*, provides definitive, comprehensive information on OpenGL and the OpenGL Utility Library. This fifth edition of the best-selling "red book" describes the latest features of OpenGL Versions 1.5 and 2.0, including:

- Storage of vertex arrays in buffer objects for faster rendering
- Occlusion queries for course-grain visibility testing
- Non-power-of-two dimensioned texture maps
- Point sprites
- Separate stencil operations for RGB and alpha
- Rendering to multiple color buffers using GLSL

Most importantly, this new edition discusses the OpenGL Shading Language (GLSL) and explains the mechanics of using this new language to create complex graphics effects and boost the computational power of OpenGL.

0-321-33573-2 · ©2006 · 896 pages

OpenGL® Shading Language, Second Edition

Randi Rost

OpenGL® Shading Language, Second Edition, extensively updated for OpenGL 2.0, is the experienced application programmer's guide to writing shaders. Part reference, part tutorial, this book explains the shift from fixed-functionality graphics hardware to the new era of programmable graphics hardware and the additions to the OpenGL API that support this programmability.

Included are updated descriptions for the language and all the GLSL entry points added to OpenGL 2.0; new chapters that discuss lighting, shadows, and surface characteristics; and an under-the-hood look at the implementation of RealWorldz, the most ambitious GLSL application to date. This edition also features 18 extensive new examples of shaders and their underlying algorithms, including

- Image-based lighting
- Lighting with spherical harmonics
- Ambient occlusion
- Shadow mapping
- Volume shadows using deferred lighting
- Ward's BRDF model

0-321-33489-2 · ©2006 · 800 pages

OpenGL® Distilled
Paul Martz

OpenGL® Distilled is a concise guide and reference covering the essential, commonly used OpenGL features professional programmers need to know to write effective OpenGL code. The book is written in a direct, how-to style, so readers can find information quickly. Topics include drawing primitive types, lighting, texture mapping, pixel rectangles, writing version and platform-independent code, best practices, and more. Debugging and performance tips, and pointers to sources of additional information, appear throughout.

0-321-33679-8 · ©2006 · 304 pages

OpenGL® Programming on Mac® OS X: Architecture, Performance, and Integration
Robert P. Kuehne and John Rosasco

This book explains how to access OpenGL on the Mac, creating and setting up OpenGL prototypes under the various APIs available. It explores the Mac-specific characteristics of performance optimization, and shows you how to integrate Mac-native APIs into OpenGL. Learn how to choose among APIs for the Mac and how to incorporate other capabilities of the Mac into OpenGL. For those moving applications to the Mac, it explains the choices available and the unique characteristics of the Mac OpenGL setup and configuration.

0-321-35652-7 · ©2006

www.awprofessional.com

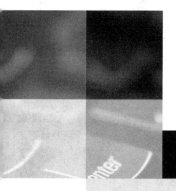

BOOKS ONLINE
ENABLED

THIS BOOK IS SAFARI ENABLED

INCLUDES FREE 45-DAY ACCESS TO THE ONLINE EDITION

The Safari® Enabled icon on the cover of your favorite technology book means the book is available through Safari Bookshelf. When you buy this book, you get free access to the online edition for 45 days.

Safari Bookshelf is an electronic reference library that lets you easily search thousands of technical books, find code samples, download chapters, and access technical information whenever and wherever you need it.

TO GAIN 45-DAY SAFARI ENABLED ACCESS TO THIS BOOK:

● Go to **http://www.awprofessional.com/safarienabled**

● Complete the brief registration form

● Enter the coupon code found in the front of this book on the "Copyright" page

Addison
Wesley

If you have difficulty registering on Safari Bookshelf or accessing the online edition, please e-mail customer-service@safaribooksonline.com.